**THE CONTEMPORARY DISCUSSION SERIES**

# Women in the World's Religions, Past and Present

# WOMEN IN THE WORLD'S RELIGIONS, PAST AND PRESENT

EDITED BY
URSULA KING

A NEW ERA BOOK

PARAGON HOUSE
New York

Published in the United States by
Paragon House Publishers
2 Hammarskjöld Plaza
New York, NY 10017

A New Ecumenical Research Association Book

**Library of Congress Cataloging in Publication Data**

Women in the World's Religions, Past and Present.

(God, The Contemporary Discussion Series)
"A New ERA book."
Includes index.
1. Women and religion. I. King, Ursula. II. Series.
BL458.W58 1986     291′.088042     86-21213
ISBN 0-913757-32-2
ISBN 0-913757-33-0 (pbk.)

# Contents

# General Introduction
## URSULA KING

Women have gained a new awareness which makes them question much of what has long been simply taken for granted. Feminist experience and thinking now challenge many aspects of culture, especially many of the traditional ideas and practices rooted in religion. An exciting new field of enquiry thus has opened up through this examination of the image and role of women in different world religions. Over recent years a considerable number of books in this area have appeared, but our global religious heritage is so vast that many more studies will have to be undertaken before we possess a full picture of women in the world's religions in both the past and the present. This publication is meant to make a small contribution to the ongoing discussion in this field.

Looking at the past, one can ask what do the sacred scriptures, the theological and spiritual writings of the religions of the world, teach about women? How far do the different religions draw on feminine symbols in speaking about ultimate reality, about the nature and experience of the spirit? To what extent do women take part in ritual and religious practices, choose to follow the religious life, or hold positions of authority in particular religions? Most important, what is the religious experience of women? Why has it been so little reflected in the official theological literature whereas it has contributed so much to the wealth of mystical and spiritual writings in different religions?

Perhaps the central question today is how far women are still hindered or, on the contrary, encouraged in giving full expression to their religious experience. Contemporary feminists often sharply criticize traditional religions and explore the meaning of religion for women in a new way. Although this challenge has barely been met by the official religious leaders of the world, in each tradition women and men are beginning to reflect on its meaning.

With one exception all the chapters in this volume were selected from a wide range of papers first given at an international conference entitled "God: The Contemporary Discussion III," held from December 30, 1983—January 4, 1984 at Dorado Beach, Puerto Rico, and sponsored by the New Ecumenical Research Association, an ecumenical project of the International Religious Foundation, Inc. One of the many sections of that conference was devoted to "Women in the World's Religions, Past and Present." Papers were invited from women and men from different world religions and nations that would deal with religious teachings on or by women from a historical, contemporary or comparative point of view, and would take into account some of the perspectives on women and religion found in current feminist literature. Each participant not only wrote a paper, but also presented a critique of another paper given in the same group.

Unfortunately, it was not possible to achieve a comprehensive coverage of the major world religions. Nevertheless, well over two dozen women and men from different religious, cultural, ethnic and educational backgrounds were present, and lively interaction occurred. As one participant wrote later: "It's phenomenal that our concerns can transcend religious, racial and national barriers. I felt so encouraged and excited by the discovery of common problems and great victories for sisters everywhere. It seems like a great victory just to be able to name the problem!"

The participants wrote and spoke from different perspectives. The discussion was always lively and challenging, sometimes provocative. It is impossible to reproduce this atmosphere and experience in print. But the different chapters of this volume, taken from papers revised after discussion, highlight the diversity of data and perspectives. They perhaps also show that men still tend to consider women as objects of study whereas women now write in a new mode as subjects about themselves. Given this marked difference in approach, it is no wonder that the different chapters reflect wide-ranging differences in thought and feeling, sensibility and perceptiveness.

Papers were selected to avoid unnecessary duplication and to provide readers with material not easily found elsewhere. Most, though not all, work on women and religion has been concerned with Judeo-Christian tradition, and to some extent this book is no exception. Readers particularly interested in this religious tradition will find here papers that will enlarge and complement material from elsewhere. This book is unusual, however, in including papers on women in African traditional religions, on women in evangelical Christianity, and on women in new religious movements, a topic hardly studied so far.

The chapters of this book can be read and discussed independently of each other. In fact, each provides an excellent background and basis for seminar discussions with students and other groups. But the chapters have been divided into three different sections wherein the different papers, in spite of their diversity, nevertheless share certain characteristics. The first section is entitled *Historical and Systematic Perspectives.* It focuses on developments in the past and points to some of their continuities in the present. The different chapters examine either specific historical and descriptive data (with examples from African traditional religions, Christianity and Buddhism) or offer systematic philosophical and theological reflections on the feminine in religion.

The second section discusses *Contemporary Perspectives.* Authors present particular case studies ranging from the role of women in the Hare Krishna movement to evangelical feminism, from the debate about the ordination of women in the Episcopal Church to women and perceptions of the feminine in Unification theology and ritual. The section also includes a description of the different religious experience of women in a particular West African society.

While feminist perspectives are mentioned in most chapters of this book, the contributions to the third section are explicitly devoted to *Feminist Reflections.* These deal with the significance of feminism within the transformation of contemporary religious consciousness, follow philosophical and literary explorations into feminist notions about self and identity, and explore the interrelationship between sex, dependency and religion from the perspective of Buddhism. An introduction to each section gives further details about the chapters in it.

The contributions to this volume, with their diverse perspectives, are a clear proof that the images, positions, activities and histories of women in the world's religions past and present furnish a most rewarding field of enquiry. The past can provide us with grounds for critique but also with elements of inspiration, new discovery and the need to rethink our position today. Above all, however, it is the challenge of the present we have to meet. Women and men, whatever their religious background or interest, need to reflect on the vast data on women in world religions old and new which are now coming to light. Their exacting analyses may perhaps help us to reach a new level of awareness concerning the religious quest.

By way of conclusion and as a suitable introduction to the main parts of this book, I would like to quote from Anne Bancroft's report on the conference group devoted to "Women in the World's Religions, Past and Present," where earlier drafts of the papers in this volume were first presented: "In the past, women from all traditions have been regarded not only as inferior beings who were not likely to have the capacity to experience ultimate reality, but also as actual obstacles to men's spiritual progress. These attitudes have left a residue of bitterness in women, especially as they see few signs as yet of men acknowledging their needs or indeed their mutual humanity. Many women are now beginning seriously to question whether the model of patriarchal religion has any place in it for them at all, or whether a different model, one more akin to that revealed by the mystics, should be adopted...

"It was on our last day together that these vital issues received most voice. Too many of us had written mere descriptions of the position of women in the different religions—descriptions which were factually correct but static, needing no comment but sadness for the plight of our sisters, particulary in the past. What we needed was an urgent discussion of the present—of the need to get beyond the fixation on sex altogether and to find ways of worshipping and being together which are *human,* life-enhancing, and transcending sexual orientation. We needed to discover how to create situations which wake up the basic insight and spiritual ardor that all humans have."

# I.

# HISTORICAL AND SYSTEMATIC PERSPECTIVES

# Introduction by the editor
## URSULA KING

This section begins with a chapter on women in African traditional religions. Friday M. Mbon looks at the role of women as healers and diviners, at the sacral power of women, and at female imagery in the religions of several peoples in Africa. There is the primordial God-Mother, a spirit agent who is the mother of every child born into this world; there is also the lunar mother-goddess, the image of the earth as mother, and the intriguing symbol of the forest as woman, an image which relates to the wild and includes the dark, cold and demonic as well as the divine. Mbon stresses the complementarity of male-female roles and relationships in traditional tribal society. However, he emphasizes that further investigation on women in African religions is necessary and, when achieved, will make an important contribution to women's issues at the global level. Other suggestions might also be examined, such as the remark in a footnote that an interesting research topic would be the analysis of the role allegedly played by woman in the supposed separation between God and man, a story found not only in African mythology but in many other creation myths of the world's religions.

The second chapter moves into a somewhat different cultural area by looking at the figure of the Wisdom Goddess, especially as she appears in the Nag Hammadi texts found in Egypt around 1945. These documents shed new light on the New Testament period as they preserve religious myths parallel to the biblical material without being part of the orthodox canon of Christian scriptures.

Rose Horman Arthur has made a special study of the figure of *Sophia,* the Wisdom Goddess, in these texts and relates her findings to current discussions in feminist theology, especially those surrounding the person of Jesus. She compares the figures of Eve and *Sophia* as found in proto-gnostic and pre-Christian documents

3

and argues that with the establishment of Christianity, focused on Jesus Christ who presents "a one-sided conception of the deity," Western religion became overly masculine in nature.

While Rose Horman Arthur develops her critique from material outside the canon of Christian scriptures, E. Jane Via arrives at an equally positive image of woman from within the New Testament itself by focusing on the activities of women portrayed in one Christian gospel, that of Luke. A detailed textual analysis highlights the important role of women as recipients of Jesus' ministry, as disciples and apostles, as active participants in the early Christian ritual meal, and as examples in the teaching of Jesus. Such a detailed study calls into question the amount of material ignored in the traditional exegesis of the Christian scriptures. Via also considers the hypothesis that the evangelist Luke may have been a woman. Such a hypothesis may not be verifiable, but neither is the traditional belief that a man wrote Luke's gospel. What has always been taken for granted may now well be questioned. The implications of this new approach to Luke's gospel still have to be developed, but as Via concludes, a church which "does not acknowledge the ministry of women has betrayed Luke's Jesus and the salvation he sought to bring." The paper is a good example of the ways the new hermeneutic of feminist theology can be brought to bear on specific biblical passages and can draw out their meaning in a new and unexpected way.

This new approach is further exemplified by Walter Gardini's paper on "The Feminine Aspect of God in Christianity." He argues that while Judeo-Christian religion received a masculine and hierarchical structure from which women were excluded, there are nonetheless sufficient elements in the tradition to which current feminist experience and its need for reinterpretation can relate. There are many passages in the Old Testament that express maternal aspects and activities of God, there is the image of *Sophia* in the wisdom literature, and there are certain aspects of the Christian doctrine of the Trinity which disclose a maternal Father and an even more feminine figure in the Holy Spirit. There is also the important figure of Mary, the abode of the Spirit and of his action in the world. Gardini mentions briefly the correspondence between the Christian doctrine of the Holy Spirit and the Hindu idea of *shakti,* the creative power of God, conceived as female in Hinduism. These ideas require further investigation but are an indication how far the new perspectives raised by contemporary

4

feminism can lead to a discovery of hidden resources and parallels in different religious traditions.

Systematic theological concerns are central to George H. Tavard's chapter on "Theology and Sexuality." What kind of questions does the sexual revolution raise for theology? Similarly, ought one to think about a theological revolution regarding the nature and meaning of sexuality? This paper considers the classical theological tradition concerning sexuality, especially in marriage. It first describes the views of early Christian and later medieval writers, but then moves to the contemporary situation. Tavard believes that theology still has to come to terms with the psycho-analytic view of human sexuality; at present the mutual dialogue between these two perspectives still seems to be in its infancy. In this, as in the preceding chapters, several ideas are open to further debate, but the basic challenge affecting our understanding of sexuality, marriage, celibacy, secular and religious life is perhaps Tavard's unanswered question: "Are maleness and femaleness two different 'embodiments-cum-ensoulments' of humanity? Or are they two aspects of humanity which are shared, though unequally, by all human persons?"

This is a general human question to which different religions give quite different answers, as is evident from the chapter on "Women in Buddhism," an insightful account by Anne Bancroft of the role of women in Buddhism from the past to the present day. Writing as a Buddhist, she highlights the ways in which the Buddha's view of women was more generous and positive than that of later misogynist monks. The Buddhist admitted women followers to his order, but the nuns were always given an inferior position to the monks, as illustrated by some quotations from the Buddhist scriptures. The nuns never possessed the same scope for teaching and consequently also never created a schism within Buddhism, whereas the monks created many different schools of thought. Of particular interest is the figure of *Prajnaparamita,* known as the Perfection of Wisdom. Her description is not unlike that of the Wisdom Goddess, *Sophia,* discussed in earlier chapters of this section. The Perfection of Wisdom was never worshipped as a goddess but became one of the celestial *bodhisattvas* or saviour figures of Mahayana Buddhism.

The chapter also includes material on women in Tibetan and Zen Buddhism; the discussion of their history is linked to contemporary considerations, especially to the way in which Zen

Buddhism has met with feminism in the West. It is suggested that "western Zen may hold the key to the unlocking of women's participation in religion at the highest level." The question of the full ordination of Buddhist nuns is as vigorously debated among Buddhists as is the ordination of women to the priesthood in different Christian churches. Anne Bancroft reflects on this with insight and radical questioning: "Why are women content to be looked upon as religiously inferior beings? This question applies to all religions. Men ordain each other in hierarchical formation. Why are women prepared to wait, perhaps indefinitely, for that grudging approval by men which will result in their feet being placed on the ladder too? Why do not women take the whole issue into their own hands and ordain each other, or start a church which has no need of ordination?"

These are important questions indeed, and some of them are taken up again in later sections of this book.

# 1

# Women in African Traditional Religions

## FRIDAY M. MBON

There is a certain relation between any religious unit and its power to direct the movement of its most precious human resource, women. . . . [E]ven though religion in Africa is principally a man's affair, its reason for being is woman, guardian of life and link between the living and the dead, between the past and the future.[1]

—Dominique Zahan

## Introduction

Literature on women and religion has been growing at a phenomenal rate in recent times. But much of this literature is deficient in the sense that even though many of the titles contain the generic term "religion," the only religious tradition that is usually discussed in many of them is the Christian. If one is fortunate, one may find passing allusions to the Islamic, Jewish, and Oriental religious traditions. To this day, however, research into the role played by women in the traditional religions of Africa is still a *desideratum*. This is why I agree with Mercy Oduyoye when she suggests that "further work on women in African religion will be a great contribution to global women's issues."[2] It is our aim in this chapter, therefore, to try in some way to offset the imbalance that usually characterizes the treatment of the subject of women in world religions. But first, a brief word about the nature of African traditional religions, in the interest of the reader who may not be conversant with them.

By way of definition, the traditional religion of a given ethnic group in Africa refers to the religion of that group before the intervention of colonialism and non-African religions such as Christianity and Islam. It further refers to a way of life of that ethnic group, characterized by the presence of a central religious focus known in the language of that people as the supreme being, whom

7

the people recognize as the supreme creator of the world and everything that exists in it, including men and women, and to whom all acts of worship ultimately go. This religious system also acknowledges the presence or reality of spirits, divinities, and ancestors who, though believed to be subordinate to the supreme being, also receive veneration in their own right, and, either as the messengers of the supreme being or on their own, exert considerable influences, for good or ill, on the religious and social life of the people.

The existence of these other deities besides the supreme being has led many students of African religious systems to the still debatable conclusion that African traditional religions are polytheistic. Other students of these religions, however, do not see these deities as being necessarily separate, *other* entities apart from the supreme being, but rather as *essential* emanations of him/her. This second category of students see African traditional religions, therefore, not as polytheistic but as essentially monotheistic. In fact, one of the propounders of this view even speaks rather interestingly of the structure of these religions in terms of "diffused monotheism,"[3] which one could transliterate "poly-monotheism." But there is no space here for either such playing with words or for the monotheism/polytheism controversy in African traditional religions.

Moreover, according to the cosmologies of traditional African peoples, the community is quintessentially religious or sacred, and is composed of both the living and the "living-dead," ancestors, elements of the material cosmos as well as spiritual forces. It is a sort of extended family in which constant communication among both the human and non-human members is indispensable for its smooth functioning and cordial, coherent co-existence. Relationships among the members of this community are founded on neatly defined systems of social and religious ethics and covenantal configurations. Any breach in these ethical and convenantal arrangements constitutes "sin,"[4] and will invariably result in serious social and sometimes economic catastrophe. This will remain in the community until removed by requisite rituals of atonement or purification, carried out by the combined efforts of the elders or leaders and the diviners of the community.

Such, then, in brief, is the nature of the religious stage on which traditional African women find themselves. They discover that it is impossible for them to remain on this stage as mere observers.

Like their menfolk, they too must play their role. It is this role that this chapter attempts to examine.

While much of what is said here no doubt applies to many African peoples, I am aware of the problem of generalization which always crops up in studies on Africa. I also realize that no matter from how many different African ethnic groups one draws one's illustrations, those illustrations cannot in every detail apply everywhere in Africa. As Swailem Sidhom has quite rightly observed, "Africa is such a large continent, composed of hundreds of peoples of several races, and it would be misleading to make general statements about 'African' beliefs and practices."[5] This caveat is worth noting. But one should at the same time not forget that in matters of religious beliefs and practices in traditional Africa one may sometimes safely speak in general terms because quite often a ruling passion, a common denominator, or what Professor Bọlaji Idowu refers to as "a common Africanness,"[6] cuts across these matters in some fashion. Indeed, I agree fully, in this connection, with Evan Zuesse when he says:

As we move from one religion to another, particularly when these are historically related or part of the same geographical area, we cannot avoid recognizing common symbolisms and rites, and especially common underlying attitudes. After devoting many years to studying African religions, we even come to sense a deep orientation uniting almost all of them, however difficult this may be to delineate.[7]

Zuesse recognizes, however, as we all must do, that "despite the common elements in African religions there are many remarkable differences and variations."[8] In the same vein, and while recognizing the physical, physiological, and perhaps cultural diversity among African peoples, Colin Turnbull concludes: "Yet there is a unity, and a powerful one, that runs through all African societies, all African peoples, and all African cultures . . . the difference is material while the similarity, the underlying unity, is spiritual."[9]

## The Role of Women in African Traditional Religions

Even to this day, the African world is still to a greater or lesser extent a man's world in the sense that woman's position in the society is still largely subservient. At least so African men think. But thanks to Western education and the influence of Western

9

women's liberation movements, remarkable improvements have occurred in the social status of the average African woman. With these Western influences, many African women can now say with a sense of relief (and sometimes the men agree with them!): "What men can do, women can also do!" Of course, one must realize that only the educated and Western-influenced women in the modern African towns and cities can say this aloud. The majority of African women are still uneducated and live in male-controlled villages. They have not yet really felt the need to sing this slogan. It is with this set of women that I mainly deal here, since they are the ones who live where the traditional religions are still most actively practiced.

While educated African women in the towns and cities today can sing "What men can do, women can also do," in the areas of political, educational and scientific achievements, the uneducated women in African villages *could* sing the same slogan (although Mercy Oduyoye might not agree[10]) in areas of African traditional religious life. Yet if they dare sing such a slogan, the menfolk may mistake it as a song of equality between them and the women and therefore a threat to their supposed divinely sanctioned superiority over the womenfolk. Only in a very few areas of African traditional socio-religious life, however, may a qualified woman not serve as the principal functionary or officiant. Such areas, which are exclusively the prerogative of the menfolk, include the leadership of the community, becoming ancestors when one passes from this world into life in the spirit-world, the slaughtering of animal sacrifices to deities,[11] the breaking of kola nuts, the physical construction of shrines, the carving of images (god-replica), and membership in certain male secret societies.

In connection with this last item, the nonreligious reason usually given why women are excluded from male secret cults is that their talkative nature precludes them from being trusted to keep the "secrets" that mostly characterize these organizations. That this is believed to be the main nonreligious reason for the exclusion of women is reflected by the fact that in exceptional cases, very old and reputable women who are not known to be careless talkers may be initiated into some of the traditional male cults, as is done in certain areas among the Ibibio of southeast Nigeria with respect to the predominantly male *Ekpo* society. Professor J.O. Awolalu observes also that among the Yoruba of western Nigeria, some secret societies, exclusively meant for men, include some category of women as traditional members, and without them the membership will be incomplete, and full operation will be impossible. Such women are those who have passed child-bearing stage and have virtually become men and are duly initiated.[12]

The proviso that the women who may be initiated into male secret societies should be past the "child-bearing stage" derives from the common belief among traditional Africans that women before the years of their menopause generally are too impure to approach sacred objects or places, particularly if they are menstruating. Many African peoples, for instance the Annang of Nigeria and the Zulu of South Africa, regard old women beyond the menopause as "man," possibly because they are "now free from the impurity that is the lot of women as a result of the menstruation,"[13] but also because these women, like their male counterparts, can take an active part in performing some of the important aspects of the traditional religions, such as divination, healing, exorcising, and officiating during important social and religious rites.

It should be mentioned, however, that women do have their own secret societies from which men are also barred. So the equation balances, one might say. But important aspects of African traditional religions—divination, healing, witchcraft and sorcery, magic, priesthood, officiating during offerings and sacrifices,[14] exorcising, apotheosization or godification (that is, being imaged as god/goddess), officiating during initiation and puberty rites—all fall within the role of both men and women.

Of those aspects of African traditional religions in which women can play an active role, probably the most common ones are divination and healing ("doctoring"). As Geoffrey Parrinder has correctly observed:

The diviner seeks to interpret the mysteries of life, to convey the message of the gods, to give guidance in daily affairs and settle disputes, to uncover the past and to look into the future.[15]

Or, in the words of Zahan:

It is the diviner who holds the code which allows the decipherment of the various messages intended for man, the society in which he lives, and all else related to his destiny, while it is the various systems of divination which fulfill the role of decoding grid.[16]

The professional diviner, Zahan further observes,

is not content to possess great proficiency in the science of interpreting common messages but also knows how to elicit others. He possesses the skill of penetrating the universe of signs, which mediates between the world and the human being, and, by ordering it according to his own method, he is able to make it clarify the situation at hand.[17]

The diviner, whether man or woman, thus performs indispensable social and religious functions in African culture. He or she is consulted on all "crucial" occasions. When the African wants to know about the exigencies of his/her circumstances—present or future—it is the diviner who is consulted. For example, if one wants to undertake a journey or build a house on a particular plot of land or get married, one would normally consult a diviner in order to know the consequences of one's plans. Even in matters concerning the determination of the sex of an unborn child, the birth of that child, naming and circumcision ceremonies, sickness and death, the services of the diviner are invaluable. Because the diviner is able to carry out these functions, he/she is often considered by members of his/her community not only the most informed about individuals and the psychological and social tendencies of the community, but "the representative of the divinity."[18] Among the Azande of South Africa, Zahan tells us, "certain women-diviners become mediators between spirits and humans" through a sort of death-resurrection mystical experience, and that "it is through this contact with the beyond that this woman acquired the ability to transmit to humans the spirits' wishes . . . ."[19] And James Macdonald informs us that "the Lubare of Uganda may be under the direction of a prophetess" considered there to be "powerful, and may determine peace or war. . . ."[20]

As I said above, the second most important role played by women in African traditional religions is healing or "doctoring." In traditional Africa, problems that need healing are basically religious problems. In this sense, healing is a religious or spiritual matter. Indeed, the belief in the power of the spirits to both cause and heal diseases, is one that is tenaciously held on to even in modern Africa.[21] In fact, in traditional African society, the healer "has always been more or less a priest, a diviner, a psychologist or psychiatrist, all rolled into one."[22] Or, as Zahan says, "like the healer and the priest, the diviner . . . possesses a significant social personality and plays a considerable role in African culture. Often the same person takes on all three functions."[23] These observations are quite true with regard to the multi-dimensional role played by some women in African traditional religions.

Obviously not all men or women can be traditional healers or "doctors." This being so, the one who is a healer must have been called by a god or some ancestor to be that.[24] Before and after the call, such a person must usually be upright in matters of observing the religious and ethical rules of his/her society, as dictated by the society's moral code. Any violation of these moral rules and regulations immediately disqualifies one from such a call or instantly brings upon the healer a divine curse which renders him/her ineffective if he/she is already in the healing business. Such a curse must be removed immediately through prescribed ritual cleansing, if the healer is to retain his/her role and function as a healer.

Primarily the healer's task is to heal physical and psychological illnesses. But because a healer can simultaneously function as a priest and diviner, he/she may also prophesy, help to recover stolen properties through divination, lead out in ritual ceremonies, give warning orders, and give advice on moral and social matters.

Another significant function performed by some women in African traditional religions lies in the central position they occupy in the practice of witchcraft. Several researchers of this phenomenon in Africa agree that "witches are mostly women."[25] Thus Zuesse, in reference to the Lele, a Bantu people of the Congo, speaks of the witches' cult's "generally female members."[26] Bengt Sundkler tells us that among the Bantu of South Africa "most of the heathen diviners are women."[27] S.O. Jedo has suggested that the main reason why "many women are witches" is "partly to protect themselves against traditional male domination."[28] Because of its diabolic and destructive influence and the usually paralyzing fear it instills in the average African, witchcraft is usually not considered to be a socially beneficial aspect of the traditional religions of Africa; yet Africans believe that it has its place in the generally inexplicable rhythm of cosmic existence involving life and death, light and darkness, good and evil.

There are other special functions performed by women in African traditional religions which I cannot discuss here for lack of space. Briefly, these include the responsibility that falls on some women, in their "clean condition," to keep certain sacred places tidy; other women are divinely called to render special services to specific deities such as preparing items for offerings and sacrifices, ministering to the traditional priests and conducting clients to them.[29] Sometimes women may serve as mediums to bring messages to humans from the spirit-world.[30] On special ritual occasions, something from the woman's body, like her hair, her nails, or a piece of her clothing, may be needed to complete the ritual. A good instance of this occurs at a special sacrifice to *Ogun* (Yoruba god of iron and steel) in which "men wear women's clothing."[31] Also, the pot of water that is said to be always available in the sanctuary (shrine) of the Yoruba arch-divinity called *Obàtálá,* or *Òrìsà-ñla,* is claimed to be always kept filled by women:

Such water is fetched very early in the morning from a spring by either a virgin or a woman who has passed the child-bearing age. She does not greet anybody on the way and she carries a bell which she rings all the way to let people know that she is on a sacred errand.[32]

And Turnbull tells us that among the Lozi of Zambia "women prepare the special beer for all ceremonial or public events; without their cooperation . . . the ceremony would be fruitless."[33] Turnbull further speaks of the important religious role played by the Zulu woman in the following way:

Through her libation of beer alone are the sins of the Zulu absolved. Among the Tswana, rain cannot come unless young maidens fill the sacred pots with water and carry them ceremonially throughout the land, sprinkling the ground with the water to bring fertility as well as rain. Women are so powerful spiritually that ordinary objects touched by them can become charged with a power of their own. For example, women sometimes seize musical instruments men use in their rituals, particularly rattles and drums, and thereby convey special power to the instruments and to the ritual, as though the ritual might be impotent without their intervention.[34]

Also, during the hunting rituals among the Oruendu Pygmies of Zaire, Zuesse informs us, the hunters' wives are needed to make cuts in their husbands' skins before each hunt, and to introduce medicinal ashes moistened by their saliva into the cuts. Of this practice Zuesse concludes: "There is a special need for *women* to make these cuts in the hunter's flesh. . . ."[35] Finally, among those African peoples where the supreme being or his/her functionaries are conceived of in purely anthropomorphic terms, some women are said to play the role of being "wives" or "daughters" to the male gods.[36] Such, then, is a picture of the multi-dimensional role that women play in African traditional religions.

## The Images of Woman in African Traditional Religions

No account of the role of women in the traditional religions of Africa can be considered complete without taking a look at the ways women are imaged in these religions. I shall therefore devote the next few pages to that purpose, if only briefly.

Let me broach this topic with the question of the gender of God, and hasten to say that this issue is not a problem in African traditional belief systems. It is mainly in the Judeo-Christian and Islamic traditions that this question has persisted as a problem, since Yahweh and Allāh in these traditions continue to be addressed in male terms and images. In African traditional religions, on the other hand, God is neither exclusively male nor exclusively female; it is both. That is to say, in these religions there are *both* male *and* female Gods. In one unique case, in fact, the Tarakiri Ezon of the Niger Delta region of eastern Nigeria refer to the supreme being of their traditional religion in feminine terms. She is called *Tamarau,* which means creator, but she may also be referred to by other names, such as *Woyin* or *Woyingi* or simply *Oyin,* each appellation meaning "our Mother." She may also be called *Ayebau,* meaning "the Mother of the world."[37]

Furthermore, the Akan of Ghana refer to God as the lunar mother-goddess. The Ashanti of the same country consider the earth as "the great-breasted goddess" who comes next to the supreme being in the hierarchy of their pantheon, and for whom Thursday is observed as her special day.[38] To the Igbo of Nigeria, the earth is acknowledged as a goddess, the daughter of the Supreme, who protects people in general and farmers in particular and helps in the well-being of the crops. This goddess is known by various names such as *Ake, Ala, Ana* or *Aja.*[39] Of the twenty-one (out of a total pantheon of seventy) gods that are believed to be independent of the *Asafo* system among the *Effutu* of Ghana, "twelve are regarded as males and nine as females."[40] But there is another sense in which African deities are believed to be *both* male *and* female, and that is in the biological sense, if one assumes that Jung's anima-animus complex also applies to African psychobiological nature.

African creation myths also make some interesting references to the images of women. Several of these myths claim that in the beginning the sky and the earth were in such a close proximity that someone standing on the ground could reach the sky. The present distance between the earth and the sky, these stories claim, came about as a result of the supreme being's anger at the irreverent, albeit unintentional, act of women. Some women were pounding their food in the traditional African wooden mortar one day, so one story goes, and each time they lifted their pestle they hit the sky, the supreme being's dwelling place. The supreme being did not like this so he/she withdrew to the present location of the sky, and that is why the sky is so far away from the earth today! Another version of this story suggests that some women even went so far as to sacrilegiously wipe their wet hands on the sky! The supreme being's reaction was, of course, the same.

These stories remind us of the old Judeo-Christian theological doctrine that it was the sinful act of one woman called Eve in the garden of Eden which introduced "distance" into the hitherto close, vertical relationship between God and man. One is not implying here, however, that the idea in African traditional creation myths that woman brought about the withdrawal of God from man, is borrowed directly, *tout court,* from the Genesis story of the fall (now unacceptable to secular minds). But these African mythical stories do have some serious implications for the place of women in the religions of some African peoples, where women are allowed to play only subordinate roles because of their alleged initial "sin" at the genesis of Creation.[41]

One of the most interesting references made to women in African traditional religions is the unconscious use of female imagery in talking about ultimate reality, or in referring to some aspects of the traditional religions. Thus the Annang and Ibibio of southeastern Nigeria speak of *Eka-Abasi* (literally God-Mother), a spirit agent to whom, they believe, the supreme being (*Abasi Ibom*) gives unborn babies in the spirit-world to deliver into the wombs of would-be mothers where they remain for "ten moons" (ten lunar months) before they are born into the physical world. Each woman in this world who has reached child-bearing age and has a healthy physiological capacity for child-bearing, the Annang and Ibibio believe, has an *Eka-Abasi* assigned to her. This *Eka-Abasi* continues to deliver unborn babies from the supreme being to her and to protect both the mother-to-be and the unborn babies in her womb for as long as she remains biologically productive.

An *Eka-Abasi,* according to this belief, is not merely a spirit agent or messenger between *Abasi Ibom* and women; she is also symbolically the primordial mother of every child born into the physical world. As such, so the belief goes, she must not be "forgotten"; she must be given periodic offerings or even sacrifices, especially when the baby is newly born and generally until the child reaches the mysterious age of seven, after which age, it is believed, the *Eka-Abasi* can no longer disturb him/her. If a particular *Eka-Abasi* feels that she has been "forgotten," she may cause the newly born child to be seriously sick or even to die. It is a common practice among the Annang and Ibibio to consult a diviner immediately in cases of a seriously sick, newborn baby to find out through divination the cause of the sickness. If this baby's sickness is caused by an *Eka-Abasi,* the baby's life can be spared if an appropriate offering or sacrifice is made to the *Eka-Abasi* involved.[42]

Sometimes, even if the appropriate periodic offerings and sacrifices are made to them regularly, "jealous" *Eka-Abasi* may still cause the death of newborn babies. This usually happens when the babies concerned are so physically attractive that the *Eka-Abasi* become "jealous" and covet them. Thus they "kill" these beautiful or handsome babies and keep them for themselves in the spirit-world. At other times, "jealous" *Eka-Abasi* may not deliver to the wombs of some women beautiful babies given to these women by *Abasi Ibom*. And if it happens that a particular woman has the fortune/misfortune of always being given such babies by the supreme being by such a "jealous" *Eka-Abasi,* who goes on keeping the babies for herself, such a woman will remain barren. However, if through divination the tricks of the "jealous" *Eka-Abasi* are found out, the physical parents-to-be may plead, through special rituals and sacrifices prescribed by the diviner, with the supreme being to change the "jealous" *Eka-Abasi* in charge of their family. When thus replaced with another, less "jealous" *Eka-Abasi,* the previous one is never again put in charge of family and, consequently, outlives her usefulness and is soon forgotten. As a forgotten deity, she no longer receives any prayers, offerings or sacrifices from the living. This point illustrates trenchantly that traditional Africans do not worship their deities indiscriminately. Rather, the worship of a particular deity depends on his/her continued utility or functionality. Once he/she ceases to be useful or becomes destructive to the people who worship him/her, that deity becomes redundant and is left unattended and finally forgotten.

On other occasions, the female imagery has been used to depict other characteristics of the supreme being. For instance, the image of the loving, caring, nourishing mother has often been used to symbolize the loving and protecting concern of the supreme being for his/her creatures. Moreover, the image of the female's capacity to give birth has also been seen as a symbol of the supreme being's creative powers.

Lastly, one interesting female image often used in African traditional religions is the image of the earth as mother. Even elements in nature are sometimes referred to in feminine terms, as when some of the Pygmies in Zaire address the moon as mother: "Mother moon, mother, mother, hear us mother, come."[43] Also, among the Epulu Pygmies of the same country, the forest and its animals are frequently referred to in feminine terms, and the hunt regarded as an erotic pastime.[44] This image of the forest as woman is particularly telling when one considers the negative side of woman: the forest can be the habitat of dangerous animals! Or, as Zuesse expresses a similar thought: "Women are somehow related to animals and the wild, which includes the dark, cold, and demonic as well as the divine."[45] And as animals, women are believed to flirt with the hunters, especially the successful and therefore particularly virile ones, in attempts to win them as husbands.[46] Moreover, the bees in the forest, for whose honey men hunt, are also a symbol of women.[47] Yet bees can also sting!

In further exploration of the symbolic relationship between women and the forest among the Epulu, Zuesse suggests that because of the sacred nature of the forest, women in themselves "are central to the culture, imply divinity, and precisely for this reason must restrain themselves" from sexual activity with their hunter husbands during the hunting season.[48] According to Zuesse, "the felt significance of the taboos underline *woman's sacral power* and link to the forest...."[49] This "sacral power" of women, Zuesse further explains, becomes conspicuous to society if they should violate any of the taboos of the society (e.g., if a woman approaches her hunter husband while she is menstruating). The consequences of such violation may include fruitless hunting for her husband, injury to him during hunting, or serious illness, genital disease or impotence. And since her husband is the family's bread winner, if he should become so ill that he cannot support the family, his children will be adversely affected. And if he becomes impotent, the entire community will be affected because he would therefore no longer be able to contribute to its replenishment. Thus, because of the "sacral power" in their possession, women can do and undo, and "their actions have tremendous consequences for all those around them."[50]

In general, however, the image of the earth as mother is usually used by those African people who conceive of God in terms of the male-female dichotomy. For such peoples masculinity is quickly associated with highness or aboveness or with the sky (after all it is only the males who are culturally permitted to climb trees!), while femininity is associated with the below—with the earth and thus with fertility. Hence these peoples refer to the mythical sky-god in masculine terms and mother-earth or the earth-goddess in feminine terms. This manner of referring to the deities no doubt has to do with the cultural ethos of these traditional Africans whereby, for them, the man is always above the woman (a *double entendre*).

Like God himself/herself, who is at once a God of love and of wrath, mother-earth has a dual nature. She is simultaneously friend and foe. As friend, she nurtures and fills nature with beauty and life (generativity). As foe, she introduces into nature the ugly and the negative—death, grief, pestilence, suffering, inequality, injustice, and the like. As earth, she synchronously represents the womb that gives birth to life, and the grave that takes away that life in the mystery of death. But these two sides of mother-earth are not to be seen as necessarily antagonistic or oppositional. Rather, they are complementary. For the joys of life become more meaningful only if one has experienced its sadness, since out of the darkness of nature's night, the eye may begin to behold nature's beauty. This double nature of mother-earth is repeated in women and their place in African traditional religions: they are at the same time useful and, in their "unclean moments," useless or even outright sacrilegious.

## Conclusion

From the preceding discussion, it is clear that women, in spite of their occasional "uncleanness," play significant roles in African traditional religions. Indeed, one could even speak of the indispensability of women in these religions when one remembers that certain rituals and ceremonies cannot be carried out without the presence or participation of women, especially the old ones who have passed child-bearing age. For example, rituals and ceremonies involving female rites of passage, ceremonies in which something from a woman's body must be used to make them efficacious, or those concerned with *Eka-Abasi*—all these aspects of the traditional religions cannot be carried out without the cooperation of women.

I have also tried to make clear that in much of the traditional religions of Africa the male-female role does not constitute any problem of dichotomy as such. Rather, the role played by one sex is to be seen as complementing that played by the other, and the male-female relationship is the ground of this complementarity. The outcome of such complementary roles is an integrated, inherently harmonious African traditional religion for a given ethnic group. This fortune in African traditional religions has saved their practitioners from the perennial hair-splitting problem of sexist rivalry over cultic life and sacerdotal or ecclesiastical office, a problem that still plagues Judaism, much of historical Christianity, and Islam in our time.

# NOTES

1. Dominique Zahan, *The Religion, Spirituality, and Thought of Traditional Africa* (Chicago: University of Chicago Press, 1979), 31.

2. Mercy Amba Oduyoye, "The Value of African Religious Beliefs and Practices for Christian Theology," in Kofi Appiah-Kubi and Sergio Torres, eds., *African Theology en Route* (Maryknoll, N.Y.: Orbis, 1979), 112.

3. E. Bolaji Idowu, *Olodumare: God in Yoruba Belief* (London: Longman, 1962), 202ff.; cf. E. Bolaji Idowu, *African Traditional Religion: A Definition* (London: SCM Press, 1973), 135.

4. For the argument whether or not there is a concept of sin in African traditional religions, see D. Westermann, *Africa and Christianity* (London: Oxford University Press, 1937), 96–97; J. O. Awolalu, "Sin and Its Removal in African Traditional Religion," *Journal of American Academy of Religion* 44, no. 2 (1976): 275–87; see the same article also in *Orita: Ibadan Journal of Religious Studies* 10, no. 1 (1976): 3–23; Francis A. Arinze, *Sacrifice in Ibo Religion* (Ibadan: University of Ibadan Press, 1970), 34; J. K. Parratt, "Religious Change in Yoruba Society: A Case Test," *Journal of Religion in Africa* 2, no. 2 (1969): 113–28; G.T. Basden, *Among the Ibos of Nigeria* (London: Frank Cass, 1966), 216–17; Albert B. Ellis, *The Tshi–Speaking Peoples of the Gold Coast of West Africa* (London: Frank Cass, 1894; reprint, 1966), 10–11.

5. Swailem Sidhom, "The Theological Estimate of Man," in Kwesi Dickson and Paul Elingworth, eds., *Biblical Revelation and African Beliefs* (London: Lutterworth Press, 1969), 83.

6. Idowu, *African Traditional Religion,* 103.

7. Evan M. Zuesse, *Ritual Cosmos: The Sanctification of Life in African Religions* (Athens, Ohio: Ohio University Press, 1979), ix; cf. Zuesse, 62, where Zuesse further writes: "it is possible at least in Africa to discern some common themes that are variously modulated by the hundreds of distinct and unique cultures throughout the continent."

8. Ibid., x.

9. Colin M. Turnbull, *Man in Africa* (Garden City, N.Y.: Doubleday, Anchor, 1976), xi, xiv.

10. See Oduyoye, "The Value of African Religious Beliefs," 112, where she complains: "But as far as the cultic aspect of religion goes, women now as before are relegated to the background."

11. It would appear here that it is not society as such that has excluded women from slaughtering sacrificial animals. Rather, women themselves seem to have shied away from this particular responsibility due, first, to the rather higher regard they have for blood as a symbol of life, accentuated by the memory of their own menstrual blood. Secondly, traditional African women seem not to have Lady Macbeth's heart!

12. J. Omosade Awolalu, "Women from the Perspective of Religion," *Orita: Ibadan Journal of Religious Studies* 10, no. 2 (1976): 100.

13. S. N. Ezeanya, "Women in African Traditional Religion," *Orita: Ibadan Journal of Religious Studies* 10, no. 2 (1976): 112; cf. Oduyoye, "The Value of African Religious Beliefs," 112, where she refers to the practice of forbidding menstruating women from participating in certain activities of the traditional religions, as "the irrational fear of blood"!

14. Cf. Richard P. Werbner, "Continuity and Policy in Southern Africa's High God Cult," in R. P. Werbner, ed., *Regional Cults* (London: Academic Press, 1977), 203–205.

15. Geoffrey E. Parrinder, *West African Religion* (London: Epworth, 1969), 137.

16. Zahan, *Traditional Africa,* 81. For the various methods of divination, see Donald C. Simon, "Efik Divination, Ordeals, and Omens," *Southern Journal of Anthropology* 12, no. 2 (1956): 223–28; Thomas J. Hutchinson, *Impressions of West Africa* (London, 1858), 156–58; Geoffrey E. Parrinder, *African Mythology* (London: Paul Hamlyn, 1967), 88–91. On the various ways of "making" diviners among some African peoples, see Zahan, *Traditional Africa,* chap. 6.

17. Zahan, *Traditional Africa,* 81.

18. Ibid., 82.

19. Ibid., 83.

20. James Macdonald, *Religion and Myth* (1883; reprint, New York: Negro Universities Press, 1969), 199.

21. See Z. A. Ademuwagun et al., eds., *African Therapeutic Systems* (Waltham, Mass.: Crossroads Press, 1979), esp. 1–46. Cf. Oku Ampofo, "The Traditional concept of Disease, Health and Healing with which the Christian Church is Confronted," *Ghana Bulletin of Theology* 3, no. 2 (1967); N. K. Dzobo, "The Sociological Situation in Ghana Regarding Health and Healing," *Ghana Bulletin of Theology* 3, no. 2 (1967); see also other articles on the subject of health and healing in Africa in this special issue of the *Bulletin*; see, too, Clive Dillon-Malone, "New Religions in Africa," in John Coleman and Gregory Baum, eds., *Concilium 161: New Religious Movements* (New York: Winston, Seabury Press, 1983), 58; Robert W. Wyllie, "Ghanaian Spiritual and Traditional Healers' Explanations of Illness: A Preliminary Survey," *Journal of Religion in Africa* 14, no. 1 (1983): 46–57.

22. E. Bolaji Idowu, "The Challenge of Witchcraft," *Orita: Ibadan Journal of Religious Studies* 4, no. 1 (1970): 14.

23. Zahan, *Traditional Africa,* 82.

24. For the ritual processes involved in the call to divinership among the Lulua and Baluba peoples of Zaire, see Haldor E. Heimer, "The Church Suited to Home Needs," in R. T. Parsons, ed., *Windows on Africa: A Symposium* (Leiden: E. J. Brill, 1971), 32, n. 1.

25. Idowu, "The Challenge of Witchcraft," 10; cf. Zahan, 93 ff.

26. Zuesse, *Ritual Cosmos,* 69.

27. Bengt G. M. Sundkler, *Bantu Prophets in South Africa,* 2d ed. (London: Oxford University Press, 1961), 353.

28. S. O. Jedo, "Witchcraft in Ilajeland," *Orita: Ibadan Journal of Religious Studies* 4, no. 1 (1970): 77. This article is the summary of Jedo's "Extended Essay," submitted in 1969 to the Department of Religious Studies, University of Ibadan, Nigeria, in partial fulfillment of the requirements of the B.A. degree in Religious Studies.

29. See Ezeanya, "Women in African Traditional Religion," 112–13.

30. Parrinder, *West African Religion,* 137.

31. Benjamin C. Ray, *African Religions: Symbol, Ritual, and Community* (Englewood Cliffs, N.J.: Prentice-Hall, 1976), 81.

32. J. Omosade Awolalu, *Yoruba Beliefs and Sacrificial Rites* (London: Longman, 1979), 22; cf. J. Akinyele Omoyajowo, *Cherubim and Seraphim: The History of an African Independent Church* (New York: NOK Publishers, 1982), 174.

33. Turnbull, *Man in Africa,* 50.

34. Ibid., 50–51.

35. Zuesse, *Ritual Cosmos,* 30.

36. See John Mbiti, *Concepts of God in Africa* (London: SPCK, 1970), 114–16, cf. Ezeanya, "Women in African Traditional Religion," 114–15.

37. J. E. Ifie, "The Tarakiri Ezon and Their Gods in the Ozidi Saga," *Orita: Ibadan Journal of Religious Studies* 15, no. 2 (1983): 90; cf. J. E. Ifie, "Notes on Ezon Religion and Culture in the Ozidi Saga," *Orita: Ibadan Journal of Religious Studies* 12, no. 1 (1978): 67.

38. Mbiti, *Concepts of God in Africa,* 115.

39. Ibid., 295, n. 10.

40. Robert W. Wyllie, *Spiritism in Ghana: A Study of New Religious Movements* (Missoula, Mont.: Scholars Press, 1980), 14.

41. An interesting area of research might be to examine in the world's religious traditions the role allegedly played by woman in the supposed separation between God and man.

42. For details of the *Eka-Abasi* sacrifice among the Ibibio of Nigeria, see Justin S. Ukpong, "Sacrificial Worship in Ibibio Traditional Religion," *Journal of Religion in Africa* 13, no. 3 (1982): 178. I disagree with Ukpong, however, when he says: "This sacrifice has died out today, as most sick children are successfully treated in the hospital . . . ."

43. Zuesse, *Ritual Cosmos,* 20.

44. Ibid., 31.

45. Ibid.

46. Ibid.

47. Ibid., 33–34.

48. Ibid., 68.

49. Ibid.

50. Ibid.

# 2

# The Wisdom Goddess and the Masculinization of Western Religion

## ROSE HORMAN ARTHUR

Nineteen eighty-three marked the publication of two important books by Christian feminists who study western religion and its effects on women in church and society. I refer to *Sexism and God-talk* by Rosemary Radford Ruether[1] and *In Memory of Her* by Elizabeth Schussler Fiorenza.[2] Ruether presents the first systematic critique of Christian theology from a feminist perspective. Working from women's experience of divinity as a principle of feminist theology, she submits that the God-talk which is usually presented as objective is predominantly codified *male* rather than *human* experience of God and reality. She questions, along with other feminists, the adequacy of the recorded experience of the male Christian savior as a symbol for women's liberation.[3]

If, as Ruether writes, "the maleness of Jesus has social symbolic significance in the framework of societies of patriarchal privilege,"[4] then her theological gerrymandering to suggest that it has no ultimate significance is less than helpful. More worthwhile is her use of the prophetic tradition of the Jewish and Christian scriptures as a paradigm for calling western religion to repentance for the sin of sexism. Ruether's own experience leads her to write chiefly with the Christian religion in view, but her vision of liberation from sexism is all-embracing and future-oriented:

Christ, as redemptive person and Word of God, is not to be encapsulated *once for all* in the historical Jesus . . . Christ, the liberated humanity, is not confined to a static perfection of one person two thousand years ago. Rather, redemptive humanity goes on ahead of us, calling us to as yet incompleted dimensions of human liberation.[5]

While Ruether looks to the future for the end of sexism, Fiorenza finds a model for that utopia in earliest Christianity. Disclaiming the mode of an apologist,[6] Fiorenza leaves the impression that she has found within the first century of the Christian era, in Palestine, and among a sectarian community including Jesus and his male and female disciples, a golden age of feminist consciousness. She reads the sources in a new way in order "to engage in the struggle for women's liberation inspired by the Christian feminist vision of the discipleship of equals."[7] She opines that present-day radical feminists who define "the best interests of women as the best interests of the poorest, most insulted, most despised, most abused woman on earth"[8] have discovered a principle espoused by the Jesus movement in Palestine without recognizing its religious roots.

Fiorenza knows that Christianity was a reform movement within Judaism and that the earliest Christian theology was the study of the Wisdom Goddess. Nonetheless, the prime character in her feminist reconstruction is the male god of the synoptic gospels rather than the mythological goddess of Sophialogy. Fiorenza knows that the earliest Christian tradition considered Jesus as the child, prophet, or revealer of Sophia. She knows that St. Paul and the writer of the gospel of Matthew actually identified Jesus Christ with Sophia. While she deals more than adequately with the transformation of what she calls the *woman's gestalt of the divine Sophia* into Christology, at no time does she suggest that this transformation was itself a defeminization of an older world view which had been non-sexist in its symbolism.

To be sure, there is no easy way out of this dilemma for feminists who root their religious faith in an historical founder who was born as a baby *boy*. Neither Ruether nor Fiorenza has met the bold challenge of Naomi Goldenberg in the *Changing of the Gods:*

Jesus Christ cannot symbolize the liberation of women. A culture that maintains a masculine image for its highest divinity cannot allow its women to experience themselves as the equals of men.[9]

## A Mythological Approach

In this presentation, I shall attempt to show how a part of the Wisdom Goddess tradition was masculinized in the name of Jesus Christ. The texts I use were found in Nag Hammadi, Egypt around 1945, and they preserve religious myths familiar to readers of the Bible. In most cases, their exegesis is not normative for orthodox Christianity. One is left with the disconcerting distinction that the same stories are *true* when found in the Bible but *myth* when found in the Nag Hammadi documents. To avoid this difficulty, I propose to treat the stories impartially as myths. My thesis supports the broader notion that early Christianity was the continuation of a kind of heterodox Judaism akin to a mystery religion.[10]

To discover the feminist roots of Christianity one needs to look at mythology liberally defined. In the introduction to the *New Larousse Encyclopedia of Mythology,* Robert Graves defines mythology as "the study of whatever religious or heroic legends are so foreign to a student's experience that he cannot believe them to be true."[11] It is standard practice to omit biblical stories from western collections of myths even when the biblical accounts closely parallel those from Egypt, Persia, Babylonia, or Greece. With the discovery of the Nag Hammadi documents, we are faced with a large collection of new texts presenting myths which parallel those of the Jewish and Christian scriptures. Because their interpretations do not blend harmoniously with what is considered normative in the West, the documents are sometimes dismissed too lightly. We need to read them with the grain, as it were, not against the grain of learned response. We need to see both the familiar and the unfamiliar interpretations as the efforts of pious Jews and Christians to reconsider old myths in the light of changes within their cultures.

Like myth itself, interpretations have two main functions: to justify changes in the culture and to ratify existing rites and customs. Because myths and their interpretations do not remain static, one is justified in searching for the change of consciousness which the revised myth or its exegesis implies. For example, at a recent para-liturgical service, a group of women crunched juicy red apples saying something to this effect, "Eve, you took from the tree the knowledge of good and evil. You made a conscious decision to find truth. For this we thank you." None of these liberated twentieth-century women considered the Genesis story as anything but myth. Their reinterpretation of the eating of the forbidden fruit is an indication of a change of consciousness within these women who no longer see themselves as symbolized by Eve, the last to be made and the first to sin.

Otfried Eberz, in his book *Sophia und Logos,* details from various cultures around the world the history of the repression of the *feminine* pole of conscious existence. Eberz claims that an integrated unity of consciousness existed in the prepatriarchal cultures of Europe and Asia, but that this consciousness has been distorted in historic times by the establishment of patriarchal, repressive societies. For him, the general historical development has been that of appropriation and reinterpretation of the older myths by masculine elements. Thus, he maintains that the cult of Demeter employing originally a bronze age matriarchal myth was reinterpreted along Dionysian lines. In Palestine, the Ishtar-Tammuz myth was replaced by the symbols of masculine consciousness represented by Jehovah. Nevertheless, he sees a powerful undercurrent of the older myths that show up occasionally even in the Old Testament, such as in Ezekiel 8:14 when women of Jerusalem are depicted as weeping for Tammuz. Eberz goes so far as to assert that the women of Jerusalem, as representatives of the oppressed elements of the ancient Palestinian society, were responsible for the formulation and the maintenance of that apocalyptic literature which he sees basically as the vision of the overthrow of the male-dominated order and the return of the bronze age double order of *Sophia und Logos*. He views the institution of the Yahwistic, nationalistic, sacrificial, exclusively male-ordered culture as a relatively late phenomenon which makes use of mythological material in a radically different way. For example, Eberz considers the Eden myth of Genesis 3 to be a retelling of an originally matriarchal narrative which represented Eve as teacher and priestess and Jehovah as a satanic figure overthrowing the old order and driving out the inhabitants from their proper territory. According to Eberz, the new masculine order stands even in danger of a *fall* back into matriarchal conditions. To prevent this, he submits that the whole history of the feminine gender in the first era becomes defamed as a fall into sin, and the history of the second age is conceived of as a punishment for the gnostic matriarchy of the first.[12]

Some of the Nag Hammadi texts indicate that the hypothesis of Eberz is correct at least with regard to the interpretation of the myth of the first woman. The document known as *On the Origin of the World* portrays Eve as a heavenly instructress, who as the daughter of Sophia wars against the personification of Jehovah known as Ialdabaoth. In a related but Christianized document, the *Hypostasis of the Archons,* Eve is interpreted as a carnal woman who eats of the forbidden fruit to her condemnation while Ialdabaoth is rehabilitated.

## The Spirit of Late Antiquity

We turn now to a consideration of the era in which the Nag Hammadi interpretation of Eve as teacher and Ialdabaoth as arrogant creator-god seems to have originated. For this study, there is still no greater master than Hans Jonas whose major work in English, *The Gnostic Religion,* first published in 1958, is already a classic.[13] Jonas writes of the age of late antiquity and of the religion called gnosticism, a movement which spread over the ancient world from about 100 B.C.E. to 300 C.E. I shall use the term *proto-gnostic* to designate the gnostic religion prior to its conflict with the so-called orthodox church in the second century. The western world is heir to a decision made against proto-gnosticism by the sexist early church fathers. We can understand better the western religious traditions if we understand the loser in the struggle for the consciousness of mankind.

The roots of gnosticism as a syncretistic religion may be traced to the conquest of the East by Alexander in 334–323 B.C.E. Alexander's victory and the spirit of the Greek world made possible the unity of East with West. By East I mean that old civilization which spread from Egypt to the borders of India. By West I mean the Greek world around the Aegean Sea. Alexander's planned unification of the two cultures is shown by the celebration held at Susa where, in accord with his wishes, ten thousand of his officers married Persian women. Racial and ethnic unity promoted religious unity. The mystery religions of the East meeting the more rationalistic religions of the West served to make the latter emotionally realizable. Contrariwise, the Greek concepts and language helped spread the ideas underlying the mystery cults.

In the first of his books about the ancient mysteries, *By Light, Light,* E. R. Goodenough proved, at least to this reader's satisfaction, that the Jewish religion, as it participated in the general syncretism of the age, became for some of its adherents in the Diaspora a mystery.[14] Along with the myths of Isis and Osiris, the Old Testament stories added warmth and depth to Greek abstractions such as wisdom and folly, life and death, light and darkness. With the appearance of the Nag Hammadi texts, we are able to give further substantiation to the thesis of Goodenough. One form of the Jewish mystery centers upon the Wisdom Goddess and makes use of the myth of Genesis to characterize the primordial god called the Light-man.

During the unification of East with West, cultures and religions changed, myths were reinterpreted, and Greek thought concerning the goodness and harmony of the cosmos was completely reevaluated. Whereas the Greeks had ranked the heavenly bodies far above mankind in their godly natures, the proto-gnostics placed mankind above the powers of the heavens. Although humans were obliged to wear the trappings of the cosmos for a time, they were essentially different from it. This difference was made clear by Plotinus, a detractor:

Even the basest men they deem worthy to be called brothers, while with frenzied mouth they declare the sun, the stars in the heavens, and even the world-soul, unworthy to be called brothers.[15]

In the proto-gnostic, anti-world scheme, the human body was considered an earthy shell worthy of respect only as it was the instrument by which the cosmic powers of fate were to be overcome. Of inestimable worth, however, was the human spirit which participated in divinity. Proto-gnostic sentiments had characterized Eastern thought prior to its blending with Greek notions. Thus, proto-gnosticism may be considered atavistic. It harked back to a non-sexist consciousness which existed in the pre-Hellenized age in the Orient.

To appreciate the reinterpretation of the Genesis myth of Eve by the proto-gnostics, one must be aware of the widespread myth of the immortal Light-man. Its characters in the Nag Hammadi rendition are Pistis Sophia (Faith Wisdom), the Light-man, and the benighted creator god, Ialdabaoth, who speaks in the words of Jehovah. The constitutive features are Ialdabaoth's arrogant boast, "I am god and there is no other," his rebuke by Pistis Sophia, and the flash of the Light-man upon the waters for the use of Ialdabaoth in making the human body.

In the proto-gnostic myth as presented in *On the Origin of the World,* the ignorant creator challenges, "If there is one existing before me, let him reveal himself so that we might see his light" (107.36–108.2). Ialdabaoth's first boast is repudiated by Pistis, "You are wrong, Samael" (103.17). His second boast is proved incorrect by a penetrating light from the eighth or feminine sphere. Within the light is revealed a human image which Ialdabaoth uses as his model in making an androgyne (108.3–9; 112.33–113.1). When the Light-man wishes to return to his original Light, he is unable on account of the "poverty which was mixed with his light" (112.10–13).

In *Hypostasis of the Archons,* the Christianized document based upon *On the Origin of the World,* the tragedy of the Light-man is less clearly presented, but the main features are there: the boast of the archigenetor (86.30–31; 94.21–22; 95.5), the feminine rebuke (87.3–4; 94.25–26; 95.7–8), the flash of the light from above (94.28–31), and the archons' creation of Adam "according to their body and according to the image of God which appeared to them on the waters" (87.31–33). Although the *Hypostasis of the Archons* does not explicitly name the Light-man, his existence is implied in the passage just quoted as well as in its continuation, "Come, let us catch him [the Light-man] in our plasma . . . so that he will see his co-image [masc.]" (87.33–35).

There shows here the anomaly that the *Hypostasis of the Archons* knows the mythological figure of the Light-man but not once explicitly names him. The co-image cannot be Eve because it is of masculine gender and therefore must signify Adam, as is clearly expressed in the parallel account in *On the Origin of the World* (103.11–21). In the following section, we shall see how Eve is integrated into the proto-gnostic myth.

No presentation of the myth of the Light-man would be complete without reference to the redeemed redeemer concept which Bultmann developed from the works of Bousset, Lidzbarski, and Reitzenstein. His construction supposes the existence of a primitive gnostic myth in which a primal Light-man falls and is divided by demonic powers. The particles become sparks of light imprisoned as spiritual beings within bodies of clay. The demons attempt to make these humans forget their divine origin, but a transcendent deity sends another Light-being who descends through the demonic spheres in deceptive bodily garments, reminds those humans of their heavenly ancestry, and gives them the passwords necessary for their return through the archontic spheres. Having defeated the demons, the redeemer re-ascends and makes a way for the redeemed spirits of mankind. When the spirits of all persons are thus collected, cosmic redemption is achieved. The redeemer is himself redeemed in that the Light-man who fell in the beginning is reconstituted.[16]

The proto-gnostic myth as found in the common material of *On the Origin of the World* and the *Hypostasis of the Archons* supports the basic hypothesis of Bultmann but indicates the need for some important changes in the reconstruction. At Nag Hammadi, the primal Light-man appears in connection with Sophia, and he is sent from the eighth sphere which is that of the feminine. Bultmann's reconstruction lacked the essential feminine deity, the personified Pistis Sophia. Bultmann's proto-Mandaean gnostic source is of dubious value. It is more likely that Old Testament speculation about personified Sophia provided the background for the myth. Moreover, Bultmann supposed the Light-man motif to have been integrated directly into Christianity, but in the common material of *On the Origin of the World* and the *Hypostasis of the Archons* the Light-man is connected with Jewish Sophialogy and Genesis midrash where Christian elements do not appear.

## The Salvific Eve

In several of the Nag Hammadi documents, Eve is characterized as the saving figure within the proto-gnostic myth. Eve's birth and her salvific role are quite clearly presented in the *Apocalypse of Adam* where they center around the creation, fall, and redemption of mankind. These themes are treated within the context of the myth of Genesis, albeit with a non-normative hermeneutic in respect to the existential questions for which, according to Clement of Alexandria, gnosis promises the answer: "Who were we? Who have we become? Where were we? Where have we been cast? Whither do we hasten? From what are we freed? What is birth? What is rebirth?"[17] These questions being central to the *Apocalypse of Adam,* it is our concern to note here how Eve is significant to the answers proffered.

To the first question, "Who were we?," Adam replies in his own name and that of Eve that they were beings of Ialdabaoth, a more exalted nature than Saklas. Their exaltation had been due to Eve's spiritual nature, her *gnosis* of the true God. Eve had given Adam a *word of knowledge* so that, united as a syzygial pair, they had been more honorable than the creator god about whom they had known nothing. Adam's praise of Eve is rendered in the context of a revelation to his son Seth:

Listen to my words, my son Seth. When god had created me out of the earth along with Eve your mother, I went about with her in a glory which she had seen from the aeon from whom we had come forth. She taught me a word of gnosi of the eternal God. And we were like unto the mighty angels of eternity, for we were higher than the god who created us and the powers which were with him—those of which we knew nothing (65.5–19).

The second question for which gnosis supplies the answer concerns the fall of mankind. To the question, "What have we become?," the *Apocalypse of Adam* states bluntly: "We became two aeons" (64.23). This unnatural state of division occurred because of the rage of the chief archon who found Adam and Eve more knowledgeable than himself. He separated Adam from the bringer of gnosis, the heavenly Eve. Gnosis left Adam and returned to "the seed of some great aeons" (65.4–5). Here, the "seed" probably refers to heavenly children of Eve who are to bring saving gnosis to the earth again within the Sethian race.

Blame for the separation of Adam from his gnostic counterpart is placed squarely upon the foolish god:

Then god, the ruler of the aeons and the powers, divided us in his rage. Then we became two aeons. And that glory which was in our heart abandoned us—thy mother Eve and me—along with that first gnosis that blew within us (64.20–28).

As distinct from the normative hermeneutic of the story in Genesis in which Adam and Eve fall into sin by reason of eating from the tree forbidden by God, the *Apocalypse of Adam* considers the fall of mankind as a separation of the man from her who *knew* better than he. Man's syzygial relationship was sundered when the archigenetor separated Adam from his heavenly and salvific partner, Eve.

The third question for which gnosis gives a response, "Where have we been cast?," is not so clearly answered in the *Apocalypse of Adam* as it is in some other Nag Hammadi documents. One may infer, however, that the first parents were no longer in a paradisiacal state when knowledge had left them. The *Apocalypse of Adam* relates that they began to act like mortals in serving the creator god and no longer like immortals in acknowledging the eternal God. Adam reveals to Seth how he had been cast from a heavenly to an earthly state:

After those days the eternal gnosis of the God of truth withdrew from me and thy mother Eve. From that time forth we learned about dead things, like humans. Then we recognized the god who had created us, for we were not strangers to his powers. And we served him in fear and bondage. And after these things we became darkened in our heart (65.9–23).

The last questions answered by gnosis concern soteriology: "Whither do we hasten, from what are we freed, what is birth, what rebirth?" The *Apocalypse of Adam* affirms that gnostics, having overcome all persecutions, will come into everlasting life:

"They shall live forever" (83.14–15) because they have been freed from corrupting desire (83.16). "Birth" seems to imply coming into being through the archigenetor and "rebirth" salvation by gnosis. Thus, rebirth would be the reacquisition of that knowledge which the heavenly Eve once gave to Adam in the aeon from which the first couple originated.

The birth of the salvific Eve is recorded in *On the Origin of the World*. It is placed just before the creation of the earthly Adam to show that the androgyne Eve obviously existed before the archontic creation. Her mother is Sophia, the Wisdom Goddess. Apparently, she had no father. Her nativity story reads:

When Sophia had cast forth a light drop, it floated upon the water. Immediately, the Man, being androgynous, was made manifest. That drop took its first form as a feminine body. Afterwards, she [Eve] took her bodily form in the image of the Mother [Sophia] which had been revealed. She [Eve] was completed in twelve months. An androgyne [Eve] was born, whom the Greeks call "Hermaphrodites." But its mother [Sophia] in Hebrew called her "the Living Eva," that is, "the Instructoress of Life" (113.22–34).

The salvific Eve appears in *On the Origin of the World* as an inviolable virgin. The pagan theme of an inviolate virgin attacked by supernatural powers is modified by incorporation into the narrative of Genesis events. In the presentation, the Light-man is feminine and is called Eva. As in the *Apocalypse of Adam* she represents that part of the androgynous Light-man that is not fallen. The Genesis story is used to make the abstract idea of salvation by gnosis come to life. The Wisdom Goddess and Eve are sometimes interpreted as the same figure. In *On the Origin of the World,* a song said to have been sung by Eve begins: "I am a portion of my mother and I am the Mother" (114.8–9), and in the same document we read of Sophia Zoe (115.12; 121.27), that is, Sophia Eve, mother of the living who caused Adam to live. Pejorative motifs surround neither Sophia nor Eve.

Eve as symbol of life is in accord with the pre-Pauline exegesis of the Genesis story; in the gospel stories Eve is not used as a basis for the etiology of evil. The dualism of the Old and New Adam in Pauline theology raises the Genesis story of the fall of mankind to the limelight, and post-Pauline exegesis presents Eve as the agent responsible for the first sin and model for the subjugation of women to men in the Christian churches.

With the Christianization of the myth of the androgyne, both male and female positive images were used of the male Christian *Silvanus* found at Nag Hammadi:

For the tree of Life is Christ. For he is Wisdom; he is also the Word. He is the Life, the Power and the Door. He is the Light, the Messenger, and the Good Shepherd (106.21–28).

That the prototypical Wisdom myth underlies the Christian myth is clear from another quotation from the *Teaching of Silvanus:*

For he, existing as Wisdom, makes the foolish man wise. She [Wisdom] is a holy kingdom and a shining robe. For she is much gold which gives you great honor. The Wisdom of God became a type of fool for you, so that she might take you up, O foolish one, and make you wise. And the Life died for you when he [Jesus Christ] was powerless, so that through his death, he who has died might give life to you (107.2–16).

Throughout the mythological presentations of Sophia and Eve within pre-Christianized documents, their imagery is feminine and valued. Within Christian documents one notices a curious twist. The Wisdom and Eve (Life) motifs are sometimes simply co–opted in the name of the male hero as the above quotations suggest. Often, however, the motifs are themselves downgraded. Wisdom is considered foolish, Life causes death, and the motif of a fallen or faulty Sophia begins to appear. Parthenogenetic conception is no longer a motif used to announce the birth of divine children of Sophia; rather, one reads of a guilty Sophia who dared to conceive without her male consort. While this secondary Sophia is not presented as a completely evil being, she is a representation of psychics, those of the middle way, who are neither the damned hylics or the saved-by-nature pneumatics. She is a weak one who needs the hot breath or great light of the male in order to attain her salvation.

In Christian gnosticism the life-giving Eve motif is reinterpreted so that Eve becomes responsible for her separation from Adam and for death. Christ came to repair the damage she had done. In the *Gospel of Philip* from Nag Hammadi one reads:

If the woman had not separated from the man she would not die with the man. His separation became the beginning of death. Because of this Christ came to repair the separation and unite them (70.9–18).

Such Christian gnosticism posits a distinction between the eschatological and the earthly being of mankind. Thus, before the original sin of the first woman, who becomes the symbol of the fallen psychic, mankind was a unity. At the end of time, it may again be united with the Christ. In the meantime, mankind is fallen and in need of salvation. When Christ is identified with the historical Jesus, when salvation is dependent upon his death upon a cross under the reign of Pontius Pilate, one is no longer in the realm of mythology. The historical presentation solidifies the myth into *his* story. Abstract terms such as Sophia, Logos, or even Christ defy gender specification even if they are personified in myth. Christian theology tends to make God male in Jesus. As Ruether remarks:

The use of the male word *Logos,* when identified with the maleness of the historical Jesus, obscures the actual fluidity of the gender symbolism by appearing to reify as male a *Son of God* who is, in turn, the image of the Father.[18]

## Conclusion

Jesus Christ, as male, is neither an adequate symbol for divinity nor for women's liberation. As male, he presents a one-sided conception of the deity which, by definition, is inconceivable and unlike anything perceptible to the senses. Theologians and philosophers have taught traditionally that God-talk is analogical, and they insist that God is neither male nor female. Christian theology, however, has made a distinction in the case of Jesus Christ, whom it professes to be God become flesh in the male sex.

Rudolf Bultmann is noted for his efforts to demythologize the New Testament, i.e., to interpret, according to the categories of existentialism, the essential message that was expressed there in mythological terms. My efforts have been the reverse. I have opted for remythologization of the God-human story in accord with a proto-gnostic unity of consciousness which denigrates neither the male nor the female. Modern attempts at remythologization need to highlight feminine motifs which have been submerged during two thousand years of the masculinization of western religion in the name of Jesus of Nazareth.

The recent works of Ruether and Fiorenza represent giant steps toward a feminist reconstruction of western religion, but with regard to the subject of God incarnated as male their approaches are basically conservative. They have not taken proto-gnosticism seriously, with its penchant for incarnating, mythologically of course, divine children of the Wisdom Goddess. Myths are never simple. They are not correctly labeled true or false. They are functional or dysfunctional. Thus, the myth of God incarnate as a male is functional for a Christian church which refuses to ordain women as priests on the premise that a woman cannot adequately represent the male Jesus Christ as an *alter Christus*. With Ruether and Fiorenza, as well as with the Roman Catholic *magisterium*, the myth of the Christian God-male is alive and well. A changing non-sexist Christology is long overdue.[19]

# NOTES

1. Rosemary Radford Ruether, *Sexism and God-Talk* (Boston: Beacon, 1983).

2. Elizabeth Schüssler Fiorenza, *In Memory of Her* (New York: Crossroad, 1983).

3. Ruether, *Sexism and God-Talk,* 122–26.

4. Ibid., 137.

5. Ibid., 138.

6. Fiorenza, *In Memory of Her,* 10, 92.

7. Ibid., xxiv.

8. Ibid., 132, and quoting "Redstockings, April 1969" in *Feminist Revolution* (New York: Random House, 1975), 205.

9. Naomi Goldenberg, *Changing of the Gods* (Boston: Beacon, 1979), 22.

10. The whole collection of Nag Hammadi documents and several related tractates from Berlin Codex 8502 are available in *The Nag Hammadi Library in English,* ed. James M. Robinson (Leiden: E. J. Brill, 1977).

11. Robert Graves, "Introduction" in *New Larousse Encyclopedia of Mythology,* new ed. (New York: Hamlyn Publishing Group, 1968), v.

12. Otfried Eberz, *Sophia und Logos oder die Philosophie der Wiederherstellung* (Munich: Reinhardt, 1967).

13. Hans Jonas, *The Gnostic Religion* (Boston: Beacon, 1972).

14. Erwin R. Goodenough, *By Light, Light* (New Haven: Yale University Press, 1935).

15. Plotinus, Enn. II.9.18 as quoted in Jonas, *The Gnostic Religion,* 263.

16. Rudolf Bultmann, *Primitive Christianity* (New York: World, 1956), 163–64. For a discussion of the gnostic redeemer myth in relation to the New Testament and to the question of an anti-Semitic stance within proto-gnosticism, see my book, *The Wisdom Goddess* (Washington, D.C.: University Press of America, 1984), 113–16.

17. Clement of Alexandria, *Excerpta e Theodoto* II.78.2. The relationship of Eve to the questions posed by Clement of Alexandria is discussed in *The Wisdom Goddess*, 28–30, 116–20, 130–31, 136–37.

18. Ruether, *Sexism and God-talk*, 58.

19. For a detailed discussion of changing Christologies, see John Hick, ed., *The Myth of God Incarnate* (Philadelphia: Westminster, 1977).

## 3

# Women in the Gospel of Luke
## E. JANE VIA

In the past decade, probably in response to the feminist movement of our time, more attention has been given to women in the Bible.[1] One result of this new interest in biblical women was the discovery that, among the four evangelists, Luke includes more passages dealing with women than other gospel writers. Leonard Swidler summarizes the statistics concisely: "Where John has eight passages dealing with women, Mark 20, and Matthew 36, Luke has 42."[2]

Although Luke's gospel is the longest of the four, the number of women present in the gospel is not merely a function of the gospel's length. There are proportionately more passages about women in Luke's gospel.[3]

Of Luke's 42 passages dealing with women . . . three are common to all four evangelists . . . nine more are common to all three Synoptics . . . another five are common to just Luke and Matthew and two are reported by only Luke and Mark.[4]

The remaining twenty-three passages about women in Luke are unique to Luke and constitute the largest number of unique women passages in any gospel.[5]

Thus both on the basis of sheer quantity and the very large number of women passages special to Luke, it is clear that Luke exhibits the greatest stress on women by far. . . .[6]

Swidler has undertaken the comprehensive task of identifying women and/or feminine imagery in Luke's gospel. This paper attempts to categorize women in Luke's gospel in accord with their function and roles and thereby elaborate upon the theological significance of women and feminine imagery in the gospel of Luke.

## Women Characters in Luke's Gospel

The largest category of women in Luke's gospel are women characters in the gospel narrative, that is, presumably historical women in the life of Jesus. Their roles range from prominent, as in the case of Elizabeth and Mary, to minor, such as the women in the crowds (e.g., 11:27–28). Their relationships to Jesus are various. The symbolisms of their presence in the gospel are both significant and diverse.

The women with the most prominent roles in Luke's gospel emerge in the infancy narratives of the first two chapters. They are, of course, Elizabeth and Mary; and, according to Luke, they are relatives (1:36).[7] Together these two women can be said to dominate much of the Lukan infancy narratives. The other woman who appears in the infancy narrative is the prophetess, Anna.[8] Because the infancy narratives constitute the introduction to the gospel, a strong, positive impression about women is suggested to the reader from the beginning. These three women share an important function in the gospel: each is a vehicle of revelation, a voice that articulates theological meaning for Jesus.

## Woman as a Vehicle of Revelation

The most obvious form in which a woman is a vehicle of revelation in this gospel is literal and biological. As the one who bears Jesus, Joshua, "the savior," Mary is a vehicle of revelation in a most primary and basic way. Without woman, this salvific event could not have occurred.

From the feminist perspective, however, this role of Mary's has demeaning implications for women, even for Mary. In it, woman is subordinate to her male child, who provides salvation of allegedly universal significance. Implicit in this role is the suggestion that man saves woman who cannot save herself. This suggestion is strengthened by a literal interpretation of the virgin birth narrative[9] and of the deity as male. The resulting picture is of a female human being still sexually inexperienced, whose womb is fertilized and made pregnant by a male deity. The passivity of woman in this interpretation deprives her of feminine sacred power. She becomes not a vehicle of salvation, but a vessel of divine semen. Her human power and dignity are negated. Rather than being impossible without woman, the saving act becomes impossible without a male deity who mercifully lowers himself to the human condition. Indeed, this concept of the divinely fertilized virgin, if viewed as mythological in character, may also constitute an early, patriarchal, Christian effort to delimit the powerful independence associated with goddess traditions of "pagan" neighbors and the virginity of the goddess.[10] Thus, although Mary's role has traditionally been an elevated one (e.g., "Mother of God"), it has also functioned as the proverbial pedestal on which woman is idealized in compensation for the oppression of real women. She is literal source for and enabler of salvation.

But Mary's role as vehicle of salvation extends beyond the literal-biological. As scholars of Luke recognize, direct address forms in Luke-Acts are used by the author to place emphasis on certain theological concepts and to effect more dramatic, direct, "audible" connections with gospel readers.[11] When Mary sings her canticle, the reader hears it as if she were singing not only in Elizabeth's presence but also in the reader's presence.

Mary's canticle, which is also objectionable from the feminist theological perspective because of its emphasis on what "God" (he) did for Mary (1:49), functions to praise the deity, "his" name, and "his" mercy to the multiple generations of those who "fear him" (Luke 1:49–50). Mary's psalm affirms the Jewish concept of deity as saving deity (1:47) and enumerates examples of "his" "mighty" acts (1:51). "His name is holy" (1:49). "He" scatters "the haughty in the understanding of their hearts" (1:51), pulls down potentates from thrones (1:52) and "exalts humble ones" (1:52), fills those who are hungry with good things (1:53), sends the rich away empty (1:53), helps Israel ("his servant") to remember mercy (1:54), and speaks with human beings ("our fathers") (1:56).

Mary's song conveys an image of deity as powerful but merciful, enemy of the human powerful and rich, but friend of human poor and special friend to Israel. As Luke structures the infancy narrative, the "truth" of this description of deity is verified in the life of she who sings it. She is humble, not haughty, nor rich and powerful; but she is chosen to carry divine mercy, exalted to a position for which potentates long. She will be blessed by future generations. Thus, Mary's voice is a theological voice and her life a theological model in this gospel.

Elizabeth is a vehicle of revelation in the same ways as Mary. In her old age, she conceives and bears a son who will contribute to the same plan for salvation of which Mary's son is the savior. Elizabeth's pregnancy and its circumstances are modelled on that ancient Israelite motif of the barren, sometimes aged woman, who ultimately conceives by divine intervention and bears a son whose life is crucial to the history of Israel.[12] Like the matriarchs of Israel before her, Elizabeth illustrates the proposition that "Nothing is impossible with God" (1:35). The reproach she bore for her barrenness rendered her, like Mary, among the humble (1:25). Elizabeth's son will not be a savior, but he will lie great in the eyes of the divine (1:15), filled with the Holy Spirit (1:15b), and will go before "the Lord" turning many of Israel's "sons" to the "Lord" (1:16), preparing "the Lord" a people (1:17). In Luke's interpretation, "the Lord" is not the deity but Jesus.

Elizabeth is also the voice through which divine words of salvation are spoken. When Mary visits Elizabeth, Elizabeth exclaims that Mary's babe is blessed and Mary is the mother of Elizabeth's "Lord." A sign of the "truth" of her words is the response of the babe in her womb to the babe in Mary's womb. The babe leaps with joy (1:41) and gladness (1:44), in symbolic recognition of the divine saving act about to be generated in the world.[13]

Another woman who functions as vehicle of salvation in this gospel is Anna, the prophetess, unknown in Christian tradition except through Luke (2:36–38). Her age and status in life as one who fasted night and day in the Temple (2:36–37), authenticate her ability to speak on behalf of the divine. Coming upon Mary, Joseph, Jesus and Simeon in the Temple, Anna gives thanks to the deity for what she sees and interprets Jesus' future in connection with the redemption of Jerusalem. To those in Jerusalem expecting redemption, she speaks about Jesus. Her prophetic voice thus characterizes Jesus' future as one dedicated to redemption.[14]

## Women as Recipients of Jesus' Ministry

If Mary and Elizabeth are the best known women in Luke's gospel, the best known class of women in the gospels are the women to whom Jesus ministers. Insofar as Jesus' ministry fulfills Luke 4:18–20 (a conflation of Isa. 61:1–2 and 58:6) and insofar as Luke gives these Isaian passages messianic significance, as the use of the verb *echrisen* in 4:18 suggests, Jesus' ministry to women is an extension of the messianic blessings to women as individual women. These women, however, symbolize all the women of Israel, indeed all women, Jewish or Gentile.[15]

Simon's mother-in-law is the first woman in the synoptic tradition to benefit from Jesus' ministry. The sequence of events in this brief story is theologically significant. As Jesus arrives at Simon's house, he is asked about Simon's mother-in-law[16] who has a "great fever" (4:38). Jesus rebukes the fever (4:39),[17] which leaves her, and rising up (*anastasa*), she serves (*diekonei*) "them" (4:39). The use of *anistemi* suggests a pun on resurrection; the use of *diekonei,* a reference to the early Christian ritual meal, which by Luke's time was associated with deacons. Peter's mother-in-law is able to deacon because she is healed.[18] In the process she is raised up. She symbolizes all of the women of Israel, sick from patriarchy, who need this illness driven from them in order to be able to serve.

The widow at Nain is the next woman to benefit from Jesus' ministry (Luke 7:11–17).[19] Jesus arrives at Nain just as her "only-begotten son" is being carried out for burial. She is alone. Luke is explicit about Jesus' motive in ministering to her: he felt compassion for her in her grief. The macarism of 6:21 comes alive in Jesus' words to her: "Do not weep" (7:13). Jesus goes to the bier where her son lies, touches it, and commands her son to rise from the dead (7:15). The young man is raised up; but the life-giving act is done, not for him, but for his mother: Jesus "gave him to his mother" (7:15). According to Luke, the crowd witnessing this act of compassion on behalf of the woman interprets it as a divine visitation on the part of a prophet "raised up" among them (7:16). For this act of compassion, they glorified "God" (7:16). At least thus far in the gospel, it appears that women are in special need of resurrection. Jesus perceives and responds to that need; and his ministry to women is a sign of divine visitation.

The penitent woman of Luke 7:36–50, despite her namelessness, is among the best known women of the gospels.[20] She is the woman who goes to the Pharisee's house where Jesus dines, washes his feet with her tears, wipes them with her hair, and anoints them with oil.[21] Her actions toward Jesus are a lesson of love for the judgmental Pharisee. His disdain for both sinners and women is reflected in his thought that if Jesus really were a prophet, he would *know* the woman to be a sinner and would prevent her from touching him (7:39). Jesus rejects the Pharisee's disdain. By use of a somewhat convoluted parable, Luke expresses the idea that those who love greatly are persons who have been forgiven a great deal (7:41–43). The woman loves Jesus more than the Pharisee (7:44–46). Her great love reflects how much she has been forgiven (7:47). Jesus judges her, not by her sins, but by the forgiveness she has received. Implicitly Luke suggests that, though the Pharisee may have sinned less, he has also been forgiven less. He is mistaken in his tacit assumption that he is saved and the woman is not. She is saved by her faith and can go in peace. The Pharisee cannot. In this story, woman is the receptor of purely spiritual salvation and its resulting peace, while "the religious leader," self-righteous in his presumed position before the holy, misses both.

Luke 8:40–56, a traditional synoptic passage about women, also associates women with resurrection in the story of the raising of Jairus' daughter. In contrast to the story of the widow of Nain, however, Jesus acts in response to a father's plea for his "only-begotten," twelve-year-old daughter who is dying (8:40–42). The father is not widowed (8:51), and no mention is made of Jesus' compassion for the father. Again 6:21 comes to life as those who weep are restored to joy (8:52). Although Jesus insists the girl is not dead but only sleeping, he is not believed (8:52). Jesus commands her to arise. She does arise (8:54–55), and Jesus commands that she be given something to eat.

The girl is described as twelve years old, old enough to menstruate and old enough, therefore, to be considered a woman. Her age is a symbol of her metaphorical identity. She represents all the women of the twelve tribes of Israel who are dying of patriarchy. If the reference to food is understood as an allusion to the early Christian ritual meal, the girl's resurrection renders her an acceptable participant in that meal. Through Jesus, divine power gives new life and nourishment to this whole class of living-dead people.

The woman with the flow of blood (8:43–48) also needs healing. She is bleeding to death. For twelve years she has been bleeding. She intercedes for herself with Jesus and is instantly healed when, in faith, she touches the fringe of his garment (8:44). Like the sinner woman, her faith saves her and she can go in peace (8:48). Her bleeding, and her resulting uncleanness (see Lev. 15:25), which separated her from the community of believers, symbolizes the perpetual bleeding of the women of Israel, flowing from the wounds inflicted by patriarchal culture. The divine power which heals her flows to her through Jesus, evoked without his conscious awareness. But once the healing occurs, Jesus recognizes it as a healing act resulting from the woman's faith. Her faith is faith in the power of the divine to heal through Jesus, a response to the divine affirmation of woman through Jesus. But it is also a courageous faith in herself in the face of patriarchal negation of the value of woman as person.

One last story of Jesus' ministry of women remains: Luke 13:10–17, the healing of the bent-over woman. This story also carries profound metaphorical significance for all the women of Israel. The infirmity of this woman is their infirmity. She is physically bent over; they are historically, socially, politically, spiritually bent over. The setting in which we find the woman, who is bent double and unable to raise herself, is the synagogue, the place of worship. There she is a captive in need of release (4:16), having been crushed by the weight of religious prejudice and political tyranny. No one intercedes with Jesus for her healing. Jesus simply calls her to him "and at once she straightened" (13:13). The response to her healing is not unlike the response of modern patriarchs when women begin to stand straight and tall in places of worship. The synagogue ruler criticizes Jesus on the basis of religious law; not even Jesus' compassion for this suffering woman excuses observance of the law. Jesus does not hesitate to respond harshly: "You hypocrites" (13:15). They treat animals better than they treat women (13:15). His words leave his critics shamed (13:16).

The context of this passage is significant for the determination of its meaning. Jesus is on the road to Jerusalem, teaching the crowds and his disciples as he goes. The themes which immediately precede the passage are the need for making peace with one's adversary (12:58), the act of not judging people by their fate (13:1–5), and the parable of the fig tree (13:6–9). The parable may illustrate the future judgment of the crowd on Jesus' life; but given the association of the fig tree with the Temple in Mark's gospel and Jesus' lament over Jerusalem in 13:31–34, the fig tree probably represents not only Jesus and his fate but Jerusalem and its fate.[22] Unable to discuss authentic manifestations of "the Kingdom of God" (13:17–21) and unable to grasp the character of authentic salvation (13:22–29), Jerusalem, which expects to be first, will find itself last (13:30). The sign of its sinfulness is the murder of its prophets (13:34). Jerusalem's house, the Temple, will be left desolate (13:35).

Since the destruction of Jerusalem and the Temple preceded the composition of Luke's gospel by nearly a decade, Luke 13 (and Luke 12) seems to function in part as a theological explanation to Luke's church of this violent, traumatic event in Israelite history. Inserted into its center, presumably not without purpose and intent, is the story of the bent-over woman in the synagogue. To be argued convincingly, conclusions regarding this passage require more extensive discussions, but the following hypothesis must be seriously entertained. For Luke, the patriarchal oppression of woman, evident in the restrictions on her presence and participation in worship at both synagogue and Temple, is itself a cause of the divine wrath acted out on Jerusalem and the Temple, the heart of unbending religious authority. The bending over of woman constitutes a failure to make peace with one's adversary, a misjudgment of another according to her fate, a misinterpretation of the reign of "God" and salvation. If this hypothesis is valid, Luke's audience is introduced to a radical interpretation of the destruction of Jerusalem and the Temple and a shocking warning for the future. If Israel's institution can be destroyed, among other reasons, for their failure to unbend woman, the same end might await the church if it bends women over as Judaism had done.[23] If this were one message Luke intended these passages to convey, the church apparently missed its significance almost entirely.

## Women and Jesus' Heritage

Elizabeth plays an important role in establishing the theological identity of Jesus which Luke wishes to convey. From Joseph, Jesus takes his royal, Davidic connections. From Elizabeth, Jesus takes his priestly heritage. It is Elizabeth, not her priest husband Zacharias, who is Mary's relative, and therefore Jesus' relative. Elizabeth is "a daughter of Aaron" (Luke 1:5).

Aaron, brother to Moses and Miriam and speaker for Moses (Exod. 4:14, 17:1), was designated high priest of Israel (Lev. 8:1–10:20). Outside the Pentateuch, the sons of Aaron are infrequently mentioned, a fact which raises some question about their historical significance, if not their historical authenticity.[24] The significance of Elizabeth's heritage, apart from problems of historicity, to Jesus' identity is symbolic. Jesus, explicitly designated prophet in the gospel of Luke, is of royal and priestly blood. In him, priest, prophet, and king converge.

## Women as Disciples

The possibility of the discipleship of Jesus' women followers and friends has been recently suggested by Lukan scholars.[25] The key passage is Luke 8:1–3, a uniquely Lukan passage, in which gospel readers are informed that women travelled with Jesus on his missionary journeys and served Jesus and others from their own possessions. These women were Mary Magdalene, Joanna, Suzanna and many others (8:2–3). That these women had possessions suggests they were women of some means. Joanna was connected to Herod's court by her husband, Chuza, who was Herod's steward. Joanna was married. (It need not be assumed she was a widow.[26]) This passage suggests that Jesus' relationships with women were socially scandalous. He travelled with women not of his family, some of whom were married to other men. He stayed in their homes (Luke 10:38–42). Women from Galilee accompanied Jesus to Jerusalem, stood by his cross (24:49), participated in his burial (24:55), and were first to receive the good news that he was risen (24:1–10). Jesus teaches women (10:39, 24:6–8) who sat at his feet in discipular fashion (10:39). Quesnell queries whether the unnamed disciple who accompanies Cleopas on the road to Emmaus was his wife.[27] This anonymous disciple might also be a woman disciple from Galilee. Quesnell argues convincingly that the women are present at Luke's supper just as they are at Pentecost in Acts.[28] *Diakoneo,* the service and preparation of the meal which, with the exception of the Last Supper, involves only the women, is a model for discipleship in the gospel of Luke.[29] Since women travelled with Jesus and were taught by him according to Luke, Luke must have intended readers to understand that women were among Jesus' disciples. This conclusion has clear support in Acts.[30] Perhaps only the bias of patriarchal "spectacles" has kept scholars from this realization until recently.

## Women as Apostles

Whether Luke counted women among the apostles is a more difficult question because of the ambiguity surrounding Luke's use of the word. Luke 6:13 seems to assume the equivalence of the apostles and the twelve chosen disciples. Luke 10:1 seems to presuppose a much larger group of apostles than the Twelve since 72 are sent out on a mission. If the Twelve are equivalent to the apostles, then women would not be among the apostles as Acts

1:21–22 suggests. Note that the definition of apostle (if it is that) in Acts 1:21–22, which requires a male who was with Jesus from the beginning, negates the possibility of apostleship beyond the era of Jesus' historical contemporaries. Luke's use of apostle to describe Paul and Barnabas (Acts 14:14) is inconsistent with the impression given by Luke 6:13.

The only solution which seems to account for all of these passages is that, in Luke's mind, three categories rather than two existed among Jesus' followers: his disciples, who constituted the largest group; the apostles of whom there were at least 84 (12 + 72); and the Twelve who were apostles and disciples but who also constituted a special and distinctive group.[31] If these categories of Christians existed in Luke's church, then use of these terms, ambiguous from the perspective of the modern reader, would have been unambiguous in the minds of the original audiences. If these were the categories of Jesus' followers as Luke understood them, and the Twelve were apostles but not all the apostles were among the Twelve, then nothing would prevent women from having been among the Twelve. Indeed, there is support for this conclusion in New Testament literature earlier than the gospels.[32]

## Woman and the Early Christian Ritual Meal

As I have argued elsewhere,[33] Luke's gospel is filled with meal imagery (use of the verb *diakoneo*, references to eating, and to eating and drinking) which Luke intended to be a critical commentary on and reflection of the ritual meal as it was practiced by Luke's church. For Luke, women are fully integrated into this meal. They prepare and serve it (4:39, 8:3, 10:40). They "hear the word of the Lord" (10:40). They are present at the Last Supper, [34] at which they are served by men. At the last supper, *diakoneo* as metaphor for discipleship (12:37, 17:8) is literalized. Roles are reversed. The men serve the women and Jesus acts as waiter (22:26–27).

These passages and themes in the gospel suggest that in Luke's church there were no problems with women claiming male roles but in teaching male disciples the meaning of service, a task accomplished in part by placing them in female roles. Historically, it is unlikely that men took over the preparation and service of the ritual meal of the early church on a regular basis until the meal became symbolic. Luke's gospel indicates s/he would have been shocked and profoundly opposed to a Christian ritual meal the preparation and service of which were performed by men to the exclusion of women. Such a practice would be neither in the spirit nor the literal character of Lukan meal imagery.

## Female Figures in the Teaching of Jesus

There are female figures in Jesus' teaching in the gospel of Luke. The first instance is in Jesus' sermon at Nazareth (4:25–26). The other instances involve parables (15:8–10, 18:1–8).

To illustrate that "no prophet is honored in his native place," Jesus appeals to Elijah and the widow of Sarepta of Sidon. In a time of drought and resulting famine, Elijah sought temporary refuge not with one of the many Israelite widows but with a Gentile widow. This example illustrates that the great prophet Elijah was a prophet to the Gentiles. Yet the reference to a woman Gentile is probably deliberate. Luke describes the widow as "a female widow" (4:26). While this phrase appears elsewhere, "widow" would suffice to convey the concept.[35] Luke's use of "female" to modify "widow" suggests Luke's conscious choice of a female Gentile in this passage.

Luke 15:8–10 is one of a series of three parables told to tax collectors and sinners (15:1) about the divine concern for those who are "lost" and the divine initiative taken to find them. In the parable of the lost coin, a woman with ten coins loses one, then lights a lamp, sweeps the house, and seeks diligently until she finds the lost coin (15:9). In the parable, she represents the deity just as the shepherd of the previous parable (15:1–7) and the father of the subsequent parable (15:11–32) do. The lost coin represents the tax collectors and sinners. The woman's industrious search for the coin represents the eager efforts undertaken by the deity to save the lost.

In the parable of the unrighteous judge, the woman represents the persistent, humble petitioner before the deity. The ultimately righteous act of the unrighteous judge, though done for the wrong reason, is the reward for her persistent pleading. The context of the parable is Jesus' exhortation to the disciples (17:22) to symbolize persistence in prayer. The unrighteous judge, badgered into a righteous act, is compared to the righteous deity from whom even more righteousness flows.

Thus woman has various roles in the teaching of Jesus. She is an image of the outcast chosen by the deity, an image of deity, a model of a persistent, prayerful posture before the deity, and the rewards for that posture.

## Feminine Imagery for Jesus' Self

When Jesus expresses his grief over what he foresees as the fate of Jerusalem (Luke 13:31–35), he speaks of Jerusalem as feminine (13:34), describing himself in relation to Jerusalem with feminine imagery. He describes his longing to protect and save Jerusalem from its destruction as the instinctive desire of a mother hen to gather her brood under her wings (13:35). Just as baby birds can resist being gathered under their mother's wing, Jerusalem did not want to be taken under the protection of Jesus (13:35). His grief is that of a mother whose young is lost.

## Other Women in Luke's Gospel

Among other women in the gospel of Luke is the woman in the crowd (11:27–28) whose macarism echoes and partially fulfills Mary's prophecy of her memory among future generations (1:48–49). Her macarism, "Blessed are those who hear the word of God and keep it," is tempered by Jesus' teaching response to it. The woman in the crowd underestimated herself. She can be as blessed or more so than the womb that bore Jesus if she responds to the word and keeps it.

The widow who gives two coins to the Temple but gives in abundance from what she has (21:1–4) is a living example of the kind of giving the deity requires and rewards. Implicit in the comparison between her gift and the gifts of the rich (21:1) is the suggestion that her gift is valued more. Herodias, wife of Herod's brother, is mentioned in Luke 3:19. She is the only woman of Luke's gospel who stands in the role in which patriarchal interpretations of Gen. 2–3 have traditionally placed Eve. She is the object, if not the cause, of Herod's sin. Still other women appear in the gospel such as the women of Jerusalem who weep for Jesus (23:27).[36]

## "Luke": A Woman Evangelist

Although not yet taken seriously by commentators of Luke-Acts, Leonard Swidler's hypothesis that the author of the gospel of Luke may have been a woman recommends itself as interesting.[37] Scholars agree that the actual authors of the gospels are anonymous.[38] It may be mere patriarchal bias, coupled with tradition born of that bias, which led to the church's conclusion that the canonical gospels were written by men. The presence of women, wealthy women, disciples throughout the gospel and Acts supports the possibility of a woman author (Luke 8:1–3; Acts 5:14, 8:3; 9:1–2; 16:14; 17:4, 12, 34; 22:4–5; etc.). Most of the passages about women special to Luke appear in sections of the gospel special to Luke (e.g., the infancy narratives).[39] The Hellenistic character of the gospel's author is widely acknowledged.[40] As Swidler argues, it is not unlikely that Jesus' women disciples preserved the stories about Jesus and women. A Hellenistic woman of some means, such as the converts at Thessalonica, or a woman like Lydia, may have been educated in the classical literature from which "Luke" draws literary forms and technique.

While such a hypothesis is not verifiable, neither, strictly speaking, is the hypothesis that a man wrote this gospel. Intellectual honesty demands consideration of this hypothesis. If, for the sake of convention and ease, Luke-Acts scholars continue to refer to this anonymous author as Luke, the use of strictly masculine pronouns in reference to this author should be avoided lest truth be obscured and the unwary led astray.

## Conclusion

This survey of the various women and their roles in the gospel of Luke indicates the following: women are significant to a full grasp of the theological meaning of Jesus' life and ministry. Women are viewed in this gospel as vehicles of revelation and voices of theological insight. They are important recipients of the messianic blessings made available through Jesus in his ministry. Women contribute by their heritage to Jesus' theological identity. Women are Jesus' disciples, perhaps even apostles. Women are full participants in the early Christian ritual meal and played a special role in its preparation and service. Women appear in the teaching material of Jesus, even in so exalted a position as the image for the deity. Jesus used feminine imagery to describe himself. And the author of this gospel may have been a woman.

This paper treats a subject some would dismiss as obvious, others as unnecessary, and some as obviously unnecessary. Unfortunately, the gospel material it treats has been neither widely acknowledged nor known. The implications of its content are yet to be developed, but the outline of such implications is evident and gaining in clarity and definition: a church that ignores ministry to women and does not acknowledge the ministry of women has betrayed Luke's Jesus and the salvation he sought to bring.

# NOTES

1. An attempt to treat biblical women in a comprehensive fashion is Leonard Swidler's *Biblical Affirmations of Women* (Philadelphia: Westminster, 1979). Phyllis Trible's *God and the Rhetoric of Sexuality* (Philadelphia: Fortress, 1978) explores, among other things, a new exegetical approach to Eve. Quentin Quesnell's "The Women at Luke's Supper" in R. J. Cassidy and P. J. Scharper, eds., *Political Issues in Luke-Acts* (Maryknoll, N.Y.: Orbis, 1983), 59–79 is a recent and important contribution to the discussion. Though not exegetical in character, Elisabeth Moltmann-Wendel's *The Women Around Jesus* (New York: Crossroad, 1982) is an interesting contribution. My paper "Luke: The Early Christian Ritual meal," presented at the 1983 national meeting of the Catholic Biblical Association for the Luke-Acts task force, examines the roles of women in the early Christian ritual meal. Women are getting more notice in the Lukan commentaries; see Charles Talbert's recent commentary *Reading Luke* (New York: Crossroad, 1982), 90–93.

2. Swidler, *Biblical Affirmations,* 254.

3. Swidler, *Biblical Affirmations,* 255.

4. Ibid.

5. Ibid. Luke has 23 unique women passages; Matthew has 10; John has 8; Mark has none.

6. Swidler, *Biblical Affirmations,* 255. Next is Matthew. Mark follows at some distance from Matthew. John is last.

7. Luke 1:5–7, 24–25, 26–56, 60–61; 2:4–7, 16–20, 22–24, 34–35, 38, 41–51.

8. Luke 2:36–38.

9. There are exegetical difficulties with a literal interpretation of the virgin birth. Jesus' Davidic origins, emphasized in Luke's description of Joseph as "of the house of David" (1:27; 2:4), in Jesus' place of birth as "David's city" (2:4, 11), in the genealogy (3:31), in Luke's adaption of the traditional title "Son of David" (18:38–39; 20:41), and in the David imagery of the infancy narratives which helps shape the theological identity of Jesus (1:32, 69) vanish. There are more references to David in Matthew's gospel (16) than in Luke's (12) and Matthew employs the title "Son of David" more frequently (nine times) than Luke (three times). Luke, however, develops the imagery of David's house (1:27, 69; 2:4) and throne (1:32). In Acts, David is viewed as

patriarch (1:16) and the author of the Psalms through whom the Holy Spirit prophetically spoke (1:16; 2:25, 29–30, 34; 4:25; 13:32–35). In Acts, the theological image of "the tent of David" is introduced (7:45; 15:16). Thus to sever the biological connection of Jesus and Joseph is to sever a theological question Luke elsewhere struggles to create.

10. In the ancient goddess traditions, the chief characteristic of the goddess was her virginity. Married or unmarried, she remained virgin, even as goddess of love. She was virgin and simultaneously "ancient and eternal Mother of God" whose divine son she preceded. She was not dependent on a husband in any way but bore divinity in her own right. Her virginity is an inner attitude. She is unconventional and independent in her virginity, "One-in-Herself," and is not defined as counterpart to a male. M. Esther Harding, *Women's Mysteries* (New York: Harper Colophon, 1976), 124–25.

11. Examples of direct address in Luke-Acts include the canticles, the announcements of the angels, and dialogues in the infancy narrative and the numerous instances of Jesus' teaching throughout the gospel.

12. Sarah (Gen. 16:1, 21:1–3), Rebecca (Gen. 25:21), Rachel (Gen. 29:31) and Hannah (1 Sam. 5:5) are biblical women in Luke's heritage whose lives reflect this pattern. Apart from its possible historical roots, this literary motif seems to have been an early Israelite myth for the birth of a great people. The same might be said of Jacob. Joseph, however, is more than a biological link to Israel's future. Joseph, though rejected by his brothers, saves his people from extinction. Samuel speaks for himself. Last of the great judges of Israel, Samuel is the architect of Israel's monarchy which will extend itself hundreds of years into Israel's future.

13. This the reader has learned from the angel's annunciation to Zacharias (1:13–18). Henceforward, except for the birth and naming of her son, Elizabeth disappears from Luke's narrative of Jesus' life.

14. As has been often noted by redaction critics in recent years, Luke structures the gospel narrative around "paired" incidents. Charles H. Talbert, *Literary Patterns, Theological Themes and the Genre of Luke-Acts,* SBL Monograph Series, no. 20 (Missoula, Mont.: Scholars Press, 1974). Frequently the pairs reflect a male-female component, that is, a male will figure in the first story of a pair of related stories and a woman in the second. This is evident throughout the infancy narrative. The appearance of the angel and announcement of Jesus' birth to Mary have their parallels in the appearance of the angel and announcement of John's birth to Zacharias. Zacharias's canticle parallels Mary's canticle. The parable of the lost sheep, in which a presumably male shepherd figures, parallels the parable of the lost coin in which a woman figures. See also Luke 4:25–26, 27; Luke 7:11–17; 8:40–42, 49–56.

15. This is true of the synoptic tradition in general but is especially true in Mark where the women are a special class of the unclean and Jesus' ministry is dramatized as a mission to the unclean.

16. "They," who ask (4:38), has no clear noun of reference in the preceding verses. Its use by Luke may indicate edition in the text. In Mark, Jesus has

already called Simon, Andrew, James, and John (1:16–20) before he goes with them (1:29) to Simon's house. To the extent that Luke has retained a call-of-the-disciples narrative, it appears after the story of Peter's mother-in-law (5:1–11). Thus the pronoun, which makes perfect sense in Mark, is vague and unclear in Luke, perhaps intentionally or perhaps carelessly.

17. *epetimesen to pureto.* The verb used is the same verb used to describe the expulsion of demons (e.g., 4:41).

18. Notice that the appearance of Peter's mother-in-law in the text points to the implied presence of another woman, namely, Peter's wife.

19. Except for the raising of Jairus' daughter and the raising up of Jesus, this uniquely Lukan passage is the only other resurrection narrative in the gospel. That it foreshadows Jesus' resurrection is a distinct possibility. Mary is portrayed as if widowed where she appears in Jesus' adult life. The reference to the widow's "only begotten son" is unlikely to refer to Jesus in view of Luke 8:19–21, unless "only begotten" is a metaphor for unique salvific experience.

20. Notice that many of the women characters in the gospels are without names.

21. A worthwhile question, which commentators often do not reach, is why was this woman crying? Was she crying in sorrow, repentance, shame? Or was she crying because she was a woman whose ultimate self-worth had never been acknowledged by any other man than Jesus? J. Fitzmeyer does raise the question, albeit in a footnote, in his exhaustive volume *The Gospel According to Luke I–IX* (New York: Doubleday, 1982), 689. He speculates her tears may have been tears of joy at the realization of her forgiveness.

22. Robert Maddox, *The Purpose of Luke-Acts* (Edinburgh: T. & T. Clark, 1982), 48–50, 54 finds in Luke 13 the theme of the judgment of Judaism for its refusal of Jesus' mission, a theme he thinks extends into the passion narrative. If one focuses on the fig tree as the central image of the chapter, however, the theme of the chapter may be viewed as that of divine judgment on Jerusalem and the Temple for failure to respond to the demands of the divine call. The reference to those killed by a falling tower and those killed by Pilate illustrate that a tragic death need not imply personal failure and guilt, a point especially important in light of Jesus' coming fate. The story of the bent-over woman (13:10–17), included in the chapter, takes on new meaning if this is the theme of the chapter. The failure of institutional Judaism, even the synagogue, to raise woman from her oppressed status is interpreted by Luke as a cause for the destruction of Jerusalem and the Temple.

23. Judith Plaskow, in her essay, "Blaming the Jews for the Birth of Patriarchy" in E. Torton Beck, ed., *Nice Jewish Girls* (Watertown, Mass.: Persephone Press, 1982), 250–54, writes of "a new myth developing in Christian circles" that the Hebrews invented patriarchy. She decries the development of this "myth" as a perpetuation of Christianity's negative picture of Judaism "by attributing sexist attitudes to Christianity's Jewish origins, (and) at the same time maintaining that Christianity's distinctive contributions to the 'woman

question' are largely positive" (250). To my knowledge, no Christian feminist takes the position that the Hebrews invented patriarchy. Rather, Hebrew religion was born at a time and in a culture in which patriarchy was assuming cultural dominance. Likewise, Christian feminists distinguish between the largely positive contribution of Jesus to the woman question, and the largely negative contribution of the apostolic and post-apostolic church. While it *is* important for Christian feminists to acknowledge the diversity within rabbinic Judaism, the emergence of rabbinic Judaism after Jesus' death, and the likely hypothesis that Jesus' liberal stand toward women came from a liberal tradition within Judaism, this does not negate the patriarchal character of Judaism, the openness of Jesus to women or the patriarchal character of the church. To argue, as Plaskow does, that the real motive behind Christian feminist presentations of Jesus' Jewish background is to present true Christian tradition as uniquely free from sexism is, in my opinion, patently absurd. Such arguments are designed to promote a greater openness to women in a modern, patriarchal church.

24. McKenzie speaks of mere passing allusions to the Aaronic exodus traditions, citing 1 Sam. 12:6, 8; Ps. 77:21; 105:26; 106:16 and Mic. 6:4; see John L. McKenzie, *Dictionary of the Bible* (Milwaukee, Wis.: Bruce Publishing Co., 1965), 1.

25. Talbert, *Literary Patterns,* 90–93. Quesnell, "The Women," 67-70. Elizabeth Schussler Fiorenza, *In Memory of Her* (New York: Crossroad, 1983), 130–40.

26. Swidler, *Biblical Affirmations,* 304–305.

27. Quesnell, "The Women," 68.

28. Ibid.

29. E. J. Via, "Woman, the Discipleship of Service, and the Early Christian Ritual Meal in the Gospel of Luke," in *St. Luke's Journal of Theology* (June 1985).

30. Acts 9:1–2.

31. Via, "Woman, the Discipleship."

32. Romans 16:7 describes Junia as "outstanding among the apostles." Bernadette Brooten writes of Romans 16:7: "Whereas for John Chrysostom the apostle addressed by Paul is a woman named Junia, for almost all modern scholars it is a man, Junias, whom Paul is greeting. . . . The earliest commentator on Rom. 16:7, Origen of Alexandria (c. 185–253/54) took the name to be feminine . . . as did Jerome (340/50–419/20), Hatto of Vercelli (924–961), Theophylact (1050–1108) and Peter Abelard (1079–1142). In fact . . . no commentator on the text until Aegidius of Rome (1245–1316) took the name to be masculine." See B. Brooten, "Junia . . . Outstanding Among the Apostles," in Leonard and Arlene Swidler, eds., *Women Priests: A Catholic Commentary on the Vatican Declaration* (New York: Paulist Press, 1977), 141–44.

33. Via, "Woman, the Discipleship."

34. Ibid.

35. William F. Arndt and F. Wilbur Gingrich, *A Greek-English Lexicon of the New Testament* (Cambridge: University Press, 1957), 889–92.

36. Also of interest are four women left out of Luke's gospel or unknown to Luke. They are the four women, three of whom are Gentile, who Matthew included in the genealogy of Matt. 1:1–16: Tamar (1:3), Rachab (1:5), Ruth (1:5) and Bath-sheba (1:6). Luke does, of course, use a genealogy for Jesus (3:23–38) which may have come from the hypothetical Q source allegedly containing the material common to Luke and Matthew but not found in Mark and John. Could Luke have known a genealogy such as Matthew's and deliberately edited from it the names of these widows? Given Luke's positive interest in both Gentiles and women, this solution seems unlikely despite the major differences between their genealogies. It is more likely to assume Matthew altered the genealogical source to include the names of these women.

37. Swidler, *Biblical Affirmations*, 271.

38. Norman Perrin, *The New Testament: An Introduction*, 2d ed. (New York: Harcourt, Brace, Jovanovich, 1982), 257, 264.

39. Swidler, *Biblical Affirmations*, 261.

40. Perrin, *The New Testament*, 293 96.

# The Feminine Aspect of God in Christianity

## WALTER GARDINI

The masculine aspect of God has predominated the history of Christian philosophy and praxis. The first truth asserted in the Nicean Creed of Constantinople is: "I believe in God, almighty Father, creator of Heaven and Earth." This almighty God dwells in heaven and speaks to man through burning flames. Man is dust (Gen. 3:19; 18:27; etc.), mere creature and servant (Pss. 115:16; 142:12 . . . ). He cannot see God and continue living (Deut. 5:25). "At his wrath the earth shall tremble" (Jer. 10:10). The prophets proclaim the strictest monotheism and struggle especially against idolatrous cults of different goddesses (I Kings 14:22–24; 15:11–14; 2 Kings 21:3–7).

This living God, terrible judge, appears again in the New Testament. He "is consuming fire" (Heb. 12:29). He will destroy sinners (Matt. 21:41). The Christian ought to attain salvation in fear of God (Eph. 5:21; 6:5) as it is "a hideous thing to fall in his hands" (Heb. 12:29). This masculine and monotheistic image of God in the Old Testament is reinforced by the doctrine of the eternal son born to a virgin in time. In Jesus Christ masculinity is given a divine status while women remain as mere creatures.

In this doctrinal context, Jewish-Christian religion received a masculine structure as only men were nearly exclusively in contact with God; they elaborated the dogmas, organized and presided over the Christian community. Women were given a marginal place. The God of Abraham, Isaac and Jacob did not turn out to be, in the same way, the God of Sarah, Rebecca and Rachel.

The hierarchy—God, man, woman—brought about a legislation of masculine privileges in the Old Testament (divorce law) and also in the New Testament (1 Cor. 14:34–35; 1 Tim. 2:12). Paul gave theological sanction to this fact with the doctrine of the "head": "I would have you know that the head of every man is Christ, and the head of the woman is the man" (1 Cor. 11:3).

This theology justifies subjection of woman to man as the body is subject to the impulses given by the head (1 Cor. 3:22–23; Eph. 5:23). According to this theory the image of God in man shares divine perfection in a higher degree than in woman, "because man is the origin of woman, as God is the beginning and end of every creature."[1] Gratian openly says, in the twelfth century, "Woman was not made in the image of God,"[2] quoting words attributed to St. Augustine.

Accordingly, ecclesiastical structures have been centered around men. In the Catholic Church this center is the parish priest, the bishop and finally the Holy Father. Authority and rights come from above while, in the lower echelons, subjection and dependence prevail. Obedience shines as a cardinal virtue, and insubordination appears as a capital sin.

In their request for a just and fair treatment, women are also asking for a change in ecclesiastical matters. Protestants and, to a lesser degree, Catholics have started to give more responsibility to women. Can theology give a ground for the requests of present feminist movements? In particular, could not the traditional image of God be an insurmountable obstacle? Ought the whole thing to be rejected? Or is it possible to undertake a new exegesis of the Bible? And to what extent?

## The Image of the Biblical God

A basic postulate of biblical exegesis is that revelation always has a historical frame and obeys the law of incarnation. The Jewish people had a patriarchal organization and the socio–cultural consequence of this was the predominance of male over female. With the foundation of cities, man gradually controlled the instruments of social power. An antifeminist attitude developed, evident in the Yahwist's biblical description of the creation of Eve, the original fall, and the later exegesis made, obviously, from a masculine point of view.

The biblical writers were not able to overcome the prevailing discriminatory patterns of their culture and projected their socio-cultural categories on the image of God presented as the guardian of the social laws of the time. The divine revelation could have been understood and accepted in no other way. This situation did not change in the New Testament and later centuries. Thus, the almighty male God is the reflection of male predominance in a society where women have a marginal place. However, this historical conditioning does not exhaust the doctrine contained in revelation. There are other aspects which create an inner tension and lead to a more complete image of God.

The first is found in the Priestly Code, written around 6–5 B.C.E., which is contained in the first page of the Bible. Opposing the antifeminist spirit of the time, the sacred author affirms forcefully: "God created man [humanity] to his image . . . male and female, he created them" (Gen. 1:27). "Male and female" are not to be understood in a hermaphrodite sense, but with reference to a couple made up of two equal beings. They are the "key" to understand the image of God. God is neither masculine nor feminine, nor a combination of the two; but the placing of the divine transcendence within human reality requires some human symbols and, among these, sexuality is one of the most important.

God created a male and a female in his image. Therefore to discover the masculinity and the femininity is like perceiving the image of God. Not only man, but also woman is the image of God. The feminine is also contained within God as its source and its prototype. It is interesting to observe that God is spoken of in a plural way: "Let us make man in our image" (Gen. 1:26). This plural expresses the majesty and wealth of God whose common name in Hebrew, as used in this text, is the plural form *Elohim*. God, being feminine and masculine, does not live in absolute solitude.

Could one invoke him as Mother in the same way as we invoke him as Father? The answer seems affirmative. One can already begin to see this in texts of the Old Testament, and it becomes more explicit in the New Testament in certain trends of theology.

## The Maternal God in the Old Testament

In the prophetic literature and the Psalms, God is represented through feminine images. This is done in contexts which express the fidelity of God to Israel and the pain he suffers because of the ingratitude of the people. To describe this situation the Bible does not find adequate analogies in masculine activity and so appeals to the image of the mother who gives birth to a son and maintains a wholehearted love to the fruit of her womb. "God as a woman in labour cries out, gasping and panting" (Isa. 42:14). "Can a mother forget her infant?... Even should she forget, I will never forget you" (Isa. 49:15).

In other passages, where the mercy of God is evoked, the image of the mother, although not named explicitly, is present in the background. "I fostered them like one who raises an infant to his cheeks. ... I stooped to feed my child" (Hos. 11:4). "Remember that your compassion, O Lord, and your kindness are from of old" (Ps. 25:6; Cf. Ps. 116:5; 22:9–11). While being Lord, God acts maternally.

The attributes of power and justice are secondary, compared to the statement that he is love and that all his actions are manifestations of his benevolence towards all men. "His anger lasts but a moment; a lifetime, his goodwill" (Ps. 30:6). To avoid the identification of his image with the one of a rigid and repressive God, he is compared to a kind and faithful husband (Hos. 2 and *Song of Songs*).

All these elements converge in the wisdom literature on the feminine image of *Sophia* who mediates in the work of creation and plays an important role in the reconciliation of man with God (Prov. 8:24–26; Wisd. of Sol. 7–9). She is a divine reality who has existed since eternity and will exist forevermore. She has come out of the mouth of the Almighty as spoken word. "She is an aura of the might of God and a pure effusion of the glory of the Almighty... the refulgence of the eternal light; the spotless mirror of the power of God, the image of his goodness" (Wisd. of Sol. 7:25). She dwells in heaven, seated next to the throne of God and lives in close relation with Him as his wife (Wisd. of Sol. 24:4; 9:4; 8:2). She was with God when he created heaven and earth and resides now in fellowship with man (Prov. 8:27–31). She leads history and is the bearer of salvation for all. Without her, God does nothing in the world.

What and who is this *Sophia*?

For some, she is simply a divine attribute poetically elaborated. According to others, she is a personification of God himself under a feminine image.[3] In reality, a close relationship is established between wisdom and woman, and a symbolic transmutation takes place between one and the other (Prov. 19:14; 31:10; 26:30). In this image certain specific characteristics of the goddesses of the Ancient Near East, as Isis or Astarte, shine through, imagined as redemptive and creative. The open-minded atmosphere of

Hellenism favored this inculturation. However, we do not advance further than a poetical figure.[4]

The image of *Sophia* disappears from orthodox rabbinical thought after the advent of the Christian era, possibly due to her use in gnosticism. On the other hand, it will be used again by Paul and John and applied to Christ, Incarnate Verb and Wisdom of God. Christian traditions in their investigations of the Trinity will apply it also to the Holy Spirit.

## The Trinitarian Image of God

Jesus revealed God as Father and made himself known as Son by the power of the Holy Spirit. The Father expresses the divine reality inasmuch as he is the beginning without origin of everything, the source from which everything comes forth and to which everything returns. The Son is that same reality, self-communicated as Truth of His own self. The Holy Spirit is the same reality inasmuch as it produces loving acceptance in the one who receives it. In the doctrine of the Trinity we speak of three moments in the only self-communication of God. The unfathomable mystery comes out of its darkness and manifests itself as light (knowledge) and shows itself as a gift (love) without losing its character of unexplainable mystery.

From this view, the title of Father that Jesus bestows on God carries a special sense: it is no longer related to the creation of the world but to the generation of the Son; it is not the reflection of a patriarchal conception, but the revelation of that inner wealth, already visible in the Old Testament, by virtue of which God begets and gives birth to a Son. All this puts us in the presence of a maternal Father. We cannot only represent God as unisexually masculine; we must consider him bisexual or transsexual. In this sense the words of St. John about the "bosom of the Father" (John 1:18) can be understood.[5]

In like terminology the Council of Toledo, in the year 675, stated: "We must believe that the Son does not come from the void nor from any other substance; he has been begotten and born from the maternal womb of the Father, that is, from his substance." This is what is proclaimed in the creed: "Begotten from the Father before all time," through which the origin of the Son from the Father is designated.

## The Feminine Aspect of God in Christianity

The Christian doctrine of the Trinity overcomes patriarchal monotheism and, asserting the maternal character of the Father, represents a first step towards overcoming the masculine language of God. It lays the foundations for that community of women and men without subordination or privileges, asserted by St. Paul: "There is neither male nor female, for you are all one" (Gal. 3:29), and also justifies the attribution of the title of "Mother" to God.

The first to make use of it was Clement of Alexandria (3 C.E.). Reflecting on the divine maternity of Mary, he states: "God is love and it is precisely because of that love that we search for him. In his ineffable majesty he is our Father, but in his compassion towards us, has become mother. In his love the Father became mother to us."[6] St. Anselm of Canterbury addresses Jesus as his Mother: "And thou, Jesus, Good Lord, art thou also Mother? Is it not true that mother is, like a hen gathers her chickens under her wings? Truthfully, Lord, thou art my Mother."[7] Juliana of Norwich, the great English mystic of the fourteenth century, in her *Revelations of the Divine Love* also refers often to God as "our loving Mother" where the love and benevolence of the Holy Spirit make up the one unique God and the one unique Love.[8] In the oriental Christian tradition Gregory Palamas and others emphasize the feminine and maternal dimension of God.

These quotations must not beguile us; generally they are isolated voices. The vast majority of writers use masculine metaphors. Only in recent decades has the God–Mother theme been taken up again within the context of women's liberation.[9] There is a consent in denouncing the conditioned thoughts of the past and in asserting the analogical character of theological language. God dwells in an inaccessible light and is beyond the sexes. He is pure spirit and surpasses all determinations including sexual ones. When saying he is "Father," one affirms and negates something about him: he possesses the conceptual perfection of paternity elevated to an infinite dimension and so he is the source of all good.

From this premise, Leonardo Boff makes reference to Carl G. Jung, who detects the presence of *anima* (feminine principle) in each male and of *animus* (masculine principle) in each woman. Every human being is simultaneously *anima* and *animus,* although in different proportions. The human being is a unity that takes form in multiple differences; it is essentially polar and multiple. In the historical salvation experience of the trinitarian God as the original, ultimate source, one can discover analogically the same structure that is found in the human being: there is a plural unity, a pluralism of ways of being and existence of the One. It is a mysterious and inaccessible depth (feminine) and, at the same time, self-communication in truth and love (masculine). "In this sense," Boff concludes, "Triune and One God, mysterious and distant, fascinating and tremendous, may be invoked as Father and as Mother."[10]

In the incarnation, the Son is humanized, assuming the masculine form and implicitly the feminine. By means of the hypostatic union, the humanity of Jesus must be considered as the humanity of God himself. In this manner, by means of the eternal Verb, the masculine was made divine and eternal, whereas the feminine was made so only indirectly.

"Can we not expect," L. Boff questions, "that also the feminine be assumed in the same way, as the masculine was in an immediate and full manner?"[11] His answer is affirmative. The Holy Spirit would be the divine person who assumes the feminine directly and makes it divine.

## The Eternal Feminine in God: The Holy Spirit and Mary

In Hebrew, the Holy Spirit is feminine (*ruah*) and is always associated with life, with creativity, with generation. Its winging over the waters at the moment of creation conveys the fluttering of a bird or of a dove. Clement of Alexandria, already quoted, identifies the womb of God with the Holy Spirit, the invisible and ineffable abyss only accessible to the Verb, the ineffability of God.[12]

The Gnostics correlated the ancient mother goddess with the Holy Spirit and saw God himself in Him in his voluntary and free fertility.[13] St. Efren, in the fourth century, referred to the Holy Spirit as mother, the eternal feminine within God.[14] St. Nicholas of Flüe, the Swiss ascetic (15 C.E.), describes a vision in which the Trinity appeared to him in the form of God Father, God Mother and God Son.[15]

The image of the Holy Spirit as mother fits with Christian dogma and makes for a clear enunciation and understanding of it. Though proceeding from the first two divine persons, the Holy Spirit is in the midst of them, since he is love and unites the Father to the Son and the Son to the Father. In this interpersonal relationship his specific role is defined as maternal character and he keeps this also in his worldly actions.

## The Feminine Aspect of God in Christianity

In the conception of the historical Christ, the Spirit and Mary do not proceed as two partners but rather *ad modum unius,* as one person, related to the Father. In the same manner as the Spirit is united substantially to the justified soul of every Christian, so is established a relationship with Mary, which some French and orthodox Russian theologians have called hypostatic and which is more commonly referred to as nearly formal self-communication of the divinity.[16] Mary is transformed into the abode of the Spirit, the place of his presence and his action in the world. The Spirit spiritualizes her and makes her divine to enable her to be the mother of God in the flesh.

This process of spiritualization, already prepared in the immaculate conception of Mary, took place in the Annunciation. From that moment, the Spirit assumed in Mary all that took place in her life until her plenitude in the Assumption. It was then, at the end and culmination of her life, that the plenitude of the spiritualization took place. The eternal feminine was joined to the feminine created to associate it eternally to the mystery of the Holy Trinity. For that same reason, Mary became Queen of the Universe, Universal Mediatrix (dependent on Christ), Lady of Heaven and Earth. She came so close to divinity that she deserved to belong to the trinitarian circle, being definitely bound to the Holy Spirit and the Son made flesh.

The proclaiming of this dogma stimulated reflection on the ultimate meaning of the feminity of Mary within the Trinity. The Dominican theologian Victor White wrote, "Maybe this definition will lead the Church to a deeper and ultimate formulation of the abyssal mystery regarding the motherhood of God. The fact is that, in the Assumption, Mary returns to the fountainhead. Not she, but God is the ultimate prototype of motherhood and feminity. As Christ's Ascension into heaven took us to the arms of God, our eternal Father, it may be that Mary's Assumption will lead us to a deeper knowledge and love of God, our eternal mother."[17]

Jung considered the proclamation of the dogma of Mary's Assumption a major event after the Reformation because it realized the demand for the deification of the female principle which can be found in the collective unconscious. It is worth noting his comment about J. Fouquet's painting (15 C.E.) where three identical masculine figures are placed together with a female figure, but this last one is placed a little lower. Jung admits that

63

Christianity never deified Mary but gave her a divine status owing to her proximity to God.[18]

This is practically visible in the manifestations of popular devotion to Mary. Sometimes these cults include deviations and exaggerations which have been pointed out by evangelical observers; but at the basis of this piety is the people's intuition of the presence of the Holy Spirit in Mary. The expressions used, surprising as they may be, are all addressed through Mary, to the Holy Spirit which dwells and acts in her. In the same way we are to understand the sapiential texts of the Old Testament used in the Marian liturgy.

According to Erich Fromm the Marian cult, which started to be propagated during the fourth century, is a renaissance of the cult of the Great Mother defeated by Yahve. This revival could be one to explain the success of Christianity. Mary nursing the child Jesus was the dominant figure of medieval Christendom. Protestantism meant a return to God the Father.[19] In practical Catholicism the image of Mary predominates, but it is openly recognized "that some expressions of her cult, although valid in itself, are less adapted to different civilizations." In a society which is already awakened to the subject of women's liberation, and where men and women in some places are enslaved by unjust political and economical systems, God's image takes the attribute of liberator from injustice, and Mary is "the strong woman, who shared poverty and suffering and knew retreat and exile; she did not hesitate to assert that God is the avenger of the poor and the humble who dethrones the powerful of this world."[20]

Mary appears to be the most adequate way to understand the material aspect of God, "the sacrament of divine tenderness" (P. Claudel), the most perfect historical expression of God's feminine aspect. She is completely related to the ultimate root and the supreme source of perfection.

## New Trends and Initiatives

The renewal of the cult of Mary parallels the re-evaluation of the maternal aspect of God. During a public audience Pope John Paul I said: "God is Father, but above all Mother."[21] His predecessor, too, had recognized that God is Father as well as Mother.

The religious activities organized on the basis of male categories have started to be questioned as relative ones. God is above the sexes. Self-revelation of God in history uses the symbol of the father, but also the symbol of the mother. There is no reason why we should not be able to call the first person of the Trinity Mother instead of Father; also, we could imagine creation as being effected by an ultimate maternal principle.

In the Catholic area an effort is taking place to make Christians conscious of this fact by means of the following invocation: "In the name of the Father and the Mother, in the name of the Son and the Holy Spirit," ending with: "God bless you and protect you. May She make his face shine upon you and may She give you peace."[22] There have been some proposals to use only the word "Mother," but this is the other extreme to be avoided. Both maternal and paternal aspects have to be involved.

Others are in search of new symbols. They consider less ambiguous and more suitable natural symbols such as "vivifying wind, water of life, light, fountainhead of all good." These symbols would not be associated with the idea of power or authority; they are more ecumenical in scope and also nearer to the expressions of Indian religions,[23] but the personal discourse, which is an outstanding characteristic of Christianity, is lost. Besides, sex categories seem to express essential aspects of human experience more adapted to approach the divine mystery. Others have noted the correspondence between the Christian doctrine of the Holy Spirit and the Hindu idea of *shakti,* the generating strength, the creative power of God, thought of as female in Hinduism.[24]

The theology of the cross, connected with the Jewish conception of theopathy, pays attention to the suffering and crucified God. The pain and passion of Christ affect the Father. "Our liberation from pain and redemption from suffering springs up from the suffering of the whole Trinity: the agony of the Son, the anguish of the Father and the patience of the Spirit. God liberates for life through suffering love. What is divine is love, not the power, superiority and omnipotence of Patriarchalism. The afflicted Mother with her son, upon her knees, the 'Piety,' would be the expression of the feminine aspect of God's suffering."[25]

It is to be hoped that investigations will increase and also concrete steps will be carried out to give women the importance they deserve in the liturgical and pastoral activities of the churches. Putting discussions aside, we must not lose sight, however, of the essential acceptance of finitude and creatureness. In the symbol of the father submission and obedience are underlined; in the symbol of the mother dependence is changed into a confidence which liberates from dread and anguish. The extremes join: power and proximity, dependence and trust, strength and mercy. The union of these symbols appears as the image of a new humanity where "There is neither Jew nor Greek; there is neither bond nor free; there is neither male nor female" (Gal. 3:28) because God "has broken down the middle wall of partition, the enmities in his flesh" (Eph. 2:14).

# NOTES

1. Thomas Aquinas, *Summa Theologica,* I,a q. 93 a 4 res. 1.

2. Decretum Gratiani, q. 5, causa 33.

3. Wilfrid J. Harrington, *Iniciaciòn a la Biblia* (Santander: Sal Terrae, 1967), 1: 405.

4. Raphael Patai, *The Hebrew Goddess* (New York: Ktav, 1967) has traced the heritage of the ancient goddess of the Near East who appears in a hidden form in Hebrew theology.

5. Phyllis Trible, *God and the Rhetoric of Sexuality* (Philadelphia: Fortress Press, 1978), 21.

6. *Quis dives salvetur* 37, 1; P.G. 9, 641–644.

7. *Oratio* 10: P.L. 158, 40–41.

8. *Revelations of Divine Love* (London: Burns & Oates, 1952), 119.

9. Mary Daly, *Beyond God the Father: Toward a Philosophy of Women's Liberation* (Boston: Beacon, 1973); Leonardo Boff, *O rostro materno de Deus* (Petropolis: Vozes, 1979); "Un Dios Padre?," *Concilium* (March 1981); M. Adinolfi, *Il Femminismo della Biblia* (Roma: Antonianum, 1981); Phyllis Trible, "Depatriarchalizing in Biblical Interpretation," *Journal of the American Academy of Religion* 41 (1973): 31–34; J. E. Burns, *God as Woman and Woman as God* (New York: Paulist-Paramus, 1976); F. Armendariz, "El Padre materno," *Estudios Eclesiasticos* 58 (1983): 249–275; A. Gibellini, *La afida del femminismo alla Teologia* (Brescia: Queriniana, 1984).

10. Boff, *O rostro materno,* 111.

11. Ibid., 113.

12. *Stromata* V, 12.81.3.

13. Cf. A. Orbe, *La Teologia del Espìritu Santo* (Roma: Gregoriana, 1966), 69–116.

14. Donald Nicholl, *Recent Thought in Focus* (London: Sheed, 1952), 90.

15. Marie Luise von Franz, *Dreams and Visions of St Nikolaus von der Flüe* (Zurich: 1957), Lecture 8.

16. M. Dupuy, "L'Esprit Saint et Marie dans l'École française," *Bulletin de la société française d'études mariales* 26 (1969): 21–38; Paul Evdokimov, *La mujer y la salvación del mundo* (Barcelona: Ariel, 1970).

17. Victor White, "The scandal of the Assumption," *Life of the Spirit* 5 (1950): 211–212.

18. Carl G. Jung, *Zur Psychologie westlicher und oestlicher Religion,* Sämtliche Werke, 11 (Zürich: Rascher, 1963), 498–499; 16, 185–186; also Jung, *Psicologia y Religion* (Buenos Aires: Paidos, 1961).

19. Erich Fromm, *El dogma de Cristo* (Buenos Aires: Paidos, 1964), 72–75.

20. Paulus VI, *Marialis Cultus* (1974) nn. 36–37.

21. Quoted in Boff, *O rostro materno,* 109.

22. Dorothee Soelle, "Padre, Poder y Barbarie," *Concilium* 163 (1981): 408.

23. Ibid., 409.

24. D. Spada, "Dio come Madre. Un tema di Teologia ecumenica," *Euntes Docete* 29 (Roma: 1976): 472–81.

25. Jürgen Moltmann, "El Padre maternal," *Concilium* 163 (1981): 388. Cf. J. Moltmann, *Der Gekreuzigte Gott* (Munich: Christian Kaiser Verlag, 1972).

# 5

# Theology and Sexuality
## GEORGE H. TAVARD

Some years ago it was fashionable in ecumenical circles to accept the slogan, "The world sets the agenda for the church." This was of course founded on the idea that the church is, by at least one of its basic dimensions, to serve God's purpose in the world. The same slogan is not so fashionable today. For one thing, one has discovered or re-discovered that the agenda of the world is not a straightforward expression of God's design; it is also, in the politics of power which dominate relations among nations, the expression of the sinfulness of human beings and of what classical theology called original sin. Whether we attribute this to the existence of a cosmic or infra-cosmic evil force—called Satan or the devil—or to the ambiguities and the demonic possibilities of all created existence, the result is the same: the church must sift through the world's agenda before it can discover what it ought to borrow from this agenda.

Among the prominent items of the world's agenda in our time, there has been a sexual revolution: a revolution in mores, in acceptability of behavior, in the gradual acceptance of divorce as normal even among Christians, in the legal, social, and even at times moral acceptance of abortion, in the leveling of Christian marriage to secular marriage. Should this also entail a theological revolution about the nature and meaning of sexuality?

This question, however, cannot be answered today without doing justice to the contemporary developments of the anthropological sciences which in turn raise some questions for theology: is an anthropocentric turn legitimate for theological thinking, which is, by definition, centered on the knowledge and worship of God? Assuming the legitimacy of such a turn, what can the cost be, that is, how many traditional doctrines or assumptions in theology and ethics will need reformulation? To what extent should the concept of God be influenced by the changing experience of what it is to be human? Is there something, in the contemporary anthropological sciences—such as psychology, depth-psychology, sociology, ethnology, linguistics, semiotics—that is of immediate interest and relevance to theological thinking? Among the human sciences that may or should influence modern theology, should we also count Marxism, which some of its adepts—at least in the most "orthodox" Communist parties—consider to be not only a philosophy, but also a science?

## The Classical Theological Tradition about Sexuality

As we try to answer such questions, it becomes apparent that the theological tradition about sexuality is in fact not well known, even among theologians. Indeed, one gets the impression from reading in the area of sexual ethics, that no theological tradition is now considered, if not normative, at least relevant. The practice in the churches has largely aligned itself with that in secular society. At the time of Tertullian it was possible to consider Christians as forming, in the Roman Empire where they lived, a *tertium genus,* a third kind of people, alongside the Jews and the Gentiles. At this time there seems to be only one kind, the secular one, with more or less sectarian pockets, like those of Orthodox Jews or Trappist Monks.

The theological tradition regarding sexuality began with the church fathers, at the time when classical Christianity shaped its interpretation of the scriptural data.[1] One finds two general orientations among the church fathers.

In the first, sexuality belongs to the universe of sin. This view itself follows two different lines. One may be identified with Augustine for whom sexuality belongs to the original creation and therefore to the primary plan for God for humankind. Yet, after the fall, its exercise is tainted with sin. On the one hand, it transmits, together with life, original sin; on the other, it is not itself practiced without some degree of at least minor sin. Marriage is tolerated rather than esteemed. Yet Augustine is able to find a triple goodness in marriage, summed up in the three words, *fides, proles, sacramentum* (mutual commitment and fidelity, procreation and education of children, sacramental grace).

The other line may be identified with that of Gregory of Nyssa. Here, sexuality does not belong to the original creation, which was sexless, but results from original sin. In both positions, the image of God is located in the human soul as such, beyond the distinction between male and female. In the concrete order, however, Gregory finds in woman no more than social inferiority, which therefore may be temporary; Augustine finds in her real inferiority, which is necessarily permanent: her only purpose as female is to assist the male in relation to *proles*.

The second orientation is a minority position, which may be instanced from Basilius of Ancyra. Sexuality belongs to the original order of creation. It is not only bodily, but also psychological. The whole female radiates sex appeal and the whole male responds to it. This is meant to serve as an inducement to procreation. In this there is, between male and female, difference rather than superiority or inferiority. At the level of *nous,* as naked souls, men and women are simply human and therefore equal. There is no special tie between sexuality and sin. Yet—we are in a Platonic philosophical climate—the perfect life is that of the naked soul, whether its body be male or female.

Modern theology has been more affected in this area by scholastic speculation than directly by patristic reflection. It was fundamentally the Augustinian tradition which prevailed in the medieval schools but in a form that was somehow distorted by Aristotelian hylomorphism.[2] Briefly, hylomorphism proposes a model which is applicable to all created reality, allowing one to understand its inner structure and, accordingly, the laws of its behavior. It is the idea that everything contingent or created is composed of two co-principles of being, neither of which is complete and subsistent in itself, each needing the other to subsist. Since being can be conceived as potential or as actual, all concrete being has aspects of potentiality and aspects of actuality. More simply: it can be and it also is. As the being comes to be, its potentialities are gathered in what is called matter, and its actualities in what is called form. It is the form that is; but the form is because of the underlying possibilities or potentialities that it makes actual.

Under the influence of the metaphysics of Aristotle, as rediscovered in the course of the thirteenth century, theologians applied this model to such Christian realities as the sacraments. In the case of matrimony, male and female were seen to function as form and matter. And since each of them, the male and the female, is a concrete being in the first place, each is also comprised of form and matter. Thus we have a female form (woman's soul) which, in relation to the male, is like matter. The female form relates to the male form as matter relates to form. If this is the case, then the male is in the realm of human nature a higher form of humanity than the female, even though each needs the other. Then it follows that, since nature spontaneously aims at perfection, the conception and production of a female have to be seen as inferior and to be explained as an accident of nature, although it is for the future of the human race a necessary accident. Hence the supposedly natural and social inferiority of woman.

To this summary of the medieval conception, one should, however, add two provisos. In the first place, scholastic theologians always affirm that, as images of God, male and female are equal. As the image of God is located in the soul, it then follows that something in the soul lies outside and above sexuality. No responsible theologian today would accept the scholastic explanation of female inferiority, or the intrinsic dichotomy by which woman would be Christianly equal, but socially inferior, to the male. Yet belief in a natural inferiority of woman has shaped the very structure of western society and, perhaps, much of the structure and canon law of the Christian churches.

In the second place, the Middle Ages in their social organization were in fact not affected by Aristotelian scholasticism, which came to Europe too late to shape the basic feudal organization of society. As a result, medieval woman was an emancipated woman when compared with her sister of the Roman Empire and, still more, with her sister of the Greek cities. In many areas she was in fact more emancipated from male control than modern woman.[3]

It is only with the Renaissance that medieval woman began to lose her position in society. And this was not caused by Aristotelian philosophy but by a philosophical rediscovery of the pagan world of the Romans and the Greeks and by a progressive return of the legal systems of western Europe to Roman law. This law now superseded the Germanic common law which had chiefly ruled social relationships in the earlier Middle Ages.

The Reformers themselves functioned in a world in transition in which the politics of power were creating the modern system of nation states. And this system is founded in a legal convention according to which woman is, if not socially inferior (there are many women of high society who are inferior to no one), at least legally subordinate. Thus the rights of property, of inheritance, of social initiative, of education, all of these traditionally recognized to medieval woman, were being eroded in the sixteenth century.

The idea, popularized by Roland Bainton, that the Calvinist tradition promoted a new role for woman by fostering a conception of marriage as companionship, is pure fiction.[4] Marriage as companionship was precisely the medieval conception, which Calvin maintained, despite the humanist tradition of the Renaissance which was congenial with him in other areas.

If we now try to sum up the classical tradition as it is found in theological thought at the start of the modern age and, I presume, still prevails in some Christian circles, we may propose the following picture. God created humanity as Adam[5] (in the original, proper generic sense, rendered in Greek as *anthropos,* in Latin as *homo,* in Old English as *manncynn,* in contemporary German as *Mensch*). This humanity, however, was divided by the Creator as male and female. The patristic view that sexuality resulted from sin is not accepted (except perhaps by some Eastern Orthodox). Sexuality is seen as belonging to God's good creation. As a result, humankind is divided between two sexes. The relationship between these two halves of humankind is generally seen as one of complementarity. While they are equal before God and, generally, in their own eyes, male and female have different functions and roles.

Fundamentally, these functions are rooted in the differences of their bodies: the one made to conceive and carry the child, and then to nurture it until it can absorb common food, the other made to provide seed for conception and endowed with the strength necessary to feed and protect the family. It is generally assumed that bodily and social functions entail spiritual differences which directly affect the soul, although it is not clear or agreed whether these differences are due only to nature or are at least partly brought about by education: these spiritual differences are usually related to aggressiveness on the one hand, and patience, kindness, and warmth on the other.

## Some Important Modern Developments

Yet this general picture, which I have tried to draw fairly, is not really true to facts. Another element, which often passes unnoticed, is special to the modern world. This is the historical conjunction, which took place between the sixteenth and the twentieth century, of the difference between male and female and another human dichotomy, that of master and slave.

The distinction between master and slave was basic to many ancient societies, if not to all of them. The distinction was slowly transformed, mostly under the impact of Christian principles. There were no slaves in the Middle Ages, but there were serfs, tied to the land which itself had an owner. As the system of serfhood vanished progressively, it was succeeded by the appearance of two new classes, that of hired servants or domestics in wealthy households, and that of manual workers and employees in the budding industries which made the growing wealth of merchants, the burghers (who lived in a burgh or city) or *bourgeois* (who lived in a *bourg*). Thus the dialectics of labor relations transformed the differences of male and female, which were assimilated to those of master and slave.

After the shameful episodes of the slave trade, the direct result of Renaissance humanism and of American slavery, in which this humanism was reinterpreted by the Enlightenment, the dialectics of master and slave was succeeded, with the growth of capitalism, by the dialectics of owner/employer and worker/employee. The convergence of the male/female difference and owner/worker relationships resulted in the assimilation of the first to the second, with the dire consequence that woman, in the context of marriage, became an unsalaried worker. Already a legal minor in the eyes of the law, she was seen as the provider for the married man of free comforts, as the unpaid keeper of his home, and as the educator of his children. The laws applying to woman were patterned more and more on the laws regulating the ownership of property.[6] This is precisely what the woman-liberation movement, in its various forms from the early suffragettes to our own days, has been reacting against.

However, this is not the whole perspective. One cannot assess the problem of womanhood as a contemporary theological problem without giving its due to the new understanding of sexuality which followed the "discovery" of the unconscious by Sigmund Freud. This is not unrelated to the master/slave dialectics, since it emerged in the bourgeois world of Vienna which would not have existed in the first place without the master/slave structure of wealth in the Austrian Empire. This is of course the reason why Freud and his followers have not been welcome in the Communist movement. Be that as it may, it is incumbent upon Christian theology to come to terms with the psychoanalytical view of sexuality.

Theology has to take cognizance of the fact that, since its inception by Freud, depth-psychology has turned—though not exclusively, in the schools of Jung and Adler or in the more recent existential psychoanalysis—to the analysis of the sexual act, of sexual fantasies, sexual abnormalities, etc. This has led to the conviction that whether it remains latent or becomes active, sexuality pertains to the deepest levels of personality, that from earliest infancy humans are sexually oriented, and that their sexual inclinations are predetermined by their earliest experiences. (Schools of psychoanalysis vary in their assessment of what is the earliest: Freud places this in the Oedipus complex, Lacan in the much earlier stage of the mirror.)[7] This has given rise to the opinion (now popularly held, and also shared by a number of psychologists) that the exercise of sexuality is normal (moral) and its non-exercise abnormal (immoral or at least personality-stifling). Theological reflection in dialogue with psychoanalysis is still in its infancy, despite the adoption of Freudian positions by a number of Catholic priests (e.g., Marc Oraison, Louis Beirnart, Antoine Vergote) and the, at times uncritical, popularity of Carl Jung in both Protestant and Catholic circles. Indeed, I sympathize with this popularity.

In the conclusion of *Woman in Christian Tradition,* I drew attention to the convergence between the position I was led to take and some of the conceptions of Jung.[8] Jung's theory of *animus* and *anima* as dimensions of the soul which are shared by all human beings, though in a sort of reversed way (the male being *animus* first and *anima* second, the female being *anima* first and *animus* second), presents a challenge to the assumed relationship of dialectical complementarity between the sexes which is commonly accepted in theology. I wish to complete this discussion with two considerations.

## The Insights of Psychoanalysis

The first relates to Freud and the basic lesson to be learned from him, although it could have been learned in other ways from basic human experience. Freud has successfully questioned the classical theological understanding of the purpose of sexuality. In this understanding, the basic mode of sexual existence is futuristic and altruistic: both sexes are turned to the future of the child to be conceived and born. Sexuality is for procreation. This is traditionally embedded in the Augustinian-Thomist approach to sex and marriage, and was expressed, in the context of the sacrament of matrimony, in the Roman Catholic code of canon law of 1921, canon 1013, §1: there is in marriage a hierarchy of purpose: procreation comes first, then mutual assistance, lastly the alleviation of concupiscence.

This triad corresponds to the three "goods" of marriage in the theology of Augustine: *proles, fides, sacramentum.*[9] But there has been a degeneration since Augustine. *Sacramentum* (grace and its symbol) has been removed from the purpose; *fides,* mutual fidelity, has been reformulated in such a way that one can hardly read love into it, as one could with the *mutuum adjutorium* of Augustine; and the strictly sexual element is so worded—*remedium concupiscentiae*—that it is treated like a disease. In a less canonical language, this expresses the theological notion that marriage and therefore sexuality have three purposes: procreation and education of children, mutual love, and sexual pleasure, the last two being subordinate to the first in the order of objective ends, though not necessarily in the order of subjective intentions.

This approach should be considerably modified. For the chief finding of Freud is precisely that sexuality is a major ingredient, not only in the procreation of children, but in the growth of personality. One could of course question the adequacy of the base on which Freud reached his conclusions. One could ask about the impact of culture in phenomena which Freud attributes to nature. That sexuality is in some civilizations, such as ours, a favorite popular medium for the expression of mutual love is undoubtedly a product of culture. Not all cultures, even today, understand and practice sexuality in that way. Yet the possibility of mutual love being experienced, expressed, and strengthened through sexuality belongs to the order of nature. I would gather from this that it also belongs to the objective nature of sexuality. As such, it is neither secondary nor subject to the procreative purpose, which is often separated from it by nature.

If this is so, the principle of Paul VI, that "each and every marriage act must remain open to the transmission of life"[10] does seem to be too absolute. The Augustinian contention that sexual pleasure may be tolerated but ought not be sought for fear of sin needs to be modified. For sexual pleasure may properly be viewed and sought, not as selfish gratification, but as mutual gift of the partners. It can no longer be relegated to the level of "concupiscence" and its "alleviation." Rather, it has the possibility of belonging to the order of love and being assumed in the order of charity.

The second consideration relates to more recent developments in psychoanalysis. I would like to draw attention to Jacques Lacan's interpretation of Freud and especially to his finding that it is essential to the sexual act that there is in fact something more than the mutual (physical, psychological, and even spiritual) exchange taking place in it.[11] There is—especially, as he maintains, on the feminine side—a basic "insatisfaction." If, as he puts it, "love is the desire to be One," it is bound to fail when it is based on "two" (sexes). The two find that they cannot be one. Woman cannot be one with man because she has maternal organs which cannot be reduced to her sexual organs and which escape sexual conjunction. Man cannot be one with woman because her maternal organs escape his impact. Then, for Lacan, the phallus of the Oedipus complex acquires further mythical dimensions, as it becomes the symbol of what is missing between the two who cannot be one. As such it feeds the language of the unconscious, which keeps calling (dreaming, in Freud) for the impossible satisfaction of impossible oneness. Lacan suggests, however, that this "insatisfaction" may be a higher satisfaction, so high that it cannot be known or, like God in mystical experience, is known only from its apparent absence.

What can this mean for a theological theory of human sexuality? Pedagogically, men and women should realize that, in sexual union, they do not try to do the same thing. They do not seek the same kind of oneness, since woman in her maternal organs preserves a part of herself that cannot be shared with the man; and they do not seek oneness in the same way, for the man thinks he owns and masters the means of unity, the phallus, whereas the woman knows that neither she nor he owns and masters it. Morally, this always-remaining gap between them should become the starting point of mutual forbearance, cooperation, and support in all aspects of their life in common. Theologically, this gap may be seen as symbolic of the fundamental unfulfillment of all human desire until Another (God) fulfills it by the gift of divine grace.

## Theological Reflections on Maleness and Femaleness

What is the central theological problem of sexuality? In the light of the theological tradition, with the ambiguity that seems to be structured in it, and of the findings of psychoanalysis, it would seem to be this: Are maleness and femaleness two different "embodiments-cum-ensoulments" of humanity? Or are they two aspects of humanity which are shared, though unequally, by all human persons? We might put the question differently: does sexuality belong to the first level or the second level of human nature? As first-level quality, it would flow directly from whatever may be called the essence of being human; as second-level quality, it would belong to the concreteness of human existence here and now. The answer to this is that sexuality is both a first-level and a second-level quality of humanity.

As first-level quality, it has little to do with male and female within humanity. It has to do with the animal order of which humanity is only one segment.[12] It expresses the continuity of the human with the animal world. Sexuality as first-level quality of human nature is the seat of a desire for life, an instinct for species survival, or, to use Bergson's phrase, an *"élan vital,"* which agitates the entire animal world where it acts as the prime motor of evolution. At that level, sexuality is participation in a nature which is older and wider than the human. We may presume that it is, in part, on account of this fundamental setting of the human in the animal that babies, according to some of Freud's findings, exhibit sexual traits long before the male-female relation can have any meaning for them.

As second-level quality, sexuality has been humanized. It is not only the outcome of an urge coming from past millennia of animal evolution. It is a meeting of male and female which involves not only their organs or bodies, but their spirit, their will, their choice, and which, among other aspects, may become symbolic and effective of love. At this level the question must be asked: are maleness and femaleness two opposite but complementary ways of being human? Or are they two aspects of humanity which are shared, though unequally, by all human persons?

If we choose the first option, then it follows that men and women are mutually characterized by *complementarity,* at least in regard to sexual and procreative functions, and possibly in life in general as regards social tasks and responsibilities, psychological processes and orientations, forms of logic, intellectual capacities, and in ecclesiastical life as regards sacramental, liturgical, ministerial, and magisterial functions. Such a perspective favors the identification of some virtues as male and others as female, and the exaltation of Mary as the ideal woman and mother. In this case, however, logic requires that male and female be defined in relation to each other. And if this logic is pursued, then advocacy of celibacy as a stable way of life makes little sense. Yet monasticism has been, historically, a major ingredient of Christian society. It still is, in the context of Orthodoxy, the highest Christian ideal. And if it never had the same central importance for the Latin West, we still would face the peculiar situation that theology would have favored the complementarity of male and female, yet also affirmed celibacy in religious orders as a Christian way of life, while canon law made it, for the Latin clergy, a requirement of ordination.[13]

Recent theology contains several variants of this position. The notion, dear to Teilhard de Chardin, of the "feminine Eternal" is among them (not, "eternal Feminine" as the translators, reversing his noun and adjective, have put it). The symbolic identification of woman with shekinah, divine wisdom, destined to receive and transform the male, is another. One finds this in Albert Frank-Duquesne's speculation: woman is a "vital principle which is complementary of the male"; it is through her that *vir,* the male, is destined to become *homo,* human.[14] Or one can cite Charles Williams' notion of woman as the revealer of the divine glory, a revelation which would take place in the process of falling in love.[15]

It is, however, the second option which, in my judgment, does justice to all the data. In this perspective, men and women are complementary in sexual activity, yet identically human in everything else. What are called male and female characteristics are stereotypes which vary from culture to culture and represent nothing more than social habits imposed from early childhood. In this case, each person has the basic capacity to fulfill the diverse roles assigned to men and women and to develop the corresponding attitudes or virtues (such as, aggressiveness and availability, strength and acceptance, reasoning and intuitive logic ...). Then, celibacy is not an anomaly or an extraordinary vocation, for personal fulfillment does not demand partnership with someone of the other sex, even though most persons would be supported by such a union, whether in marriage or in friendship.

In *Woman in Christian Tradition,* I proposed "identification" as the proper category for the harmonization of masculine and feminine, conceived not as two modes of human nature or two ways of being human, but as two dimensions of every human person, the balance of each dimension varying from person to person. A point can now be added. When they do not simply identify with each other as human, but encounter each other in the expression of love or friendship, male and female stand to each other in a position, not of complementarity, but of *supplementarity*. Each brings to the other a supplement of humanity, a surplus, which enriches each.[16] What it is then that enriches one's life and how such enrichment is offered and received are matters for further exploration on the basis of cultural patterns and individual experiences. I would suggest that exploration of the what and the how of this supplementarity has constituted the central topic and the chief inspiration of poetry since the rise of the earliest oral and audial cultures.[17]

# NOTES

1. This point is developed in my volume, *Woman in Christian Tradition* (South Bend, Ind.: University of Notre Dame, 1973), 3–121.

2. See Kari Børresen, *Subordination et Equivalence. Nature et rôle de la femme d'après Augustin et Thomas d'Aquin* (Oslo: Universitetsforlaget, 1968); English translation: *Subordination and Equivalence: The Nature and Role of Women in Augustine and Thomas Aquinas* (Washington, D.C.: University Press of America, 1981).

3. See Joan Morris, *The Lady Was a Bishop* (New York: Macmillan, 1973); Régine Pernoud, *La Femme au temps des cathédrales* (Paris: Stock, 1980).

4 Roland Bainton, *What Christianity Says about Sex, Love, and Marriage* (New York: Association Press, 1957), 91–102.

5. That this implies the basic identity of male and female was not lost on earlier theology. A striking expression of this identity was included, presumably by Hincmar, archbishop of Reims, in the acts of the synod of Douzy in 860. In a context which refers to social responsibility, the synod provides this explanation of the expression, *primus homo* (the first man): *quia et Eva ipsa est Adam* (Migne, P. L., 126, 125). This somewhat tautological proposition can be rendered as "for Eve herself is also Adam," or "for Adam is also Eve herself." The Renaissance rediscovery of pagan antiquity later split what earlier Christian thought had joined.

6. This is especially true of the Napoleonic Code, which embodied the spirit of the French Revolution in a more systematic way than the Revolution itself had been able to do.

7. Jacques Lacan, *Écrits;* vol. 1 (Paris: Editions du Seuil, 1966), 89–97; Anika Lemaire, *Jacques Lacan* (London: Routledge and Kegan Paul, 1977), 79–81, 176–78.

8. George H. Tavard, *Woman in Christian Tradition*, 227–29.

9. *De Bono Conjugali,* chap. 24, in *Oeuvres de saint Augustin,* vol. 2 (Paris: Desclée de Brouwer, 1937), 93. The Code of Canon Law of 1983 slightly modifies the formulation of the Code of 1921: "The matrimonial covenant, by which a man and a woman establish between themselves a partnership of the whole of life, is by its nature ordered toward the good of the spouses and the procreation and education of children; this covenant between baptized persons has been raised by Christ the Lord to the dignity of a sacrament." Can. 1055, §1, *Code of Canon Law. Latin-English Edition* (Vatican: Typis polyglottis, 1983), 387.

10. Encyclical *Humanae Vitae,* n. 11.

11. Jacques Lacan, *Encore* (Paris: Editions du Seuil, 1975).

12. See Abel Jeanniere, *Anthropologie sexuelle* (Paris: Aubier-Montaigne, 1969).

13. Undoubtedly the complementarity of sexes dominates many statements on Christian anthropology made by recent popes, from Pius XI to John Paul II. It does seem strange that no discrepancy has been detected in such "official" theology between this view and the traditional promotion of consecrated virginity and celibacy "for the Kingdom." For an ecumenical attempt to face the problem, see the statement of the Anglican–Roman Catholic Conversations, USA: "Reflections on Christian Anthropology," *Origins* 14, no. 30 (Washington, D.C., January 5, 1984), 505–12.

14. Albert Frank-Duquesne, *Creation et procreation. Metaphysique, théologie et mystique du couple humain* (Paris: Editions de Minuit, 1951), 15–49. See Henri de Lubac, *L'Éternel féminin. Étude sur un texte du Père Teilhard de Chardin* (Paris: Aubier, 1968). The text of Teilhard is in the collection of writings entitled *Écrits du temps de guerre, 1916–1919* (Paris: Ed. du Seuil, 1965), 253–62.; English trans. René Hague, *Writings in Time of War* (New York: Harper & Row, 1968). That *"éternel"* is the noun and *"féminin"* the adjective is made clear by the parallelism of this expression with *"l'attraction féminine,"* where *attraction* cannot be anything else than a substantive. The mistranslation into "the eternal feminine," in which "feminine" is the noun, and "eternal" the adjective is of course due to contamination from Goethe's *"das Ewig-Weibliche"* in the translator's mind. But, as de Lubac (*L'Éternel féminin,* 53–54) makes clear, Teilhard's conception does not derive from Goethe's. See Tavard, *Woman in Christian Tradition,* 140–47.

15. See Mary McDermot Shideler, *The Theology of Romantic Love: A Study in the Writings of Charles Williams* (New York: Harper, 1962).

16. This would need to be supported by an analysis of love; see my volume, *A Way of Love* (Maryknoll, N.Y.: Orbis Books, 1977).

17. See Antonio de Nicolas, "Audial and literary cultures: the Bhagavad-Gita as a case-study," *Journal of Social and Biological Structures* 5 (1982): 269–88.

# 6

# Women in Buddhism
## ANNE BANCROFT

The aim of this article is to give an outline of the role of women in Buddhism up to the present day. Since the area of both the geography and the time-scale involved are huge, the article gives a general survey rather than a detailed account. The survey is based on research, personal observation and dialogue. It is divided into four sections: the Hinayana School, the Mahayana School, the Theravada (Hinayana) through the present, and the Mahayana through the present.

### The Hinayana School

The essence of the Buddhist goal is liberation. Although such a statement may seem a truism since this is the goal of most religions, the liberation hoped for may take different forms. To a Buddhist liberation means a radical freedom not only in future worlds or planes of existence, but very much in this world too.

The advent of Buddhism into Hindu society of the sixth century B.C.E. was a turning point for both men and women of India, but particularly for women. The Hinduism of that time meant that women could not have any status apart from that of wife and mother, nor could they, whatever their rank or status within marriage, achieve the *moksha*—spiritual freedom—of upper caste men (lower caste men could not achieve this either). Nevertheless, the Buddha taught that *nirvana* (liberation) was within the reach of anyone from robbers to kings prepared to live out the Four Noble Truths. The Buddha saw no harm in preaching to women, too, and it was not long before women requested to be allowed to enter the Sangha as nuns. Although Buddha seems to have been strangely reluctant to accept women in the robe, large numbers of

Indian women had become Jain nuns. This circumstance may have encouraged him to assent to a women's order, although apparently with considerable foreboding:

If, Ananda, women had not received permission to go out from the household life and enter the homeless state, under the doctrine and discipline proclaimed by the Tathagata, then would the pure religion, Ananda, have lasted long, the good law would have stood fast for a thousand years. But since, Ananda, women have now received that permission the pure religion, Ananda, will not last so long, the good law will now stand fast for only five hundred years.[1]

What part of these gloomy words was the Buddha's own and what part was inserted by monks at a later date, it is hard to decide. Certainly women were regarded as a great deal less fortunate than men (and therefore presumably not ready for the religious life) because of the suffering entailed by childbirth, menstruation and menopause. Few women received any education, and a woman's greatest merit was to be reborn as a man. It was generally thought (although not by the Buddha) that women could not achieve enlightenment, and this trend of thinking continued for a long time after the Buddha's death. The nun, Soma, (during the Buddha's lifetime) comments on this belief, upholding a deeper view—the voice of a woman claiming that her true being lay deeper than sexual difference:

She was taunted:
That vantage-ground the sages may attain
Is hard to win. With her two-finger consciousness
That place no woman is competent to gain.

She replied:
What should the state of woman do to us,
Whose mind is firmly set—or do to anyone
Who, knowledge rolling on, discerns the dhamma?
Am I a woman in these matters, or
Am I a man, or what am I then?
To such a one are you, sir, fit to talk![2]

The Buddha himself, in answer to a question whether women could attain Arahantship or not, replied that it was possible for them to do so. From this we can know that the Buddha saw nothing inherently inferior in a woman's mind, although the wandering life might be difficult for her physically. It was because he

believed that they could attain Arahantship that he permitted them
to become *bhikkhunis* (nuns). This institution led to a new liberation for women in India and meant that life was perceived as having worth in itself. To become a nun meant entering on a career of
sorts. Marriage and motherhood were no longer seen as the
inevitable fate for having been born a female, and a new drift was
set exclusively towards religion. A dowry and an arranged wedding need no longer preoccupy a family. Buddhist laywomen
were allowed to travel freely to hear the Buddha preach.

This change had its effect on marriage itself, which became a
more equal arrangement between partners; the Buddhist wife now
shared authority in choosing a child's career. Her consent, as well
as the father's, was needed if a child wanted to enter a monastery.
Married Buddhist women could inherit and could manage their
property without interference. Widows were not expected to
commit sati or become recluses; indeed, on the death of a husband, a wife could enter the Sangha and expect to find religious
companionship, or she could stay in the world, remarry, and
manage her own affairs. It is interesting to note that marriage
required specific duties of men as well as women. The wife owed
her husband faithfulness, watchfulness over his earnings, hard
work and the use of her skills, and hospitality to his parents; the
husband owed the wife respect, courtesy, faithfulness, the giving
of adornments, and the relinquishing of authority over her.

Nevertheless, although a much greater freedom for women per-
tained generally at the time of the Buddha than had gone before,
the new *bhikkhunis* were restricted by eight important curtailments
of liberty. There is considerable debate today whether these eight
were actually pronounced by the Buddha or were later inserted by
monks. They are excessively chauvinistic, and it is difficult to
imagine the Buddha, having agreed to the possible Arahantship of
women, giving voice to some of them. But they have played and
continue even today to play a major role in the customs of
*bhikkhunis* towards *bhikkhus* (monks). So we should take a brief
look at what they are.

1. "A *bhikkhuni* who has been accepted even for a hundred years
must pay homage to, get up for, reverentially salute and respect-
fully greet, a *bhikkhu* accepted even that day." This means that
a senior *bhikkhuni* must bow down three times to even a
newly ordained *bhikkhu*. The nun Gotami is said to have asked
that juniors, male or female, pay respect to senior *bhikkhus* or

*bhikkhunis* without distinction. The Buddha, however, replied that no *bhikkhu* should pay homage to a *bhikkhuni*. The Ven. Khantipalo suggests that the Buddha took into account the way this matter would appear to laypeople. At the time of the inception of *bhikkhunis,* men in lay society hardly acknowledged female ability and certainly did not bow to it. Thus, to permit this would cause too strong a rift between lay and religious people and might lead to the downfall of Buddhism.

2. "A *bhikkhuni* must not spend the time of the rains in a place where there are no *bhikkhus*." This was one way in which *bhikkhunis* were made dependent on *bhikkhus,* but it was also done for the safety of the *bhikkhunis* since molesting a nun was by no means unknown.

3. "Every half month a *bhikkhuni* is to await two things from the Sangha of *bhikkhus,* the asking of the date of the Uposatha ceremony, and the time when the *bhikkhu* will come to give an exhortation." The *bhikkhus* were to calculate the phases of the moon, and every half month a learned *bhikkhu* should give a *dhamma* talk to the *bhikkhunis*. The fact that a teacher from the men would give a fortnightly talk did not mean that the *bhikkhunis* had no teachers among themselves, however. The *bhikkhunis* who were declared "foremost" in the *Book of the Ones* were famous teachers; these enlightened *bhikkhunis* also had many beautiful verses in the *Verses of the Elder Nuns.*

4. "After keeping the rainy season the *bhikkhuni* is to enquire whether any fault can be laid to her charge before both Sanghas (men and women) with respect to three matters, namely what has been seen, what has been heard and what has been suspected." Apparently the faults imputed to the *bhikkhunis* were investigated by both the Sanghas, although there is no evidence as to which body had priority in apportioning punishment. But it is clear that to begin with the *bhikkhunis* were not allowed to decide solely for themselves.

5. "*Bhikkhunis* who have been guilty of a serious offense must undergo discipline towards both the Sanghas." *Bhikkhus* were subject to thirteen possible offences, but *bhikkhunis* seventeen. If she confessed, the punishment for a *bhikkhuni,* however, was the same as for a *bhikkhu*—practicing a penance for seven days plus a period of probation equal to the time of concealment, if the offence had been deliberately concealed.

6. "When a novice *bhikkhuni* has been trained for two years she is to ask leave for ordination from both Sanghas." If a would-be *bhikkhuni* was given acceptance merely from her own branch, she would not be considered fully ordained. Her acceptance had to be passed by the male Sangha too.

7. "A *bhikkhuni* is never allowed to revile or abuse a *bhikkhu*." According to Khantipalo the aim of this rule was to stop malicious gossip and promote concord between the Sanghas. A *bhikkhuni* could report a *bhikkhu* to his teacher if his actions went against the rules, but she could not speak directly to him or behind his back.

8. "From henceforth official admonition by *bhikkhunis* of *bhikkhus* is forbidden, whereas the official admonition of *bhikkhunis* by *bhikkhus* is not forbidden." As I. B. Horner comments:

This last rule is another instance of the placing of women in a position of definite inferiority to men, and of a refusal to grant them independence to manage their own Order, with the power to ratify their own proceedings. That they were permitted to enter the Order at all, and were not precluded from full membership, were doubtless concomitant of the times in which they lived. Although preceding epochs had been slightly relieved by the cult of the mother, they were otherwise depressingly uniform in their branding of women as inferior to men, never to be considered as anything but as a man's property. Even with the improvement of their status under Buddhism, still young when these rules were formulated so far as the records indicate, to permit women complete equality and complete independence would have been unexpected. But the advance made by women was patent and definite. With the exception of the necessity for the wife to gain her husband's consent, they were allowed to enter the Order on the same conditions as the men, and although once in the Order they would find both as individuals and as members of their Chapter that a certain amount of subservience was expected of them by the *bhikkhus,* yet the permission granted them to enter the Order at all was a fact of momentous significance.[3]

The Buddha compared these eight rules to an embankment; one can rightly ask what was the flood which he hoped to prevent by means of them. As Khantipalo points out, all eight have one point in common: they deal with the variations of conduct between *bhikkhunis* and *bhikkhus,* either as Sanghas or individually. So the flood the Buddha hoped to stem was probably unregulated, even innocent, conduct between the two sexes, which might give rise to gossip. In the Vinaya there are many examples of laypeople, who were not Buddhists, thinking that the *bhikkhunis* were the *bhikkhus'* wives.

Once fully ordained, a *bhikkhuni* was (and is) subject to 311 daily rules, while a *bhikkhu* need only observe 227. Nevertheless, during the time of the Buddha many thousands of women from all walks of life became *bhikkhunis,* including many of pronounced spiritual attainment and vigor. The scriptures are sprinkled with the stories of women Arahants, and some of their great understanding is recorded in the *Verses of the Elder Nuns.*

By the first century B.C.E., however, when the Pali Canon was first recorded in writing, the Buddhist view of women as equal marriage partners, and of *bhikkhunis* as having equal abilities for enlightenment, had long since abated. The Pali Canon, from which these rules have descended, was written and edited by scholarly monks who undoubtedly had come to regard themselves as the only real Sangha, and whose attitude toward women appears to have been one of abhorrence. In the *Jataka Tales* (stories about the Buddha's life which were recorded at this period) women were portrayed as ugly, blind and wretched, and having voracious sexual appetites, whereas men were seen as noble, loyal, generous and holy, betrayed by their wicked wives.

In this way the Hinayana literature of this period came to make women obstacles to the liberation of monks. Buddhist monastic life became as fixated on celibacy and the evils of sex as any Christian puritanical sect. Unmarried women were regarded as a menace and the only good wife was the chaste wife, with her freedom much curtailed. Her position came to resemble that of her Hindu sister—she should be totally submissive, use only sweet words, and obey all her husband's wishes.

It is interesting to speculate on the extent of fear which women seemed then and still seem to engender in men. They are regarded as not only personal but universal obstacles, preventing the spiritual progress of humankind and even filling the Buddha with fear that they would bring about the fall of the Sangha. Denise Carmody takes the view that "early conservative Buddhism (Theravadin) linked their desire and productive becoming with samsara, the realm of change and endless redistribution of the life-force. Since samsara was the enemy and the trap, so too was femaleness. Thus women took on symbolic force as epitomising karmic bonds."[4]

Indian Buddhism and Hinduism shared many common beliefs and one of these was certainly a strong misogynistic strain. As Carmody points out, "unless a woman is neutralised by marriage to a controlling man, Hindu imagination conjures up for her such images as the snake, death, the underworld, hell's entrance, the prostitute, the adulteress."[5] In much the same way the young Siddhartha, on the point of leaving the palace for a wandering life, fell asleep while beautiful dancing girls were performing for him. When he woke, he saw them lying all around him asleep too— saliva trickled from their mouths; they were covered with sweat; some ground their teeth; some snored; the garments of some were in disarray, so that they repulsively showed their private parts. This sight so filled Siddhartha with disgust that he likened the banquet hall to a charnel ground full of corpses.

An attitude later ascribed to the Buddha, but probably of monk-ish origin, is given in this dialogue:

"How are we to conduct ourselves, Lord, with regard to womankind?"
"As not seeing them, Ananda."
"But if we should see them, what are we to do?"
"No talking, Ananda."
"But if they should speak to us, Lord, what are we to do?"
"Keep awake, Ananda."[6]

Reference has been made to later editing of the Buddhist scrip-tures by monks, and perhaps a clarifying word should be added here. The ancient Indian teaching tradition was to pass on knowl-edge by word of mouth, which meant the encouragement of good memory. The way in which the Buddhist scriptures came to be written down reflects this reliance on memory, since the endlessly repetitive style of the utterances was the way by which a student came to learn the sutras and sayings and then to pass them on.

This tradition continued until some 400 years after the Buddha's death, when the scriptures came to be written down in Sri Lanka and India (it should be remembered that we are dealing only with the Hinayana school here). Thus at some date far removed from the Buddha's life his supposed words were committed to palm leaf, and there is no scholarly doubt at all that the sayings were largely edited. A monk would have no hesitation in doing so since he would be acting, as he believed, in the spirit of Buddhism. Richard Robinson states: "Modern philologists in the West, India and Japan, have done sufficient work on the Pali Canon (the records were written in Pali, a language which the Buddha would not have spoken) to discredit the orthodox Theravada view as to its authorship and literal reporting of Sakyamuni's words."[7] I. B. Horner remarks:

So long as the monk-editors were ready to ascribe to Gotama a genial and full character, with warm sympathy open to the troubles of every man, they could not deny that he was ever accessible to the laity. This may be partly the reason why the stories have survived. But how far he was accessible to the *bhikkhunis* appears to be a matter of some doubt—a doubt which is increased and not diminished by the fact that the texts were written down, glossed and edited by men who had little historical sense and little sympathy with the doings of women.[8]

From what we know of the Buddha's references to the *bhikkhunis,* there is no doubt that some of the humiliating restrictions of their lives were created at a later date by monks who regarded women as inferior. For example it is certain, according to Horner, that *bhikkhunis* were told they must treat *bhikkhus* with a deference close to humility. Complaints from the *bhikkhus* had led to it being regarded as an offence by a *bhikkhuni* if she sat on a seat or even on the ground in front of a *bhikkhu* without asking leave, unless she were ill; it was also an offence if she asked him a question concerning the *dhamma* without first begging permission to ask it.

In two other matters her position was different from the *bhikku's*. A *bhikkhuni* could not create a new school of teaching; only a *bhikkhu* could do that. The implication, according to Horner, appears to be that

a *bhikkhuni* could not become a sufficiently powerful, original, or heterodox leader of religious thought to create altercations, discord, divisions, quarrels, disunion, separations, schisms among the Sangha. If the *bhikkhuni* did not preach to the *bhikkhus* nor to other *bhikkunis* but only to the laity, it is easy to see that they would not have the maximum scope for the expression of religious sentiments which would be either in keeping with the training set forth by the Buddha, or against it, and that their sphere of influence would be limited. But if a dissenter should arise, and in private conversations make her position clear, being only a woman, her words and teaching should not have any weight attached to them. There are in fact no records of any women who managed to create a schism, or of any who attempted to do so; and since this disability figures in the Milindapanha and not in the canonical literature, it may be taken merely as further proof that by the time this work was written down women were again relapsing into a degraded position, and greater differences between them and men were again darkening the horizon.[9]

The second matter was a *bhikkhuni's* goal. Horner says:

Again, despite her strivings as a religieuse, a *bhikkhuni* could not hope to attain to the highest state of all, to Buddhahood. At the end of the round of becoming, it is said: "A woman will not become a Buddha, absolutely holy and perfectly enlightened . . . nor a universal monarch." The second follows from the first, for a man born with certain marks will become one or the other according as he leaves the world for the homeless state, or remains in it. The Majjhima, not content with asserting that a woman can be neither a Buddha nor a universal monarch, makes a thorough denial of the potency of women to rise to the pinnacle in any of the realms: "It is impossible for a woman to be an Arahant, all-enlightened; but it is possible for a man to be. It is impossible for a woman to be a Sakka, or a Mara, or a Brahma; but it is possible for a man to be any of these."[10]

Horner sums up the position, as she has discovered it in the scriptures, of what the Buddha actually did and said in contrast to later insertions by monks:

It is said that the Buddha won enlightenment for both *bhikkhus* and *bhikkhunis,* laymen and laywomen, and taught the *Dhamma* equally to all four branches of his flock; that the virtuous or bad behaviour of the members of these four branches would have an analogous effect on the persistence or disappearance of the *Dhamma,* and would affect the community for good or ill; that women may have the same spiritual limitations or the same mystic powers as men; that *bhikkhunis* may grow and become as much as the *bhikkhus* may; that Gotama would not die until he had gained wise and disciplined *bhikkhus* and *bhikkhunis,* laymen and laywomen as his disciples; that women may conform to the same type as men in their relations to the Buddha.[11]

As well as the sayings from which Horner has derived her summing up, there are stories which bear out the Buddha's fairness of mind towards women, including laywomen. He is recorded to have said about the *bhikkhuni* Nanda that she has by the complete destruction of the five bonds that bind people to this world become an inheritor of the highest heavens, there to pass away entirely, thence never to return and that the devout laywoman Sujata is assured of final salvation. There is also the *Jataka* story which ascribes the statement to him that no disciples, male or female, who seek refuge in the Three Gems are ever reborn into hell and like states: but released from all rebirth into states of suffering, they pass into the realm of devas and there receive great glory.

## The Mahayana School

The distinctly anti-woman attitude of Hinayana *bhikkhus* was not shared to such an extent by the Mahayana school (the two different aspects of Buddhism developing within two centuries after the Buddha's death). Mahayana consistently stressed that all human experience, male or female, is the very ground of enlightenment. *Prajna,* or wisdom, sees no divisions or boundaries. All things share one life because no single thing can stand on its own without the rest; nor is any one thing absolute—all is relative.

The understanding of this truth, resulting in the realization that this one shared life is mysterious in its origin, came to be personified in Mahayana as the Supreme Wisdom, *Prajnaparamita,* the feminine principle. *Prajnaparamita* is a wisdom supremely compassionate, rescuing humans from their ignorance and consequent suffering. Because "she" is nurturer and sustainer but also liberator, empty of clinging and defilement, she is not worshipped as a goddess. But faith in *Prajnaparamita* will lead the disciple to release many fears and to see that there is no division between matter and spirit, the world and *nirvana.*

*Prajnaparamita,* commonly known as the Perfection of Wisdom, can be seen to be feminine not only from the grammatical form of her name but also from the many statues and images where her feminine body is not in doubt. Edward Conze remarks that:

The Mahayana believed that men should in their meditations complete themselves by fostering the feminine factors of their personality, that they should practice passivity and a loose softness, that they should learn to open freely the gates of nature, and to let the mysterious and hidden forces of this world penetrate into them, stream in and through them. When they identify themselves with the perfection of wisdom, they merge with the principle of feminity (Jung's anima) without which they would be mutilated men. Like a woman, the "Perfection of Wisdom" deserves to be courted and wooed, and the Sutras on Perfect Wisdom constitute one long love affair with the Absolute. Meditation on her as a goddess has the purpose of getting inside her, identifying oneself with her, becoming her. In the later Tantra, a sexual attitude to *Prajnaparamita* is quite explicit. Disguised by the use of ambiguous terms it was already present in the older *Prajnaparamita* Sutras themselves.

And it is interesting to notice that these writings show many feminine features, in which we learn to participate by their recitation, and by meditation on them; argumentations almost entirely rely on intuition and attempts at reasoning are scanty and far from conclusive. The Sutras win over by fascination and not by compulsion. Timeless, they are not obsessed with time, but ignore it. They urge on to a contemplation of the world, and not to its conquest by manipulation. They show some of the amoralism which later on hardened into the antinomianism of the Tantra, and which did not fail to provoke protests from the more tight-laced monks. They are indifferent to sensory facts, and in vain do we search through the thousands of pages for one single "hard fact." And in her ultimate core the *Prajnaparamita* is described as for ever elusive, not possessed by anyone, but absorbing all.[12]

The course of the Mahayana school which, as we can see, is almost the antithesis of the Hinayana in many respects, was summarized by the Ven. Sangharakshita in the following way. In its differentiation from the Hinayana it was

a) progressive and liberal minded, caring more for the spirit than for the letter of the scriptures, willing to write fresh ones whenever the need of recasting the outward form of the teaching arose; b) more highly emotional and devotional in attitude, with a deeper understanding of the value of ritual acts; and c) more positive in its conception of Nirvana and the Way; d) while continuing to cherish the monastic ideal it gave increased importance to a dedicated household life; and e) it developed the altruistic aspect of Buddhism and preached the Bodhisattva ideal.[13]

In India and then Tibet a number of feminine deities arose in Mahayana, after 400 C.E. Though there never was a feminine Buddha, the *Prajnaparamita* became a celestial *bodhisattva,* and others were added as time went on. The most famous of these and perhaps the most popular and beloved was the Tara, of which there are many versions. Tara is the savioress and mother of the world who exists to protect and reassure us and fulfill our spiritual hopes. Other feminine powers of the time were concerned with the personification of magical spells such as the Five Protectresses and the Dakinis, or Sky-Walkers. They were visualized by practitioners in intense meditation. Worship of the Perfection of Wisdom resulted in the following, typical poem:

Eight maidens form the boat of the three refuges.
My body is compassion, emptiness my mistress.
I have crossed the sea of existence like an illusion, like a dream.[14]

As well, during the sixth to tenth centuries C.E., a number of Mahayana Crazy Wanderers—wandering saints—appeared. They were "long-haired, mad, endowed with magic powers, and singing of the bliss that dwelt within the human body." They took the Perfection of Wisdom as the Great Whore, for she opens herself to every man who seeks her. "They sang in puns and riddles, made love to the spontaneous maiden within them, and preached a world turned upside down." One such was Kanha, and the following verse typifies their stance, with reminders of the Spanish mystics:

As Kanha goes off to marry the Whore,
The Whore is married and birth is eaten up.
The dowry is the highest Law.
Day and night pass in lovemaking.
The night is brightened with my Lady's flame.
The yogin who is devoted to the Whore
Does not leave her for a moment: he is drunk with the spontaneous.[15]

During the course of early Mahayana considerable faith was put in mantras and magical procedures. A synthesis of all these diverse elements was made in the Buddhist universities under the Pala dynasty (750–1150 C.E.). Then, after about 1200 C.E. Buddhism, and with it the Mahayana, disappeared from India although the Mahayana had already put roots in China, Korea, Vietnam, Tibet, and Japan, whereas Hinayana had migrated to Sri Lanka, Burma, and Thailand.

The effect of the Mahayana school on the position of women was favorable from the beginning. Little emphasis was laid on celibacy and the idea of women as "temptation" barely arose. Mahayana agreed to the possibility of enlightenment for laypeople, and thus for married people. This led to the position of women as equal life partners. It emphasized the view that nothing in this world was to be despised, fled from or rejected; rather, it was to be accepted, understood, and fully experienced. The mystery of the Void was to be looked for at the core of all experience.

By the eighth century C.E. Buddhism in India was largely on the wane, replaced by the original Hinduism and additionally hastened on its way by Islam. As Mahayana developed in other countries, two chief schools arose, the Vajrayana and Zen.

Vajrayana (the Thunderbolt Vehicle) was the product of Tibet. The use of the senses in pure awareness was encouraged throughout Buddhism. But whereas in Hinayana all attachment to the body was to be strongly rejected, in Vajrayana the attachment was to be seen through rather than rejected, and it could only be seen through if it was experienced. In other words, wisdom was to be found by using appropriate and skillful means rather than by any form of rejection. Yoga, particularly sexual yoga, was one of the means although Tantra, meaning sensual experience, was concerned with all the senses and not just the sexual. In sexual yoga, the Hindu and Taoist attitude was that of treating the female as a tool for man's advancement. In Tibetan yoga, however, the female could not be used one-sidedly in this way since both wisdom (female) and skillful means (male) were equally necessary. So we see in this meditational act of Buddhism a strong inclination towards the equality of woman, to imitate the cooperation between *Prajnaparamita* and skillful means.

Zen, the other main school of Mahayana, developed in China (where it was known as Ch'an) and spread to Korea and Japan. It was known as the school of sudden awakening, and its knowledge of emptiness depended more on intense insight gained through meditation, koans, and the guidance of a master than the sensual awareness of Tantra, although realization through the senses still played a large part. Women in Zen fared well—sudden enlightenment, by its very nature, was available to the human race and not merely to men. Nevertheless the main Vinaya rules were still adhered to within the Sangha—but we will return to this presently.

## The Theravada (Hinayana) Through the Present

Theravada (Teaching of the Elders) was one of the schools developing from Hinayana and is the name used commonly by the countries of the Southern School both today and for many centuries past, probably since 346 B.C.E.

The order of *bhikkhunis,* which included a number of Arahants, lasted for a considerable time after the Buddha's lifetime. Respect for them was sufficiently great that many of their inspired discourses and poems were included in the predominantly male work, the Pali Canon.

The *bhikkuni* Sangha flourished in Sri Lanka for many centuries, and the construction of convents continued until the reign of Kassapa IV (898–914 C.E.). *Bhikkhunis* were treated with respect as the king's wards and consequently their convents were in the Inner (royal) City. When the island was conquered by the Cholas from India in the tenth century C.E., they became more vulnerable to destruction, for they were clustered in the few towns and cities. The *bhikkhus* could survive as they spread throughout the country, but the *bhikkhunis* were entirely extinguished. When peace returned later on, the new kings did not restore the *bhikkhuni* Sangha, either through indifference or because there were no ordained *bhikkhunis* left who could ordain others. There is even less record of the *bhikkhunis* in India, and it is not known whether they continued till the end of Buddhist teaching there.

However, long before the fatal attack of the Cholas, *bhikkhunis* had travelled to China and had established a Sangha there which has continued to this day. Consequently, if you wanted to find a Theravada *bhikkhuni,* you could do so in Hong Kong or Taiwan, South Korea or Vietnam. Their rule has altered, however, in that they are now ordained only by the *bhikkhus,* which casts a question on the strict Theravadin whether they are really *bhikkhunis* or not.

Nowadays, in the more familiar countries of Sri Lanka, Thailand and Burma, there are no *bhikkhunis* at all. Since they were destroyed in Sri Lanka, none has been ordained. These are male-dominated countries with man as the final arbiter. Khantipalo raises the question whether women will ever again be able to be recognized as *bhikkhunis* in Theravada lands. He says:

It is difficult to see how this could be done. A Sangha of *bhikkhus* led by responsible Theras (elders) would have to recognize that the *bhikkhunis* are not quite extinct and then reordain them in Theravada tradition. Many problems would arise since there have been no *bhikkhunis* for such a long time and ways of doing things have been forgotten. More serious than this, however, would be the danger of causing a schism in the Sangha.[16]

This may strike the observer as rather specious reasoning since the ways of doing things, far from being forgotten, are written down in minute detail, and one does not think it would take a great deal of effort on the part of the Sangha to introduce *bhikkhunis* once more. Therefore it seems obvious that the intention is lacking. If a schism could be caused by an order of *bhikkhunis,* then the attitude towards women as obstacles to spiritual growth must still be in operation.

Meanwhile, women have lived fairly comfortably outside the full Sangha by becoming nuns who are not fully ordained, but who take either eight or ten precepts, shave their hair and wear robes of differing colors according to their country of origin.

They live mainly in special sections of *viharas* (monastic compounds) or establish their own nunneries. Among them are many learned and wise women, highly developed in meditation. In Sri Lanka they are known as *Silmatavaru*—mothers (honorific) observing the precepts; in Thailand as *mai chees*—mothers (an honorific for women) who are ordained; in Burma as *Thila-shin*—possessors of the precepts.

Their status in these countries is considerably lower than that of the *bhikkhus*. In a mixed *vihara* they sweep and cook for the men and generally take on all household duties, rarely being given education or spiritual teaching. When on their own, they must rely on lay supporters who are a great deal less generous to them than they are to the *bhikkhus,* and thus many nuns continue to receive some support from home. These attitudes are beginning to change as more attention is being paid to nuns and their education.

There is a big gap between the Thai or Burmese nun and a western woman who thinks perhaps of joining them. Westerners who go East are usually well educated and have enquiring minds. But Asiatic nuns may have had very poor education and have led much more sheltered lives. Khantipalo says that "great patience and perseverance, as well as adaptability, are needed by a western woman to succeed as a nun." He also says that humility is important and proposes an argument that, to say the least, does *not* include humility for a man: "For myself I take the attitude that there is nothing in the world except *nama* (mind, mental states) and *rupa* (body, material qualities) and therefore if offence arises at having to pay respect first to a man, then it is only the ego that is offended or unhappy."[17]

Such an attitude was brought home to a party of English people who went to a forest monastery in Thailand recently. The women discovered that they were separated from the men (sometimes wife from husband), their living quarters a half-hour's hot walk from the monastery. They had to wait for a meal until the men had finished theirs, and it was then their duty to clear everything up. In similar style a young English woman who had spent two years meditating in India came to Thailand with the intention of joining a nunnery. At one *vihara* she was invited to speak about her experiences in India. But when the time came to give the talk, it was discovered that there was nowhere for her to give it, since she was not allowed to be higher than the *bhikkhus* and thus could not mount the platform. Although she was prepared to discard her talk, in this case the abbot made an exception (probably because she was a foreigner), and she was allowed to mount the platform. She did not, however, persevere in her plan to join a nunnery. What discouraged her most deeply was the fact that if she wanted to ask a question or make a comment to any *bhikkhu,* however young and recently ordained and however lax in keeping the rules (the very young ones were smoking, lounging about, etc.), she had to go on her knees to him. The first of the eight Vinaya rules in which a woman must physically show some subservience to a man is the one which seems to have been vigorously upheld in all Buddhist countries.

In England, a group of western *bhikkhus* who have all spent years in Thailand under the tuition of Achaan Cha, have established a monastery at Chithurst in Sussex. They have attracted a small group of nuns—*mai chees.* I asked one of the *mai chees,* a French ex-ballet dancer, what they felt about their inferior status. She said they tried not to think about it, because it would cause so much resentment. The abbot, an American, is conscious of their position, however, and considers that in the twentieth century it is an anachronism. He hopes to alter it so that they will be able to take the full ordination. But he has to work slowly in order not to offend the Thai community which helps to support them. In the meantime, the *mai chees* said, they find real help in meditation, which reconciles the opposites, bringing out compassion in men and strength in women. One hopes that it is not just strength to do the washing up!

## The Mahayana Through the Present

### a) *The Tibetan Vajra School*

Modern Tibet, in the year 1931, was described by Charles Bell, the researcher of Lamaism, as follows: "Politically and socially, Tibet is in the condition of Christian Europe in the Middle Ages, but the Tibetan woman's level is, and long has been, consistently higher than what Europe could then show."[18]

Perhaps due to their physical surroundings, Tibetan women have always been strong in character and body, and social custom has given them considerable independence, including polyandry, the practice of having more than one husband.

Tantric beliefs have also led to women becoming gurus or adepts, since the feminine aspect of spirituality was rated highly. Such women received the title of *siddha* and were believed to be perfectly enlightened. They themselves frequently cast aside social conventions and both preached and practiced "crazy wisdom," a belief that at a certain stage of adeptness one's actions, however socially strange, will be correct.

Nevertheless, the Indian sexist influence has made it hard for a woman to become a guru, even in Vajrayana. The story of Laksminkara illustrates this situation. Laksminkara, born in North India in the ninth century C.E., was taught Tantric practices from early childhood. But she was of royal blood and was therefore betrothed at an early age to a neighboring Hindu ruler. When she later came to his palace, however, she was received coldly because she was a Buddhist. She saw a hunting party returning with a slain deer and was so shocked that she pretended madness (a frequent Tantric device), gave away her dowry, jewels and clothes, and wandered about naked until she was locked up. She escaped and wandered in poverty for seven years, still feigning madness. Eventually she received deep enlightenment and came to be followed by many disciples.

In present-day Vajrayana the same situation exists for the Theravadin *bhikkhunis;* there is no full ordination. Even if fully ordained, however, a nun would still have to sit below a monk. In Tibet, too, education for women is lacking although from time to time a wise nun does become a lama (learned and high on the spiritual ladder). The usual set-up in a convent existing only through endowment by a rich family, however, is that the poor and uneducated nuns wait on and serve the richer ones.

Tibetan life is based on both feudal blood lineage and spiritual hierarchy. Women in general are considered inferior to men, although the ex-nun I talked to told me that a married *tulku* (an incarnation) had tried to sit below her at a meal, obviously considering her to be his spiritual superior. There is more flexibility than in Theravada as there is more affectionate jostling and play, including bowing contests, at meal times and other occasions, to vie for lower seating. This playful and loving spirit extends up the hierarchy, although it is considered a social embarrassment to sit above a spiritual superior. The ex-nun felt that inferiority was not exacerbated, even though it exists.

The first rule of the eight is kept, and nuns, although they do not have to kneel or go on the ground, do have to bow to a monk. The ex-nun felt that there was a certain amount of double dealing with women, particularly with regard to celibacy. The doctrine is puritanical, but there is a large area of hypocrisy where a blind eye is turned. In general she felt that although the spirit of Vajrayana is good in that the Tantric status of the feminine is very high—there is a Tantric vow never to speak ill of a woman—yet reforms, particularly towards education and spiritual teaching for nuns, are necessary.

## b) The Zen School

A more complex position exists in Zen. The main countries involved are South Korea, Japan, and now America, since a number of masters have settled there and have large followings. Both Korea and Japan are still strongly male-oriented countries, where the head of the family does the thinking and the decision-making for the family. Neither country is wholly Buddhist although Buddhism has been the official religion periodically. It is possible to say that Korea appears to give more freedom within the family situation to women but that there do not seem to be many, if any, outstanding women within religion. Nuns must bow to monks in Korea; but in Korean Zen, as practiced in America, women teachers are given the seal of approval equally with men. In Japan families are tightly knit and women quite subservient; yet Zen nuns are appreciated, and a number have become famous during the centuries.

Nothing has yet been said about China, a grave omission because Chinese Buddhism has been one of the most important of the branches. It includes not only Zen but also the Pure Land school, which also flourishes in Japan. However, modern China is only just reviving religiously, and the position of Zen there is quite undefined. Another ten years and we will know more. We can, however, say briefly that during the history of Chinese Buddhism there seems to have been a minimum of chauvinism and Chinese nuns have shared with monks the religious teaching. During the eighteenth century nuns were renowned for their invincibility in Kung Fu competitions, and the very fact that they took part in them shows a much more liberal attitude than would have occurred in Japan at that time. A fairly modern record of a girl entering a Buddhist nunnery appeared in the prominent Buddhist periodical *Hai Ch'ao Yin* (Sound of the Tide) in 1923. Apart from her parents' disapproval all was straightforward, and in the end her parents provided some money for her.

The Pure Land school, which is now quite active in Japan, does not seem on the surface to have much respect for women. In its main sutra it states: "In the world made up of the wholesome roots of Mahayana (i.e. Pure Land) all are equal. Here, objectionable designations do not exist: women and those with defective senses and those belonging to the lineage of the two vehicles are not caused." Women do, however, play an active role in its practice.

To return to Zen. Throughout its history there has been no reason, except for cultural ones, why women should not have become teachers. The famous thirteenth-century Master Dogen made this plain:

What is more worthy about a male? Emptiness is emptiness; the four elements are the four elements: the five skandhas are the five skandhas. It is the same with the female; and actualising the Dharma is actualising the Dharma in either case. Simply you should revere and honour the one who actualises the Dharma and do not consider the matter of being male or female.

Various formidable nuns are mentioned in the Zen scriptures, and their teaching is acknowledged in some instances to have been superior to a master's, as in the following story: Gutei, the famous master, while he was first living in a small temple had a visit from a travelling nun who came into the temple without removing her headgear, not saying a word and ignoring the presence of Gutei. Carrying her staff with her, she went three times around the meditation chair in which Gutei was sitting. Then she said to him, "Say a word of Zen and I shall take off my hat." She repeated this three times, but Gutei did not know what to say. She was about to leave, when Gutei suggested: "It is growing late. Why not stay here overnight?" The nun answered, "If you say a word of Zen, I shall stay." As he was still unable to say a word, she left. This was a terrible blow for Gutei, who said to himself, "I was born a man and I was called a man, but I am useless as a man. Perhaps I am not a real man." He felt ashamed to be a monk so he made up his mind to leave the temple and travel and study more.

That scene took place in China, towards the end of the T'ang dynasty, but there are also stories of equally determined and awesome Japanese nuns. It is hard, though, to imagine such a scene taking place in Japan today although there is no doctrinal reason why they should not become *roshis* (masters). An English woman, Peggy Kennett, was made a *roshi* in Japan some twenty years ago.

Zen in America is perhaps the most hopeful of all for the participation of women. Whereas the western Theravada, as at Chithurst, is very slow to change and wants any change that does take place to be as little remarkable as possible, in American Zen the spirit seems quite the opposite. Zen masters in Japan are still surrounded by formality and mystique; in America the formality is much in abeyance. One, Sokei-an, did baby-sitting when he first arrived. Another, the Korean Seung Sahn, worked in a launderette. The spirit of the original Chinese Zen was always practical. From the beginning the monks look after themselves, growing food and cooking, cleaning, etc. Soto priests marry. All monks handle money, unlike the *bhikkhus,* and travel alone freely. In this milieu the acknowledgement of women as equal, both in the robe and as laywomen, is not difficult, and it is possible that western Zen may hold the key to the unlocking of women's participation in religion at the highest level.

Susan Murcott, editor of a journal on women and Zen and also an American Zen practitioner, thoughtfully discusses in a paper, "The Feminine in Zen Buddhism," certain aspects of the *form* of Zen. She considers that some of the Zen form may be inappropriate "for a community of western practitioners who stand behind the full equality of women in their respective sanghas" in spite of its freedom.

She defines the areas in which the feminine form is likely to be inappropriate: the Buddha himself, the Buddha legend, lineage, and the popular stereotype of Zen training. About the Buddha, she says:

Feminist theologian Carol Christ emphasizes that religions centered on the worship of a male god create moods and motivations that keep women in a state of psychological dependence on men and male authority. A woman can never have her full sexual identity affirmed as being in the image and likeness of God, an experience available to every man and boy in her culture.

While Zen does not hold the Buddha out as god, but as a man and a teacher, he is nevertheless the embodiment of the teaching. As a man, he is the centerpiece on many of our altars. The essential teaching is "When you meet the Buddha, you kill the Buddha" [to avoid clinging and attachment to a form]. But there he sits. He is revered as the first of the three Treasures—the Buddha, the Dharma and the Sangha. [The first of the three bows we perform each day is to his nature, which is our nature.]

If Carol Christ's point is valid, this obvious, but overlooked fact has significant psychological overtones for women practitioners.

About the myth, she says:

The core Buddhist myth is also problematical for men and women who consider themselves feminists. The Buddha's spiritual quest—seeking teachers, going beyond what these teachers could tell him, sitting alone, and making the supreme effort, finally attaining enlightenment by himself—is mythically akin to western attitudes of individualism, hard work and achievement. Minus the gender difference it is also close to some aspects of a woman's search for her liberated self—even the same word, liberation, is used. The woman who has looked to outside authority, to men—father, husband, lover or employer—has rejected these authorities, and makes a lonely personal journey.

Other aspects of the Siddhartha myth are more difficult to reconcile, both with prominent Yankee attitudes or with key elements of the potentially liberated woman's journey. The glorification of the life of renunciation over and against the realm of domesticity and the secular world is a tension that is implicit in the Buddha myth. The Buddha did not seek his enlightenment together with his wife. He did not act as father to his child. . . . [W]e should honestly acknowledge that this is not a myth that supports a father's daily care and responsibility for his child. I have known more than one instance of a man leaving his family either temporarily or permanently to practice Buddhism. Furthermore, I have known women encouraged not to come to practice while they raise small children. We live, not necessarily in every facet, according to the myths we choose. These myths do affect our behaviour at a profound level.[19]

The third area, lineage, may be an unfamiliar term outside Zen. It is the passing on from the master to his successor the essence of his teaching. Murcott comments that although coming from a Christian context and from a situation of struggle for the ordination of women, she was delighted to find that women could be teachers in Buddhism, at least potentially, because there was no dogma which prevented it. Nevertheless, the historical reality is that the lineage of teachers has been of men. Considerable power is attached to such men by their pupils, a power which is occasionally abused sexually in America, at the expense of women.

She suggests that the solution can be found through a more independent attitude to the relationship with teachers, that a practice "which truly fits" should not allow the teacher alone to be the mediator.

The final point about Zen training is the popular image of the hard and austere life, which she calls "samurai Zen." She believes that this image should change and that Zen can be practiced in all circumstances. She ends by saying:

In closing, I want to speak of the potential I feel is implicit in this new religious consciousness to meet the spiritual needs of many people of genuine religious yearning who are currently alienated from a spiritual home. There are two striking absences in our Judeo-Christian heritage as I and others may have experienced it.

One is a clearly defined method that gives back to the ordinary, non-professionally religious person, her or his own religious experience. This is experience we all have intimations of, if not in dramatic flashes of perfect and complete enlightenment, in a moment of loving another person or walking late on an ephemeral spring night. It is an experience of being one with the whole universe, an experience that can be returned to us through the method, through the essential elements of Zen practice. . . .

A second felt lack in the Judeo-Christian heritage is its inability to truly come to terms with women apart from strictly limited stereotypes of virgin, whore, mother, etc. Furthermore, patterns of dominance and submission, of God to believer, spill over into relations between men and women. There is probably not one person . . . in our current culture who doesn't struggle to find balance and harmony in their [sic] male/female relationships. By extension, we are unwilling to settle for a spirituality based on an authoritarian god whom we approach in submission and humility. Zen integrated with the insights of feminism offers a means to find that god is not outside, a nature one with our own nature, and to assure a *form* that acknowledges and balances the integrity of women and men, alone and together.

I see Zen influenced by the insights of feminism has the potential to speak to that need, if it can identify and hold fast to its treasure and not cling to forms no longer appropriate for western culture.[20]

To conclude this survey, we can say that western Mahayana Buddhism possibly gives the greatest freedom to its women teachers of almost any recognized religion, that in Japan and Korea the potential for this state of affairs is there if not acted upon, but that Theravada Buddhism lags well behind. Nevertheless, a recent Buddhist women's conference in Rhode Island (June 1983) brought together women teachers from all the schools—western,

Korean, Japanese and Theravadin—with a view to finding "an American expression of Buddhism." They included Master Dharma Teachers from Seung Sahn's Korean school, Roshi Maureen Freedgood, and a woman tulku from the Tibetan school—all women have risen to the top of the ordination hierarchy in their particular schools.

Yet, why are women content to be looked upon as religiously inferior beings? This question applies to all religions. Men ordain each other in hierarchical formation. Why are women prepared to wait, perhaps indefinitely, for men's grudging approval which will place their feet on the ladder too? Why do women not take the whole issue into their own hands and ordain each other, or start a church which has no need of ordination? These are random questions, yet they apply to much of Buddhism as well as to other religions and might be carefully considered by the reader.

# NOTES

1. Frank Lee Woodward, *Some Sayings of the Buddha* (Oxford: Oxford University Press, 1973), 82.

2. Mrs. Rhys Davids, *A Manual of Buddhism* (London: Sheldon Press, 1932), 269.

3. Isaline Blew Horner, *Women Under Primitive Buddhism* (London: George Routledge and Sons, 1930), 159.

4. Denise Lardner Carmody, *Women and World Religions* (Tennessee: Parthenon Press, 1979), 51.

5. Ibid., 51.

6. Ibid., 52.

7. In Kiyota Minoru, ed., *Mahayana Buddhist Meditation* (Honolulu, Hawaii: University Press, 1978), 129.

8. Horner, *Women Under Primitive Buddhism*, 308.

9. Ibid., 291.

10. Ibid., 291.

11. Ibid., 287 f.

12. Edward Conze, *Thirty Years of Buddhist Studies* (London: Bruno Cassirer, 1967), 81.

13. Bhikshu Sangharakshita, *A Survey of Buddhism* (India: Indian Institute of World Culture, 1957), 250.

14. Stephen Beyer, *The Buddhist Experience* (California: Dickenson Publishing Co., 1974), 260.

15. Ibid., 258.

16. Bhikkhu Khantipalo, *Banner of the Arahants* (Sri Lanka: Buddhist Publication Society, 1979), 183.

17. Ibid., 187.

18. Charles Bell, *The Religion of Tibet* (Oxford: Clarendon Press, 1931), 26.

19. Susan Murcott, "The Feminine in Zen," *Kahawai: Journal of Women and Zen* 5, no. 4 (Fall 1983): 22–27. The quotations are on 23 f. and 24 f.

20. Ibid., 27.

# II.

# CONTEMPORARY
# PERSPECTIVES

# Introduction by the editor
## URSULA KING

There exists a vast body of literature on women in the Judeo-Christian tradition, but relatively little is known on women in new religious movements. This section contains two contributions in this area, women in the Unification Church and in Krishna Consciousness. Both movements have their origin in the East (Korea and India, respectively) but a considerable following as well in the West. Both are indebted to long-established religious traditions: while the beliefs and practices of the Unification Church are predominantly shaped by the Christian tradition, Krishna Consciousness is deeply rooted in the Hindu tradition. Both also share a universal outlook. The position of women is quite different in both movements but has some interesting parallels.

The section opens with a chapter on women in the Hare Krishna movement. Drawing on her recent study of this movement, Kim Knott compares the role of women devotees with that of men, beginning with a description of a Krishna Consciousness morning service in Boston, Massachusetts, performed by male renunciates. Their ubiquitous activites raise the question of what role women have in this religious movement. In many respects men and women perform the same functions, such as working in the kitchen, cooking, cleaning, distributing literature about the movement, etc. Earlier sociological studies have emphasized the inferior status of women in the Hare Krishna Movement. But what appears to be the case from a purely external, Western point of view possesses in fact quite a different reality and dynamic for the insiders, the committed members of the movement. Their starting point is the equality of all souls before God, so that the prime characteristic of every devotee, whether male or female, is complete service and surrender to God. Thus problems of different levels of meaning arise in the interpretation of the beliefs and practices of the movement. While the writings of the founder of the Hare Krishna Movement include negative comments about women, these must be seen in a wider context. Evidence shows that women from different social and educational backgrounds join the movement, and current leaders affirm that in principle women could become presidents of temples, take renunciation, or be gurus like men. (Thus far this has not happened.)

The second chapter provides a detailed survey of the rise of feminist thinking in American evangelical Christianity where one would perhaps least expect it. Richard Quebedeaux begins his contribution with a brief discussion of recent changes in family life, employment and education which have affected American women during the last two decades. While the development of the women's liberation movement and of Christian feminism have been frequently described, the rise of feminism within American evangelicalism is much less well known. This history is traced here, and its nature and significance are explored within the broader context of the evangelical tradition. "We're on our way, Lord!" was the conference theme song of the first full-fledged feminist conference of the evangelical movement held in November, 1975. Developments since then have shown that evangelical feminists "are catching up fast" and are well on their way "into modernity and its concomitant, equal opportunity with men."

The following chapter by Harriet Erica Baber is explicitly concerned with a philosophical analysis of the arguments which have been brought against the 1976 decision of the Episcopal Church in America to ordain women as priests. She examines the logical implications of various arguments, especially the thesis that men are a natural symbol of Christ. According to her, "there seems no plausible reason to hold that men are natural symbols of Christ, and hence can function as priests while women are not and therefore cannot." She also argues that the archetypal images of man and woman underlying much of the debate are ambiguous and need transcending, especially as gender in our society has lost much of its symbolic import. While in the past it may have been proper or even obligatory to exclude women from the priesthood, there are currently no compelling theological reasons to exclude them, and philosophical arguments based on the inability of women to function as "natural symbols" of Christ are shown to be illogical.

Following this philosophical debate is a discussion of Unification theology and ritual, examined from the perspective of a woman member. Its author, Sarah Petersen, joined the Unification Church in 1973 and married another member in 1982. Her contribution provides one of the few accounts available on women in the Unification Church. It begins with a discussion of images of the feminine in Unification theology, especially the basic polarity of femininity and masculinity in the understanding of God. While this has been discussed in other studies on Unification theology, this contribution looks specifically at the spiritual practices of women church members, their important contribution to the development of the movement and their comparative invisibility in the official, written accounts of Unification Church history. Descriptions of rituals undertaken at the time of engagement, marriage and childbirth and of teaching materials used by the Unification Church will be new to most readers. Church literature is examined with regard to its image of women, to mysticism, and to other aspects of doctrine. The chapter concludes by discussing the results of a brief survey undertaken among church members which point to a situation of ambivalence regarding the role of women in the Unification Church. As in other religions, the image of woman is blurred, unclear or tentative in Unification thought and practice, "but its presence is acknowledged perhaps more powerfully than in the Judeo-Christian tradition out of which the Unification Church arises. Whether the Unification approach will finally liberate the face of femininity for both male and female will not be decided now—salvation is both an event, and a process."

The last contribution to this section provides a rather different perspective within the context of contemporary thinking. Christian Gaba examines the traditional place of women in the religious experience of one African people, the Anlo from West Africa, and discusses its contemporary significance. He describes Anlo religious beliefs and practices and shows how menstruation taboos play a central role in determining and limiting the ritual position and activities of women. Women are subordinate to men, but once they have reached the menopause, they can achieve a similar ritual rank as men. He includes fascinating details about marriage practices, child-bearing and premarital sex. The ambivalence towards womanhood among the Anlo people reflects women's close association with blood, but from a wider perspective it is equally related to the duality and ambivalence of life in general. The practices of Anlo society are commented upon in relation to the perception of the sacred in traditional societies. This raises the question how far traditional views will be maintained once Anlo society becomes industrialized. It is Gaba's contention that the traditional religious world-view will allow women to find a holistic solution and that feminism will not take the same virulent form in African traditional societies as in the modern industrialized societies of the West.

One could argue with several statements in this and other chapters of this section, especially if one takes into account various feminist reflections found elsewhere in this book. It is hoped that the following chapters will give readers food for thought and discussion and will encourage further study of the perspectives presented.

# 7

# Men and Women, or Devotees? Krishna Consciousness and the Role of Women

## KIM KNOTT

It is central Boston, and it is early morning.[1] A day breaks in the service of Sri Krishna. For the *brahmacharis*—the young, celibate, male devotees—the early hours are spent in ablutions, in worshipping Krishna in the first of the day's religious services, and in chanting the *Hare Krishna mantra,* the holy names of God. As most of Boston is thinking of rising for work, the *brahmacharis* gather in the temple to greet the Deities.[2]

The curtains open. Lying prostrate on the floor in homage, the *brahmacharis* pay their obeisances to Radha and Krishna. The music begins, and the devotees, standing close to the Deities, admire their clothes, and the jewels and garlands with which they are adorned. Some of the *brahmacharis* are swaying, others standing quite still, all transfixed by the beauty of Radha and Krishna. Then, with the beat of the *mrdanga* and the clash of the *kartalas,* *guru-puja* begins. The *guru* or spiritual master is honored with offerings of incense, light, cloth, water, and flowers. Each *brahmachari* offers a handful of petals at his feet. Songs of praise are sung, and the peaceful and reverent mood gradually changes to a mood of ecstatic celebration: the swaying turns to energetic dancing; the slow tempo accelerates to a fast and lively rhythm. Everyone is fully involved, happy to be worshipping and serving Krishna and His representative. The *puja* is followed by a class—a reading and discourse on a passage from scripture. As time is precious, hearing the class is combined with other activities: the young *brahmacharis* prepare vegetables for the day's meals or make garlands, carefully selecting and sewing together the carnations, roses and lilies for tomorrow's offering. After class, and a vegetarian breakfast, the day's work begins, the *brahmacharis* dispersing to the kitchens, the *ashram* or the streets, to cook, to clean or to distribute literature.

The devotional life of Krishna Consciousness is not a life for *brahmacharis* alone. These acts of worship and service are also performed by married men, and women, both married and single. Thus, it might seem a little odd to have begun an account about women and their lives in this religious movement with a description of men and what they do. The reason for this is that we can learn a great deal about the position of women in the Hare Krishna Movement if we start by looking at the men. In this case it can help us to appreciate the perspective from which the issue of gender is approached within the Hare Krishna Movement itself. Looking back to the short description of the morning program at the Boston temple, we can see that the activities of a *brahmachari* are hardly what one might call "masculine" in type. *Brahmacharis,* like other men and women, engage in singing and dancing, sewing, cooking, dressing the Deities, praising and admiring clothes and flowers, all in a submissive and obedient manner. Roles which have traditionally been assigned to women are here adopted by both sexes.

## Devotees on the Role of Women in Krishna Consciousness

According to accounts by women in the Hare Krishna Movement, however, their role is not restricted to these activities. When asked about this, one devotee replied,

Some [women] are designers, writers, accountants, teachers, housewives, secretaries, cinematographers. I know one who's a landscape architect, one who runs an art gallery. Their roles are no different from women outside the movement. The difference is their consciousness.[3]

Another woman commented,

There are no exclusively female vocations in the movement. Both men and women cook, clean, and raise children. And rather than remain homebound, our women are strongly encouraged to be assertive as missionaries and preachers.[4]

Women devotees have also been eager to stress other aspects of their equality with men: "The scriptures do describe women as a cause of material entanglement for men, and that's true. But scripture balances that out by describing that men are also a material entanglement for women"; ". . . unmarried women . . . live as celibates within the protection of the temple community, living the same ascetic, devotional life as the male disciples."[5]

Furthermore, these women do not seem to have turned their backs on the subject of the exploitation and oppression of women in general. One woman writes of contemporary society, "[It] is pervaded by a perception of women as sources of satisfaction—especially sexual satisfaction—for men."[6] Another, while giving the final authority to God, writes,

Of course, this doesn't mean we should give up trying to protect ourselves, trying to right the wrongs of an inequitable society. (I have been in a number of places, from the jungle villages of Bengal to the streets of New York, where I wished my karate was in better shape.) Surely we should use the machinery of democracy to help the exploited minorities. . . . [W]e can appeal for the help of the greater social body; we can use our intelligence to fight for the cause of just government. . . .[7]

## Sociologists on the Role of Women in Krishna Consciousness

This phenomenon of spiritual and practical equality does not readily conform to the picture of Krishna Consciousness presented to us in the sociological literature. In the earliest and most detailed account of the Hare Krishna Movement, J. Stillson Judah described the place of women as follows:

The position of women in the Society may not appeal to Americans interested in women's liberation. Swami Bhaktivedanta says that all women other than one's wife are to be considered as one's mother, and yet he regards them as prone to degradation, of little intelligence, and untrustworthy. They should not be given as much freedom as men, but should be treated like children; they should be protected all during their lives, by their fathers when young, later by their husbands, and in their old age, by their sons. . . . This view is largely consonant with the traditional one found in the ancient Indian law books. Females may not become presidents of any temple, nor occupy positions of authority. They may do the cooking, help with the devotional services and maintenance of the temple, and prepare the flower offerings for Krishna.[8]

This view was reiterated by Francine Daner: "Ideally, the woman must be completely submissive and a constant servant to her husband"; Vishal Mangalvadi: "The strongest opposition to it [the Hare Krishna Movement] has come from the feminist movements, because of the low position it gives to women"; and John Whitworth and Martin Shiels: "Women are regarded as being at

113

once childlike and dangerous as it is their nature to tempt men from the paths of virtue, and are felt to be less intelligent than men and hence less reliable."[9]

## An Introduction to the Debate

Clearly, more than one issue is being raised in these comments. Not just what women should do and how they should do it are described here, but the fundamental nature of women according to Hare Krishna teachings is also discussed. Is it possible to square the account given by the devotees themselves with this sociological critique? Are women and men in the movement really treated as so radically different, the one so low and the other so far superior? Why then do the Boston devotees, both female and male, share the same tasks and behave in the same way?

To answer these questions in full it is essential for us to have detailed, objective information on both the beliefs and practices of Krishna Consciousness concerning the issue of gender. In addition, to comprehend the debate more fully it is important to gain some insight into the problems of interpretation which revolve around the issue of women in the movement. To achieve these objectives of description and explanation would require more space than is available here. The remainder of this account, therefore, will confine itself to an attempt to isolate some of the areas of controversy and misunderstanding which have arisen from the Hare Krishna Movement's teachings on the nature and role of women.

The International Society for Krishna Consciousness, or the Hare Krishna Movement as it is better known, despite having been established only in 1966, is concerned to spread the beliefs and practices popularized in India in the early sixteenth century by Chaitanya Mahaprabhu. As such it comprises an active part of the Indian tradition of *vaishnava bhakti,* loving devotion to Krishna or Vishnu. Although it is new to the West, it is familiar to Indians and is seen by them as a legitimate form of Hinduism. In its early days in the West those who joined were nearly all young.[10] It is helpful to remember that although they were quick to learn, they did not at first have a sophisticated understanding of the teachings of the movement or its founder, A. C. Bhaktivedanta Swami Prabhupada. This resulted in a great many disputes and misunderstandings, some of which are reflected in the sociological observations quoted above. Although there are undoubtedly still a number of devotees, both male and female, who consider women to be physically weaker than men and, in general, less desirous of pursuing managerial and administrative positions, there are few who would go as far as the girl interviewed by Judah in the early 1970s:

Well, spiritually, we have an equal position. . . . We're subordinate now in Kali Yuga, but it doesn't mean we're inferior necessarily. Actually we are. . . . I can see that women tend to flip out a lot more than men. They are more emotional. Women's lib tries to gloss over all of the very obvious differences . . . and it's nonsense. . . . On the whole we are less intelligent, our attention is not so good. . . . So we take our orders from the men and it's nice. They're very nice. It's no problem. You're protected and you're given instruction, and you don't have to make the decisions; it's really pleasant. . . . The boys really have propensities for administration . . . that we just don't have. So it must be my female body, but I'm very pleased not to have to make very many decisions anymore.[11]

Generally speaking both female and male devotees in Britain and America reject these views. The spiritual leadership teaches a view of equality, and practical opportunities for advancement are there for any person who has the propensity and desire to take them up.[12] How this view of equality is understood and practiced, of course, is conditioned by a range of complex psychological, social and historical considerations. These are general issues in the contemporary feminist discussion, and do not need to be reiterated here. Let us consider instead the background to the equality which is apparently both taught and used as a guide to social practice in the Hare Krishna Movement.

## Equality and the Soul: The Starting Point

Women themselves have to transcend the bodily conception of life and become liberated from the mundane social sexual rat race. And of course men have to raise *their* consciousness. Spiritual life begins with the realisation that one is not the material body but an eternal spiritual soul and the designations "male" and "female" refer only to the material body. So ultimately they have nothing to do with the soul or self.[13]

The majority of the articles written on the subject of women in Krishna Consciousness by devotees themselves make this their focus of attention.[14] Judah also mentions this: "Regardless of their social positions, the souls of female devotees are to be considered of equal value with their male counterparts."[15] While this priority can be confusing to those outside the movement who are not acquainted with Krishna Consciousness philosophy or its language, it is central to those within it. Like many religions, then, this movement teaches spiritual equality. All the selves or souls *(jiva)* are of the same quality and nature. They are distinct from one another, and are both one with and different to the supreme soul, God or Krishna.[16]

The self-realization sought in Krishna Consciousness is not primarily the liberation of the soul from the round of rebirth *(samsara),* although this is a by-product of this process, but the attainment and perfection of a relationship of loving service to God. *Bhakti* or devotional service is both the path and the goal. It is a path open to anyone. It is a path whose success is dependent not just on the regulative principles (abstention from meat, alcohol, illicit sex and gambling) but particularly on a "service attitude," a position of surrender to Krishna, the spiritual master or *guru,* and all the other devotees. Egoism, pride, envy, and greed, whether they are directed to material or spiritual attainments, are signs of deviation from the realization that one is by nature a servant. In Krishna Consciousness it is essential to recognize the dutiful nature *(dharma)* of the soul as well as the body. While the latter is dependent on one's social position and stage of life, the former is eternal *(sanatana).* It is the constitutional nature of the soul to be a servant of God. The perfection of this natural role is exemplified by Radha, the consort of Krishna.

This then explains why devotees writing on the subject of women return again and again to this philosophical starting point. This is where their concept of equality has its roots. What is more, the success of the self-realization of the soul is measured against the "service attitude" of Radha. Therefore, in theory, it is not that the women on the path of Krishna Consciousness must practice a male-oriented spirituality but that all devotees, whether female or male, must adopt what might be called a "female" approach to spirituality.[17] This "female" approach is essentially an attitude— spiritual, mental and physical—of surrender and service to others, and ultimately to Krishna.

To call this a "female" approach, of course, begs all sorts of questions. The important point, however, is that it is an approach to which all devotees aspire, and with which, by virtue of their social and cultural conditioning, women are generally more at home. Women, in the West as well as in India, are better practiced at adopting a "service attitude," a role of submission and obedience, than men. Many men find it difficult, for example, to surrender to a spiritual master, and there have been innumerable battles in the history of the movement over the issue of serving God through his representative. Women seem to have less problem accepting this aspect of the philosophy or the practical consequences of obedient and submissive behavior. There are, of course, a number of women who, while attracted to some aspects of the philosophy, find the notion of submission initially objectionable on the grounds that it reminds them of the oppression that as intelligent women they are trying to escape. It will be pointed out to them, however, that there is a difference between material submission and spiritual submission: material submission leads to oppression while spiritual submission leads to liberation.

The philosophy of Krishna Consciousness concerning the soul can be seen to be fairly straightforward, and although it can be problematic for some men and women, it is unquestionably a philosophy of equality. What about the philosophy of the body, though? Is this where the issue of inequality, and thus the sociological critique, arises?

## Equality and the Body: "A Can of Worms"?

Although the soul is eternal and the body impermanent in the philosophy of Krishna Consciousness, the body is not ignored. The body is there to enable the soul to serve God. Unlike the souls, bodies are different, each one having a different *dharma* or duty. This duty differs according to one's social situation *(varna)* and stage of life *(ashrama)*. [18] This, it seems, is where some of the confusion arises both in critical circles outside the movement and also within the movement itself. The disparity of views on the issue of material, as opposed to spiritual, equality is related to three factors: a confusion of levels of meaning concerning social duty *(varnashramadharma)*, a mistaken comparison between ideal and empirical considerations, and the problem of decontextualized appraisals.

### The problem of levels of meaning

These factors need to be explained. The first stems directly from the teachings on *dharma* as they relate to women, and concerns three distinct levels of meaning. Because these are not always clearly distinguished, they have led to a certain amount of confusion both inside and outside the movement. The first question is, what is meant by *dharma?* To be more explicit, what is meant by *varnashramadharma,* one's duty according to one's social situation and stage of life? Following this, what are the implications of this for women in the movement? Is their duty defined by ancient Indian texts? Do they behave like other Hindu women? Are they trying to live out a philosophy derived centuries ago in a different social and cultural context? Both Judah and Whitworth and Shiels mention "Hindu theology," and Daner uses the phrase "Vedic ideals."[19] What is the Krishna Consciousness understanding of duty, particularly the duty of women, and how does it relate to Hindu theology and Vedic ideals?

Krishna Consciousness philosophy, as we have seen, is commonly understood by outsiders to be prejudicial to women and by insiders to be fair to women. This can be explained if we distinguish between the three definitions of *varnashramadharma* which might best be designated "Vedic," "Hindu," and "Krishna Conscious."[20] Although devotees frequently refer to what they call the "Vedic" way of life, at the theological level a distinction is drawn between the Vedic way of life per se and the ideal, "Krishna Conscious" way of life.

The "Vedic" way of life is specific to a particular period of time and a particular people, who lived out their relation to God in a particular social form.[21] In Vedic *varnashramadharma* men served God through their spiritual masters, and women served God through the men who protected them: their fathers, husbands, or sons. Because they understand it to have been operated in a different time and place, and by a people who knew perfectly how best to serve God, the devotees do not see this arrangement as unequal or oppressive. The men did not abuse their positions by using them as mechanisms for the pursuit of power over women, and women served God by supporting the male members of their family. In this arrangement, the husband was the wife's spiritual master. This view of social life has a historical reality for devotees which we will return to shortly.

The "Hindu" concept of *varnashramadharma* also has a historical reality, but it relates to a different historical period. Indian religion operates with the concept of *yugas* or ages. The devotional view conceives of the Vedic period as constituting the end of the previous age, *dvapara yuga*. The current age is *kali yuga,* the dark age. The "Hindu" social system is a function of this age. During this period Indians have continued to live by the social rules of Vedic *varnashramadharma,* but these have become distorted. In *kali yuga* the path of spiritual life has become obscured, and people resort to the lesser goals of material and sensual gratification. What was once a spiritually legitimated system of social organization becomes a means of oppression and hierarchical division. Women are still expected to serve but, instead of offering spiritual guidance and protection, the men use and oppress their "chattels."

The "Krishna Conscious" view is an attempt to apply the Vedic "service attitude" to *kali yuga,* the dark age. The aim is not to copy the Vedic system, but to use it for guidance in a troubled period. This cannot be achieved by introducing the system wholesale and expecting it to work. This, as the devotees see it, is the failing of the "Hindu" system. For this reason, in the "Krishna Conscious" system, men and women are seen not only as spiritually alike but also materially alike in the sense that they are ultimately responsible for their own spiritual welfare. Both men and women take *gurus,* and when they marry, although the women are responsible for bearing and raising children and the men for supporting them in this, both are expected to serve Krishna and the spiritual master in the best way they can, be this cooking, teaching, sewing, writing, designing, painting or whatever. Women are not seen as less intelligent or less able. In some practical situations it is expected that the man will have more propensity to guide the family; in others it is quite clear that the wife is more capable in these matters.

Following the Vedic ideal in this dark and dangerous age of *kali yuga,* then, does not mean that women should submit to the whims of their husbands but that both parties should do whatever is best for serving Krishna. In the Vedic period this would naturally have meant service through the husband; in *kali yuga* it means service to the spiritual master by whatever means is most conducive. If a woman feels that her spiritual life is best practiced through serving her husband she should focus on this; if she feels that she can serve best through "cooperative independence" she should cultivate her career in conjunction with looking after her family.

The ideal to which devotees aspire is not the Vedic *varnashrama* system of old but the Vedic *varnashrama* system accommodated to *kali yuga,* to here and now. This can be extremely misleading as devotees continue to refer to both systems as "Vedic." For this reason, the latter, the ideal Vedic system, is referred to as the "Krishna Conscious" system of *varnashramadharma.* [22]

Needless to say these complex levels of interpretation have led to many misunderstandings among both commentators and devotees. The view that has been held at times by members of both camps, that the philosophy of Krishna Consciousness is either uncompromisingly "Vedic" or uncompromisingly "Hindu," is inaccurate. The founder of the movement, Bhaktivedanta Swami, made a philosophy available to women that had once been largely closed to them, allowing them material equality with men and the opportunity to serve in the same ways and by the same means. [23]

## Mistaken comparisons

The disparity of views on the issues of women's material equality is further compounded by the problem of comparison. Commentators outside the movement and exponents inside the movement make frequent use of the device of comparison in order to underline the differences between the relative situations of women. Sometimes a writer seeks only to observe a difference; at other times he or she may seek to show that one situation is superior to another. Both intentions are perfectly legitimate, when and where appropriate, if and when they compare like with like. In the sociological accounts attention was given to the practical restrictions placed on women in the movement. Judah, for example, stated that, "Females may not become presidents of any temple, nor occupy positions of authority. They may do the cooking, help with the devotional services and maintenance of the temple, and prepare flower offerings for Krishna." [24] Reading this we feel that women in the Hare Krishna Movement in the early 1970s had a particularly difficult situation. In terms of practical role equality within the movement, they did. However, if we think of women in American society as a whole in the early seventies, we remember that the situation was not so different. Few women were in important managerial positions or were engaged in activities other than those traditionally assigned to women. There were welcome ideals concerning the equality of women and their career entitlements, but these had not filtered through to the practice of working life and domestic life in general.

The implicit suggestion is that the practice of gender roles in Krishna Consciousness differs radically from the ideal of gender roles in liberated American society. This is true, but is it a fair point of comparison? Devotees writing on this subject are equally prone to the rhetorical device of comparing like with unlike. "When Krishna, or God, is at the center of our relationships, we can live in perfect harmony with those around us. This principle is basic to the entire Krishna Consciousness Movement. Without a spiritual foundation a marriage stands a good chance of deteriorating into the 50 percent of recent U.S. marriages ending in divorce."[25] Here, the "principle" of Krishna Conscious marriage is compared favorably with the "empirical observation" of the poor success rate of American marriages in general. But are Krishna Conscious marriages always true to the ideal? Do they never fail? Are there not laudable sentiments concerning love and marriage even in secular society which, if they could be adhered to, would provide the basis for a higher rate of success?

These mistaken, and I am sure unconscious, comparisons of principles or ideals with practices or empirical observations tend to exacerbate the disparity between the views of women inside and outside the movement. The "life" of women in the movement, therefore, can seem and has seemed restrictive by the "standards" of those outside. The same kind of problem can arise, but for different reasons, from the third of these factors.

### Decontextualized appraisals

"Ideally, the woman must be completely submissive and a constant servant to her husband."[26] This was how Daner described the theoretical role of women in the Hare Krishna Movement in the mid-1970s. From what we have seen of the philosophy of Krishna Consciousness there is some truth in this. It would be true also to say that the man must be submissive, and a servant to his wife. (The suffix, *"dasa"* or *"dasi,"* which all devotees take after their names, denotes "servant.") The important point, of course, is that everyone is a servant of God, and must be submissive, particularly to the spiritual master, but also to all other *vaishnava* devotees.[27] Daner's comment is not incorrect but, by making no reference to the philosophy which produces this ideal, it suggests that women are subordinate.[28] The female devotees themselves inevitably encourage this view in their speech and behavior because they are attempting at all times to develop their humility (as indeed the men should do). It would be unlikely, for example, for a woman in Krishna Consciousness to deny the importance of service to her husband. What she might neglect to point out is that he is also expected to serve her.

The teachings of Krishna Consciousness concerning the body and material life have produced a number of problems of interpretation. As we have seen some of these have resulted from the complexity of the teachings themselves. This itself has been compounded by the fact that, as a young movement with an old theology, its members are still learning the task of articulation. The other problems are related not to the teachings directly but to the way in which they have been expressed by those describing the movement. In some ways they are only minor points but they have had an important effect on our understanding of the teachings concerning the role of women in Hare Krishna. Whereas the souls are equal and the same, in Krishna Consciousness bodies are equal but different. The souls have the same nature *(dharma)*; bodies have different natures, depending on their social situation (which itself depends on *karma*). It is not the case, however, that women's bodies and minds are of lower status than the bodies and minds of men. Neither is it the case that the souls which inhabit women's bodies must be born again in men's bodies in order to achieve liberation. As far as it is possible to tell, the philosophy of Krishna Consciousness attributes spiritual and material equality to women and men. This is not to say, however, that women and men use this potential, or have been allowed to use this potential in the same way.

## Bhaktivedanta Swami on Women

The final area of debate which needs to be examined in relation to the philosophy of Krishna Consciousness is why, if it is true that Bhaktivedanta Swami made such provision for women, he regarded them, according to Judah, "as prone to degradation, of little intelligence, and untrustworthy."[29] It is undeniably true that in both the texts translated by Bhaktivedanta Swami and the works written directly by him women are periodically described in the most unflattering terms. In *Krsna: The Supreme Personality of Godhead,* for example, he wrote, "never put your trust in a diplomat or a woman," and referred to women as "less intelligent."[30]

In order to understand why someone who upheld such an apparently sexist view should choose to open his movement to women, we must again return to the focal point of the philosophy, the equality of the souls. Bhaktivedanta Swami clearly saw all his disciples as equal. He did not, however, see those outside the Krishna Consciousness Movement as necessarily equal, although they had the potential to be so once they saw themselves as spiritual rather than material entities. To put it another way, according to the "bodily conception" of life there are men and women; according to the "spiritual conception" there are only souls. When two female devotees asked Bhaktivedanta Swami if they would make slower progress than the male devotees, he replied, "Yes . . . if you think of yourselves as women, how will you make any advancement? You must see yourself as spirit-soul, eternal servant of Krsna."[31]

Until Bhaktivedanta Swami's arrival in the United States in 1966 his religious training and his empirical experience had encouraged him to describe women in this way. In the *vaishnava bhakti* tradition of which he was a part, the emphasis had previously been placed on the spiritual progress of men. Certain women, renowned for their great spirituality, were mentioned favorably in the texts, but they had no place in the ritual practices or the *ashrams* of this tradition.[32] In addition, the normal role of women in Indian society was one of domestic subservience, with few women given the opportunity to attain higher material or spiritual positions. For men engaged in spiritual life, women, because they were thus rather inevitably bound up with things of a material nature (the family, the health of its members, its income, food, clothes, etc.), were to be kept at a distance. When Bhaktivedanta Swami came to the United States, however, his empirical experience altered. In a talk to the residents of Vrndavana, India, several years after his arrival in America, he reported, ". . . in the Western countries there is no distinction. They [boys and girls] are given equal liberty. In our country there is still discrimination."[33] Because of this he saw it as appropriate to allow both men and women to enter his movement, to become disciples on the path of Krishna Consciousness.

Like the issue of women's social duty, this aspect of the teachings is rather complex. In summary, while Bhaktivedanta Swami understood all souls to be equal, he understood material bodies to be different. As he saw it, women's bodies, and their traditional maternal roles, were more constraining than men's bodies and roles insofar as they were more effective in binding the soul to its material covering and the body to the material world and material relationships. When he arrived in America, however, where he was soon greeted by female as well as male devotees, he saw that young women there had been encouraged to develop their intelligence, their skills and their independence, and were thus more able, materially and intellectually, to pursue a spiritual path than most of their Indian sisters.

## The Debate: Conclusions

As we have seen, it is not altogether surprising that the Hare Krishna Movement has been commonly understood to be a sexist organization. The sociological studies have described it as largely unfavorable to women. Its texts have referred to women both as a danger to men and as less spiritually oriented than men. Even some of the devotees have suggested that as women they are subordinate to men. It has this much in common with other religions. That these views can be explained, however, does not let the movement "off the hook." It is apparent that the understanding of the issue of gender in the Hare Krishna Movement depends first on one's standpoint, and secondly on whether one is responding to the philosophy or the practice of Krishna Consciousness. The first proviso, one's standpoint, depends on whether one is an observer or a devotee. It is not impossible, as an observer, to understand the movement's attitude to the question of gender, but it is difficult, because it requires pushing through what at first sight seem to be deeply sexist obstacles. Constantly one is subliminally comparing one perspective with another, the Hare Krishna perspective with the contemporary western perspective. The Hare Krishna perspective comes off badly in this comparison. But like all religions Krishna Consciousness has its own dynamic, its own history, and its own criteria, on the basis of which the perspective comes more clearly into focus. Most of the devotees approach this issue from within this framework. This is what I have tried to do here.

The second determinant of one's understanding of this issue is brought about by the data themselves. Is our observation, comment or criticism directed at the beliefs or the practices of Krishna Consciousness? Here, the emphasis has been placed on the philosophy espoused by the devotees of the Hare Krishna Movement. After close scrutiny of the criticisms levelled at the philosophy, it would appear that, although the issue is complex, women and men on the path of Krishna Consciousness are afforded equality, both spiritually and materially. Had the emphasis been placed on the practice of this philosophy, the conclusion may have been different. As in most areas of western society practice has still to catch up with belief. The principles are there, but the empirical evidence points to a certain reluctance to put them into practice. Had Judah said, "women *are not* presidents of any temple" rather than "women *may not become* presidents of any temple," he would have been more accurate.[34] At present, although there is no philosophical barrier to their progress, women are not temple presidents, members of the Governing Body Commission, or spiritual masters. The barriers, as in other social and religious organizations, are historical, social and psychological. It is certainly the case that women are pursuing varied and interesting careers in the Hare Krishna Movement, and it is also true that the issue itself—of women, their practical roles and spiritual advancement—is currently given much serious attention. There is definitely room for women, in practical terms, to become "more" equal.

There are many interesting and important subjects for discussion in relation to women and the practice of Krishna Consciousness: e.g., women and renunciation *(sannyasa),* the role of women in spiritual teaching, attitudes of men to women and their roles, segregation of the sexes, and recent developments in the awareness of women and men in relation to feminism.[35] For devotees, however, the primary issue is the philosophy, the teachings of Bhaktivedanta Swami and his predecessors concerning the path and the aim of self-realization, loving service to God. For them, this is the natural starting point in any discussion. They are assured that it does not matter whether one has the body of a woman or a man. Loving service is open to all. How one practices this will depend on the body, whether it is old or young, rich or poor, healthy or sick, female or male. It is the soul, however, which engages in the relationship of loving service, and the soul is not bound by these external conditions. Those in the Hare Krishna Movement, then, distinguish between men and women, and devotees. Men and women see a material world filled with bodies; devotees see a spiritual world inhabited only by God and souls.

# NOTES

1. The sources for this account were miscellaneous articles concerning the role of women and related issues in *Back to Godhead,* the magazine of the Hare Krishna Movement, and interviews with devotees in Boston, Mass. and Watford, U.K.

2. The Hare Krishna devotees refer to the temple forms of Radha and Krishna as "Deities," as God is said to inhabit his various consecrated forms at prescribed times. I have used the term "Deities" in the text without explanation because it is my intention to provide a phenomenological account of the role of women in the Hare Krishna Movement. This issue has been the source of some controversy between commentators and devotees, and the latter have had little opportunity to explain their philosophy on this subject. The aim here, then, is to present this philosophy from their perspective. In order to do this I have focused on the critical questions which have arisen in the sociological literature.

3. Satarupa dasi, "I am not this body," interview in *Who Are They?* (Los Angeles: Bhaktivedanta Book Trust, 1982), 16.

4. Sitarana dasi, "What's the role of women in Krsna Consciousness? A Krsna Conscious woman explains," interview in *Back to Godhead* 17, no. 12 (1982): 26.

5. Ibid., 26.

6. Ibid., 11.

7. Nandarani dasi, "How a Krsna Conscious woman achieved liberation: a queen of Vedic India found freedom in dependence," *Back to Godhead* 15, no. 12 (1980): 28.

8. J. Stillson Judah, *Hare Krishna and the Counterculture* (New York: Wiley, 1974), 86. This account of the Hare Krishna Movement remains the most thorough and detailed account available. Although I have tried to highlight some of the problems which have arisen in the observers' accounts of the role of women in Krishna Consciousness, it is not my intention to imply that these accounts are of no interest or worth. Both Judah and Daner (see below), in particular, combined detailed fieldwork with serious historical and sociological analysis to provide excellent accounts of this movement in the early 1970s.

9. Francine Daner, *The American Children of Krsna* (New York: Holt, Rinehart and Winston, 1976), 68. Vishal Mangalvadi, *The World of the Gurus* (Delhi: Vikas, 1977), 98. John Whitworth and Martin Shiels, "From across the black waters two imported varieties of Hinduism—the Hare Krishnas and the Ramakrishna Vedanta Society," 161, in Eileen Barker, ed., *New Religious Movements: A Perspective for Understanding Society* (New York: Edwin Mellen, 1982), 155–72.

10. For more information on this early period see Judah, *Hare Krishna;* Satsvarupa dasa Goswami, *Srila Prabhupada-lilamrta,* 6 vols. (Los Angeles: Bhaktivedanta Book Trust, 1980–83) and *Prabhupada* (Los Angeles: Bhak-

tivedanta Book Trust, 1983); also Kim Knott, *My Sweet Lord. The Hare Krishna Movement* (Wellingborough, Northamptonshire: Aquarian Press, 1986).

11. Judah, *Hare Krishna*, 87.

12. The present *guru* for Britain, Bhagavandas Goswami, is frequently asked about the role of women in the movement. At a festival in August 1984 he said there was no reason why women should not be heads of departments within ISKCON, or temple presidents. On another occasion he was asked whether a woman could become a renunciate or even a guru. He replied that "Sannyas is ultimately a renounced mentality whereby one understands, 'Everything belongs to Krsna and nothing is mine; therefore what do I have to renounce?' Anyone who is firmly situated in this consciousness is qualified to be a guru and engage you in devotional service" (ISKCON, *Gurudevamrta*, unpublished newsletter, 2, no. 34 (1984): 20).

13. Sitarani dasi, "What's the role of women," 11–12.

14. See also, Satarupa dasi, "I am not this body," 17; Visakha dasi, "Women in Krsna Consciousness: Questions and Answers," *Back to Godhead* 16, no. 3–4 (1981): 6.

15. Judah, *Hare Krishna*, 86.

16. This philosophical stance is called *acintyabhedabheda*. For further discussion, see Steven J. Gelberg, ed., *Hare Krishna, Hare Krishna: Five Distinguished Scholars on the Krishna Movement in the West* (New York: Grove Press, 1983); O. B. L. Kapoor, *The Philosophy and Religion of Sri Caitanya* (Delhi: Munshiram Manoharlal, 1977).

17. This is described by Friedhelm Hardy in *Viraha-Bhakti: The Early History of Krsna Devotion in South India* (Delhi: Oxford University Press, 1983).

18. The Krishna Consciousness view of *varnashramadharma* is described by A. C. Bhaktivedanta Swami Prabhupada in his purports to the verses of the *Bhagavata Gita*, in *Bhagavad-gita As It Is* (Los Angeles: Bhaktivedanta Book Trust, 1983).

19. Judah, *Hare Krishna*, 86; Whitworth and Shiels, "From across the black waters," 161; Daner, *American Children*, 68.

20. These designations were explained to me in an interview with Garuda dasa, who discusses this issue in "Dharma: nature, duty, and divine service," *Back to Godhead* 15, no. 12 (1980): 7–13. The distinctions between these different philosophies of behavior are further underlined, though not described explicitly, by Satsvarupa dasa Goswami, *Living with the Scripture*, vol. 1 (Philadelphia: Gita Nagari Press, 1984), 61, and Sitarani dasi, "What's the role of women," 26.

21. The Vedic period, held to form the latter part of the previous age, *dvapara yuga* (circa 5,000 years ago), is explained in more detail below.

22. The relation between the "Vedic" and "Krishna Conscious" systems of *varnashrama* is discussed by Garuda dasa, "Dharma," 10–11.

23. This is certainly the theory. It does not answer all the questions, however. The issue of renunciation *(sannyasa)*, for example, is one which remains unclear. If women have material equality, why have they not been given formal recognition as *sannyasinis?* Is it simply that none of them have been desirous of taking *sannyasa?* Is it explained by the fact that women become informally renounced rather than formally renounced? If this is so, why then do men need to undergo a formal initiation in order to be recognized as renunciates? The issue of women and *sannyasa* is discussed in relation to modern Indian religious movements by Ursula King, "The effect of social change on religious self-understanding: women ascetics in modern Hinduism" in K. Ballhatchet and D. Taylor, eds., *Changing South Asia: Religion and Society* (London: Centre of South Asian Studies, School of African and Oriental Studies, 1984), 69–83.

24. Judah, *Hare Krishna,* 86.

25. Satarupa dasi, "I am not this body," 17.

26. Daner, *American Children,* 68.

27. Hare Krishna devotees, for example, regularly pay their obeisances, not only to Krishna and the spiritual master, but also to the other devotees.

28. Both this problem and the one of implicit comparison are well illustrated in Janet Jacobs' article, "The economy of love in religious commitment: the deconversion of women from nontraditional religious movements," *Journal for the Scientific Study of Religion* 23, no. 2 (1984): 155–71. In this article she not only uses those who have left New Religious Movements (de-converts) to illustrate the attitudes of these movements to women's roles, but she also neglects to give any consideration to the religious beliefs held by the groups. The inevitable result is that Jacobs concludes that for women in "nontraditional" religious movements "a submissive self image also becomes inseparable from the goals of spiritual growth" (158). This is certainly true for Krishna Consciousness, yet we read it without realizing that this goal, and the image attached to it, is shared by both men and women.

29. Judah, *Hare Krishna,* 86. Mangalvadi also mentions Bhaktivedanta Swami's comments on women, *World of the Gurus,* 98.

30. A. C. Bhaktivedanta Swami Prabhupada, *Krsna: The Supreme Personality of Godhead,* 3 vols. (Los Angeles: Bhaktivedanta Book Trust, 1970), 7, 21.

31. Satsvarupa dasa Goswami, *Srila Prabhupada-lilamrta, Vol 3: Only He Could Lead Them, San Francisco/India 1967* (Los Angeles: Bhaktivedanta Book Trust, 1981), 150.

32. The consorts Radha and Sita are examples of this position. There are very positive accounts of Queen Kunti and Draupadi in the *Bhagavata Purana* and *Mahabharata.* In the Chaitanya tradition itself a good example is provided by Jahnavi, the wife of Chaitanya's brother, Nityananda, in the *Caitanya-caritamrta.*

33. Satsvarupa dasa Goswami, *Srila Prabhupada-lilamrta, Vol 5: Let There Be a Temple, 1971–5* (Los Angeles: Bhaktivedanta Book Trust, 1983), 21–22.

34. Judah, *Hare Krishna,* 86.

35. Some of these issues are discussed briefly in Knott, *My Sweet Lord: The Hare Krishna Movement.*

# We're on our Way, Lord!: The Rise of "Evangelical Feminism" in Modern American Christianity

## RICHARD QUEBEDEAUX

The narrow defeat of the Equal Rights Amendment (ERA) to the U.S. Constitution in 1982 was a true disappointment to the feminists who had created and led the much publicized "women's movement" of the 60s and 70s. But this defeat should not obscure the fact that the status of women in American society has risen significantly during the last two decades. The principal cause of this changing status of women, which has altered both their conception of themselves and social attitudes toward them, is their increasing engagement in activities hitherto inaccessible to them. Today there are more options open to women—in family life, employment, education, and politics—than at any time in the past. And this freedom to choose has brought with it profound changes in the way modern Americans, women *and* men, live their lives.

Social transformation in the status of women has been *most* apparent in the whole area of family life. The increasing accessibility and social acceptance of birth control, the legalization of abortion, and the wider availability of child care facilities outside the home have all contributed to the ability of wives to seek and maintain gainful employment. Economic necessity itself has reduced the social stigma against "working wives," and the elimination of social and legal barriers against divorce has resulted in more women than ever maintaining their own households, earning an independent income, and rearing their children themselves. At the same time, the traditional "patriarchal authority" associated with the nuclear family has been modified, with an ever increasing number of husbands who share domestic and child care duties with their wives.

In the area of employment itself, women have made significant gains in the last two decades. By 1968, 30 percent of all American women had entered the marketplace. By 1973, it was 44 percent.

Working wives constituted 42 percent of the employed women in 1976, as opposed to 31 percent in 1960. In addition, better educational opportunities for women during this period have made better jobs more available to them.

The increased participation of women in higher education can be seen in the following statistics: In 1966, 40 percent of the American undergraduate population was made up of women; by 1977, it was 49 percent. Only 3 percent of all law degrees went to women in 1963; that number had increased to 13 percent by 1975. With respect to doctorates, 13.3 percent were awarded to women in 1970; by 1975, 21.3 percent of those degrees were given to women.

Family life, employment, and education have all been affected by the changing status of women in American life. But so has the world of politics. By 1979, there were 41 major political organizations for women, who have gradually come to see that their increasing demand for social equality with men must, ultimately, be worked out—and legislated—in the political arena.

## Women's Liberation

Whence, then, came all of these new opportunities for women and their consequent rise in status? Because many of these options have traditionally been the exclusive prerogative of men, the development of the same opportunities for women has involved the demand for equality, a demand articulated by the feminist leaders of what became a reborn movement for women's rights. It was their movement which was the catalyst for the profound social change to follow.[1]

With the ratification of the Nineteenth Amendment to the U. S. Constitution in 1920, giving women the right to vote, militancy on behalf of a single issue diffused into a number of women's political groups, such as the League of Women Voters (1920) and the National Council of Negro Women (1935). Organizations like these supported a variety of liberal reforms related to the rights of both women and men.

The modern movement for women's rights, however, began during the 1960s, and was encouraged by significant feminist studies such as *The Second Sex* (1953) by Simone de Beauvoir[2] and *The Feminine Mystique* (1963) by Betty Friedan,[3] and by a general intellectual and legislative climate favorable to minority rights and antidiscrimination movements. Militant women's groups were formed, and "women's liberation," manifested in the mass media's coverage of the demonstrations of radical feminists, became a household word.

Women's liberation was a social rather than political movement which raised the awareness of the United States to the prevalence of discriminatory beliefs and practices within American society as a whole. More significantly, however, political organizations emerged which developed into a full-fledged feminist movement by the 1970s. These included the National Organization for Women (NOW), formed in 1966, under the leadership of Betty Friedan, and the National Women's Political Caucus (1971), composed of such nationally known feminists as Gloria Steinem, Bella Abzug, and Shirley Chisholm [4]

At its first national conference, in Washington, D.C., in 1967, NOW adopted a "Bill of Rights" for women, the articles of which summarize the major goals of the modern women's movement in America. It demanded the following: (1) An Equal Rights Amendment to the Constitution; (2) Enforcement of laws banning sex discrimination in employment; (3) Maternity leave rights in employment and in Social Security benefits; (4) Tax deductions for home and child care expenses for working parents; (5) Child day care centers; (6) Equal and unsegregated education for women and men; (7) Equal job training opportunities and allowances for women in poverty; and (8) The right of women to control their own reproductive lives.

## Christian Feminism

The changing status of women in America during the last two decades has been manifestly apparent, as we said, in family life, employment, education, and politics across the nation. The question remains, however: what about religion? To what degree, if any, has the women's movement and it concomitants had an impact on religion?

Within "mainstream liberal" Protestantism and Catholicism, feminist intellectuals began to advocate the issue of women's rights by the 1970s. They began to question male-dominated theological assumptions, including the beliefs that the subordination of women has been ordained by God, that woman (as opposed to man) is evil by nature, and that God is male. These assumptions *had* been challenged within the churches of America earlier, but in less noticeable ways. For instance, a few of the "sectarian" holiness and pentecostal denominations had acknowledged the rights of women for more than a century (or from the time of their founding). In 1950, the World Council of Churches, founded only two years earlier, established the Commission on the Life and Work of Women to study the role of women in its member denominations. Then, in 1955, the Presbyterians, and in 1956, the Methodists, gave full clergy rights to women. (The Episcopal Church waited until 1976, giving in only after a long battle on the issue.)

One of the first important articles in the area of feminist theology was Valerie Saiving's "The Human Situation: A Feminine View," published in 1960.[5] Her contention was that the theologian's sexual identity has much to do with how he or she perceives the proper role of theology, and that historically theology has been based on a male perception which has not only ignored the uniqueness of women's experience, but also strengthened the usual stereotype of women as inferior to men. This article was ahead of its time, however; most of the Christian books and articles on women and religion in the early and middle sixties were more conservative and traditionalist in tone.

Then, in 1968, came the first widely publicized book on the role of women in the church that hinted at the formulation of a specifically feminist theology—Mary Daly's *The Church and the Second Sex*.[6] Building on the classic work of Simone de Beauvoir, *The Second Sex*, she maintained that the Catholic Church has encouraged the view of woman as inferior (a "defective male," as St. Thomas Aquinas expressed it), and that it has become a leading instrument of the oppression of women.

In the years following the publication of Daly's book, the market has been flooded with writings on feminist theology—from mainstream Christian perspectives, Catholic and Protestant, to mother goddess worship and witchcraft—by intellectuals as diverse as Letty Russell, Sheila Collins, Naomi Goldenberg, Carol Christ, Starhawk, and the premier feminist theologian of them all, Rosemary Radford Ruether. The themes and perspectives of "feminist theology" are as broad as the women's movement itself. Furthermore, this theological genre has had no single organizing theme, no obvious focus, no sharply identifiable set of objectives. To be sure, it is unified in its opposition to the maleness of

God and tradition, and the consequent subordination of women. But it has lacked a clear-cut model for dealing with these issues. It has often been divided on the question whether, for example, these problems should be solved by the reinterpretation or complete rejection of male language, by the renewal or overthrow of religious tradition, by cooperating with or snubbing the male sex, and so on.[7] Unified or not, however, feminist theology has had a major impact on the American theological academy for over a decade, and, more indirectly, on the structures of mainstream church life which had excluded women for most of their history.

## The Evangelical Tradition

The movement toward Christian feminism among mainstream liberal religious thinkers has become well-known within the theological academy and denominational hierarchies in the United States itself and elsewhere in the world. But far less familiar is the parallel movement within American evangelicalism, which is the central focus of this essay. Evangelicalism has most often been associated with the doctrine of salvation by faith in Jesus Christ alone. During the Reformation in Europe the followers of Martin Luther, stressing this singular faith, were generally called "evangelicals" to distinguish them from the Calvinists, who were designated as "reformed." A good number of Lutheran synods both in Europe and in America still use the term "evangelical" (from the Greek *euangelion,* "good news") in their official nomenclature.

The "evangelical revival" in the eighteenth century was represented by pietism in Germany, Methodism in England, and the Great Awakening in America. Since that time, especially in English-speaking countries, evangelicalism has been looked upon as the school of Protestant Christianity which affirms salvation through faith in the atoning death of Christ, and denies any saving efficacy either in good works or in the sacraments. The evangelical movement also has regarded as central tenets of the Christian faith the inspiration and authority of the Bible, the sinfulness of humankind, and the (more or less) symbolic nature of the sacraments. In its worship, moreover, heavy importance has been placed upon preaching for conversion and the reading of Scripture.

With the division in American Protestantism early in the twentieth century, between "modernists"—who became the liberal mainstream—and "fundamentalists"—the conservatives, evangelicalism took on another shade of meaning. After 1940, what was then termed "neo-evangelicalism" became recognizable as a strong force within conservative Christianity—one which held firm to what it believed was "biblical" or "historic" orthodoxy but at the same time repudiated the theological unsophistication and cultural excesses of fundamentalism (then, as now, a mass movement of marginalized white Christians, centered in the South of the United States). Led by a small group of young intellectuals who later gravitated around the revivalism of Billy Graham, modern evangelical Christianity was born out of fundamentalism and separated itself, more or less, from the parent movement.

In *The Young Evangelicals,* I defined contemporary evangelicalism as that school of Christianity—socialized, for the most part, in the American revivalist tradition—which is strongly committed to (1) the complete reliability and final authority of the Bible in all matters of faith and conduct; (2) the necessity of a *personal* faith in Jesus Christ as savior from sin and Lord of one's life (i.e., being "born again"); and (3) the mandate for evangelism, the urgency of seeking the conversion of unbelievers to Christ.[8]

But what of the role of women in modern evangelical Christianity? Here it is crucial to remember that feminism has been a movement largely of highly educated and professional women. Lacking a well-educated constituency, evangelicalism accommodated much less quickly to intellectual concerns in the wider society than did mainstream liberal Christianity; and it has put up considerably more resistance to the emergence of feminist theology than has its more intellectually oriented, liberal counterpart. In fact, until the emergence of evangelical feminism, American evangelicalism—even among its intelligentsia—was characterized by an almost complete acceptance of the subordination of women to men in church, in the home, and in society at large. Except for a few pentecostal and holiness denominations, females were not ordained to the ministry. The ideal evangelical woman married, became a housewife and mother, and put her husband's and children's welfare before her own. The very notion of evangelical feminism was unthinkable.

134

## Evangelical Feminism: History

At this point it would be well to sketch the origins and development of evangelical feminism as a movement within modern American Christianity. This account will serve as an introduction to our later discussion of the nature and significance of this new feminist stance.

In 1957, a ground-breaking study of the role of women in Christianity was published by Eerdmans, then, as now, a highly respected evangelical publishing house. The book, *Woman in the Church: A Restudy of Woman's Place in Building the Kingdom,* was brief but to the point. Its author, Russell C. Prohl, had written the work to encourage his own denomination, the very conservative Lutheran Church—Missouri Synod, to adopt an egalitarian stance on women in the ordained ministry. He insisted:

The time has come to declare that since the public activity of a woman is no longer considered as a breach of the marriage vow and since the law of the land no longer denies to woman the right to act independently . . . women are eligible candidates for any office in the church of Christ. . . . In other words it is time for the Lutheran Church to support the 1955 resolution by the Presbyterians that "there is no theological ground for denying ordination to women simply because they are women."[9]

Needless to say, *Woman in the Church*—years ahead of its time—was not well received either by the Missouri Synod Lutherans (who still do not ordain women) or by American evangelicals more generally. Prohl died shortly after the book's publication, and it was quietly forgotten.

Almost ten years later, Letha Scanzoni, a free-lance writer and one-time Dixieland jazz band leader, published a couple of new articles with moderate feminist sentiments in *Eternity,* one of the most prominent evangelical magazines. The first, entitled "Woman's Place: Silence or Service?," came out in February 1966; the second, "Elevate Marriage to Partnership," was published in July 1968.[10] In 1969, Scanzoni began corresponding with Nancy Hardesty, a Ph.D. student in church history at the University of Chicago, who was then teaching English at Trinity College, Deerfield, Illinois, a well-known evangelical institution. The result of this correspondence was a scholarly book-length manuscript by both of them, finished in 1971, on the compatibility of feminism with an evangelical approach to the

Bible. But there was not yet a market for such a book, and the manuscript was rejected by six publishers in the following three years.

The early 1970s saw the publication of a few more seminal articles on the role of women by feminist evangelicals—one by Hardesty in *Eternity* ("Women: Second-Class Citizens?," January 1971)[11]; Ruth Schmidt in *Christianity Today, the* leading evangelical periodical ("Second-Class Citizenship in the Kingdom of God," 1 January, 1971)[12]; Virginia Ramey Mollenkott in the *Christian Herald* ("Woman's Liberation and the Bible," December 1972)[13]; and Hardesty's pivotal "Women and Evangelical Christianity" in *The Cross and the Flag* (1972),[14] a collection of essays by left-leaning evangelicals. These were all seeds of the movement which was to follow.

Then, in November 1973, a group of socially concerned professors, writers, and "activists" of various sorts who were politically liberal to radical—persons I later called "young evangelicals"—met at the Wabash YMCA in downtown Chicago to formulate a "Declaration of Evangelical Social Concern," a document that would receive much more media attention and a more favorable reception than its framers expected. The declaration condemned evangelical complicity with militarism, racism, and the unjust distribution of the world's goods and resources—to the neglect of the poor. Only a few women had been invited, Nancy Hardesty and Sharon Gallagher, editor of *Right On* (now *Radix*), originally a Jesus People magazine, among them.

At the conference, these feminist women "caucused" and insisted that a clause on women be included in the declaration—a demand that resulted in the following lines being added: "We acknowledge that we have encouraged men to prideful domination and women to irresponsible passivity. So we call both men and women to mutual submission and active discipleship." Encouraged by their success, the members of this first small evangelical women's caucus kept in touch and gradually formed a larger network of like-minded women in North America to deal with their concerns.

Because its formulators and early signers included evangelical leaders whose credentials could not be questioned, the Chicago Declaration "legitimated" the leftward trend among the evangelical intelligentsia. More conferences and publications expressing the new "evangelical left" position (my designation in *The Worldly*

*Evangelicals*[15]) would emerge during the mid 1970s. In 1974, Letha Scanzoni and Nancy Hardesty's work on evangelical feminism was finally published as *All We're Meant to Be: A Biblical Approach to Women's Liberation* by Word Books, a major evangelical publishing house.[16] That year as well, *Post-American* (now *Sojourners*), the most important voice of the young evangelicals, did an entire issue in August–September supporting the feminist stance, and a follow-up conference was held in November again to begin implementing the concerns raised by the Chicago Declaration.

A significant number of women were invited to *this* gathering, and following the example of the women who attended the first conference, they also formed a "women's caucus" as one of the six "task forces" attended by participants. This women's caucus made proposals on feminist lifestyles, removing sexism from Sunday school and other Christian education materials, encouraging colleges and seminaries to help women develop their full potential, equal job opportunities for women, feminist "consciousness raising"—and support for the ERA. Conference participants as a whole were also introduced to a new evangelical feminist bimonthly, entitled *Daughters of Sarah.* Founded by Lucille Sider Dayton, and published by a collective, this little magazine (the first issue—November 1974—was mimeographed) gradually took on increasing typographical and editorial sophistication, and in recent years has enjoyed a growing readership among mainstream liberal Christian feminists as well as evangelicals.

In 1975, Eerdmans published Paul K. Jewett's highly controversial *Man as Male and Female,*[17] which represented a more "liberal" interpretation of scripture on the role of women than was seen in *All We're Meant to Be.* And by the end of the year, evangelical feminism had become a visible movement. In November, the "Evangelical Women's Caucus" (EWC) met on its own for the first time at a conference in Washington, D.C., entitled "Women in Transition: A Biblical Approach to Feminism." More than 350 women and 20 men attended the gathering which endorsed the ERA (as its parent task force had done in Chicago a year earlier) and the ordination of women. The spirit of the meeting as the beginning of a new movement was caught in the color-splashed banner at the front of the auditorium where the people were sitting. It depicted the launching of a huge balloon and announced the words of the conference theme song: "We're on Our Way, Lord!"

In the years following, the concerns and development of evangelical feminism paralleled those of the larger women's movement in America. But at the same time, it continued to identify with and reflect upon the evangelical distinctives that had been so much a part of the lives of its constituency. New books broke further ground for the new breed of Christian feminist. These included Virginia Ramey Mollenkott's *Women, Men, and the Bible*[18] and Patricia Gundry's *Woman Be Free!*,[19] both published in 1977; Scanzoni and Mollenkott's sometimes bitterly contested *Is the Homosexual My Neighbor?* (1978),[20] which took a positive approach to lesbian and gay relationships; Virginia Hearn's *Our Struggle to Serve* (1979),[21] the first collection of "testimonies" and life stories of evangelical feminists; and Mollenkott's *The Divine Feminine: The Biblical Imagery of God as Female,*[22] published in 1983. By the early 1980s, Scanzoni and Mollenkott, an orator of note and professor of English at William Paterson State College in New Jersey, had emerged as the most prominent leaders of the movement.

In due course, a number of magazines serving the larger American evangelical community became more open to women's role in the church and the expansion of society. *Daughters of Sarah* itself had over 3,000 subscribers by 1983. In the fall of 1977, the Evangelical Women's Caucus published its first newsletter, *EWC Update,*[23] which, by 1980, had emerged as a full-scale quarterly devoted to news and views of the movement.

The EWC held its second plenary conference in June 1978, in Pasadena, at Fuller Seminary. There were over 800 registrants; and after the conference, attendees voted to adopt bylaws, incorporate, and become a dues-paying organization. Other national gatherings were convened in Grand Rapids, Michigan, at Calvin College, in 1979; Saratoga Springs, New York, in 1980; Seattle, in 1982; and Wellesley, Massachusetts, in 1984. By 1983, the EWC, with headquarters in San Francisco, had over 500 members nationally, and local or regional chapters in Albany, New York; the Greater Boston area; Detroit; Fresno, California; Minneapolis; Newark, New Jersey; Portland, Oregon; the San Francisco Bay Area; and the Southwest (Southern California, Arizona, and Nevada).

## Evangelical Feminism: Nature and Significance

Now is the time to ask about the ideological and social character of evangelical feminism and its wider significance. Very simply, we can say that it is largely a product of the secular women's movement of the late sixties and seventies. Evangelical feminists are almost all white, upper-middle-class intellectuals and activists, who are students and professionals, whether single, married, or divorced. (A 1978 reader survey conducted by *Daughters of Sarah* indicated that 65 percent of the respondents had been to graduate school[24]; by 1981, the number had risen to 71 percent.)[25]

The ideas of evangelical feminists are reminiscent of those of the early secular feminists in the modern movement. Theirs has been a practical, task-oriented approach, concerned with the problems of career women and those who wish to be freed from the confines of housework—a program that would make them fit well into a moderate wing of NOW. Only a very few of the evangelical feminists share the ideas of socialist feminists—their special interest in the poor, Third World and working-class women, and their critique of capitalism as a major oppressor of women. Fewer still have much in common with the sectarian, lesbian wing of modern feminism. As a whole, moreover, these women (and men) tend to be Christians first and feminists second. They have not made a religion out of their feminism.

For evangelical feminists, the three basic teachings pertinent to a proper biblical understanding of women are (1) the first creation account—Genesis 1:27—declaring that God created human beings, male *and* female, in his own image (thus God has both masculine and feminine qualities); (2) the revelation of the life of Jesus, a true feminist in the context of his own patriarchal society; and (3) St. Paul's words—the "major biblical statement" on the issue—in Galatians 3:28: "There is no such thing as Jew or Greek, slave and freeman, male and female; for you are all one in Christ Jesus."

Evangelical feminist scholars like Virginia Ramey Mollenkott and Paul K. Jewett write that the New Testament conveys liberation for all people and was not intended to oppress modern women by imposing a first-century patriarchal social structure on them. In *Man as Male and Female*,[26] Jewett concludes that passages which *appear* to contradict the major biblical statement on the matter of women are, in fact, contradictory. The particular statements are wrong, but the general statement is right. He finds that St. Paul's teachings about women (except Gal. 3:28) were influenced both by his male-dominated culture and by rabbinic traditions representing no more than a time-bound authority not applicable to later Christians in other cultures. This use of broad cultural analysis on the scriptural texts in question was bold for an evangelical theologian of Jewett's stature in the mid-seventies, and it aided evangelical feminists in their quest for legitimacy, since even mainstream liberal Christians could accept *this* approach to the Bible and its results.

Evangelical feminism emerged as a modern movement because of (1) the ever-increasing use of higher critical methods of biblical study and broad cultural analysis by evangelical academics during the late 60s and 70s; (2) the growing interest in social ethics (including "women's studies") among evangelicals during that time; and, to a lesser degree, perhaps, (3) the new historical studies (especially those of Donald W. Dayton) linking feminist sentiments to a number of nineteenth-century evangelical reformers. Included here were Charles G. Finney, the famous revivalist; Angelina and Sarah Grimke, Quaker abolitionists; Luther Lee, an early leader of the Holiness Wesleyan Church; A. J. Gordon, Baptist namesake of the prominent evangelical Gordon College and Gordon-Conwell Theological Seminary in Massachusetts; Jonathan Blanchard, founder of Wheaton College in Illinois, Billy Graham's alma mater; William and Catherine Booth, founders of the Salvation Army; and Frances Willard of the Women's Christian Temperance Union.[27]

There are, in fact, similarities between the ideals of nineteenth-century evangelical feminists and their counterparts of the 1970s and 1980s. But we should not make too much of this connection, since nineteenth-century evangelical feminist women acted out their stance in different ways and for different reasons than their modern counterparts. They used a legitimate activity for them, voluntary church work, where they joined the church's struggle against the world. Their activities here gave them experience and expertise which some of them used later in the emerging feminist movement. These women's initial plunge into active public life, however, did not entail feminist sentiments; they merely wanted to do God's will as it was defined by the church.

Modern evangelical feminists operate in a different way. The vast majority of them have, or are in the process of training for, active professional careers. They have learned from the larger women's movement to articulate their theological and lifestyle concerns in a feminist way, and are trying hard to change the evangelical churches' attitudes about women so that church doctrine will more nearly fit the reality of their lives. Evangelical feminists did not carefully examine the biblical texts, consult theology books and their ministers, *then* declare themselves feminists. Rather, there was something about the secular women's movement's articulation of what it means to be a woman in American society that seemed true to them. They took a leap of faith, claiming to be feminists despite the contrary teachings of their churches. Their biblical and theological work came later.

Evangelical feminism as a movement has distinguished itself from secular feminism, however, and even from mainstream Christian feminism, by its insistence on the centrality of biblical authority on the issue of women in church and society. Its adherents often call themselves "biblical feminists." (The movement can also be distinguished from the more radical feminist sentiments, secular and Christian, by its conciliatory attitude toward men—stressing the *mutual* submission of all Christians to each other.) Yet despite their commitment to the full authority of the Bible, evangelical feminists share a traditionally "liberal" methodology in dealing with that authority. They emphasize the relativity of traditional orthodox doctrinal formulations, insist that personal experience (as well as "propositional truths" in scripture) can inform Christian ethics, and believe that appropriate Christian behavior can be learned from the world as well as from the Bible and the church.[28]

And how important has evangelical feminism been? Although the movement represents only a *tiny* intellectual elite within the larger community of American evangelicals, it has had more significance than meets the eye. Evangelical feminism's impact can best be understood when we identify the chief role of intellectuals in any given society—including evangelical society—as "symbol manipulators" who help people structure their everyday reality. Intellectuals are the aggregate of individuals in a society who employ in their expression and communications, with higher frequency than other members of that society, symbols of general scope and abstract reference concerning man and woman, the social order, nature, and the cosmos. Intellectual interests arise from the need to perceive, experience, and express—in words, colors, shapes, or sounds—a general significance in particular, concrete events. They emerge from the need to be in cognitive, moral, and appreciative contact with the most general or "essential" features of the world and the cosmos. This need is deeply, indeed constitutively, rooted in human nature, albeit unequally distributed among individuals.[29] Even evangelicals have to have intellectuals manipulate the symbols of their faith.

Only a decade ago there was no such thing as "evangelical feminism" as represented by the modern movement. The concept was foreign, and the words themselves seemed contradictory even to the most sophisticated evangelical theologians of the time. But through the study and scholarly production of a handful of self-professed evangelicals who also identified themselves as feminists, those two words were manipulated to form a new concept in which "feminist" and "evangelical" *could* go together. This fresh interpretation of the Bible's teaching on women gradually took hold in the leading evangelical colleges and seminaries, eventually finding sympathy in even some of the most conservative institutions. Thus, if the vast majority of evangelical laity and clergy, *do* still hold to the subordination of women to men in the family, the church, and society at large, the ever-increasing evangelical upward mobility is bound to change all that. Furthermore, even conservative, evangelical women in America enter professional careers and are exposed to the secular culture around them, and as their children attend Christian and secular colleges and graduate schools committed to the basic feminist stance, their opposition will be weakened and rendered obsolete.

Despite the ERA's defeat in 1982, modern life in America increasingly demands and will achieve a more egalitarian status for women, especially professional women. The mainstream of American Christianity, which evangelical theologians used to castigate for being "modernist," accommodated to the reality of modernity more quickly and more emphatically than evangelicalism has done. But evangelical *feminists,* at least, are catching up fast. They're on their way, Lord—into modernity and its concomitant, equal opportunity with men—into the same joys and discontent faced by *all* thinking religious believers in a post-religious world shaped by that modernity.[30]

# NOTES

1. Mildred Navaretta, "Women and Modern Society," *Academic American Encyclopedia* (Danbury, Conn.: Grolier, 1981).

2. Simone de Beauvoir, *The Second Sex* (New York: Knopf, 1953).

3. Betty Friedan, *The Feminine Mystique* (New York: Norton, 1963).

4. Mildred Navaretta, "Women's Rights Movements," *Academic American Encyclopedia*.

5. Valerie Saiving, "The Human Situation: A Feminine View," *Journal of Religion* (April 1960): 100–112. Reprinted in C.P. Christ and J. Plaskow, eds., *Womanspirit Rising: A Feminist Reader in Religion* (New York and London: Harper & Row, 1979), 25–42.

6. Mary Daly, *The Church and the Second Sex* (New York: Harper & Row, 1968).

7. Deane William Ferm, *Contemporary American Theologies* (New York: Seabury, 1981), 77–94.

8. Richard Quebedeaux, *The Young Evangelicals* (New York: Harper & Row, 1974), 2–4.

9. Russell C. Prohl, *Woman in the Church: A Restudy of Woman's Place in Building the Kingdom* (Grand Rapids, Mich.: Eerdmans, 1957), 80.

10. Letha Scanzoni, "Woman's Place: Silence or Service?," *Eternity* (February 1966): 14–16; Scanzoni, "Elevate Marriage to Partnership," *Eternity* (July 1968): 11–14.

11. Nancy Hardesty, "Women. Second-Class Citizens?", *Eternity* (January 1971): 14–16, 24–29.

12. Ruth Schmidt, "Second-Class Citizenship in the Kingdom of God," *Christianity Today* (1 January 1971): 13–14.

13. Virginia Ramey Mollenkott, "Woman's Liberation and the Bible," *Christian Herald* (December 1972): 17–18, 21–22, 24.

14. Nancy Hardesty, "Women and Evangelical Christianity" in R. G. Clouse, R. D. Linder and R.V. Pierard, eds., *The Cross and the Flag* (Carol Stream, Ill.: Creation House, 1972), 65–79.

15. Richard Quebedeaux, *The Worldly Evangelicals* (San Francisco: Harper & Row, 1978).

16. Letha Scanzoni and Nancy Hardesty, *All We're Meant to Be: A Biblical Approach to Women's Liberation* (Waco, Tex.: Word Books, 1974).

17. Paul K. Jewett, *Man as Male and Female* (Grand Rapids, Mich.: Eerdmans, 1975). Jewett is a professor of theology at Fuller Theological Seminary in Pasadena, California, America's best evangelical academic institution.

18. Virginia Ramey Mollenkott, *Women, Men, and the Bible* (Nashville, Tenn.: Abingdon, 1977).

19. Patricia Gundry, *Woman be Free!* (Grand Rapids, Mich.: Zondervan, 1977). Gundry's husband, Stanley, was dismissed from the faculty of Chicago's Moody Bible Institute in 1979 for his feminist sentiments.

20. Letha Scanzoni and Virginia Ramey Mollenkott, *Is the Homosexual My Neighbor?* (San Francisco: Harper & Row, 1978).

21. Virginia Hearn, ed., *Our Struggle to Serve* (Waco, Tex.: Word Books, 1979).

22. Virginia Ramey Mollenkott, *The Divine Feminine: The Biblical Imagery of God as Female* (New York: Crossroad, 1983).

23. *EWC Update* (formerly Evangelical Women's Caucus). P.O. Box 3192, San Francisco, California 94119. Quarterly. 1977–.

24. "Survey Results," *Daughters of Sarah* (July-August 1978): 15. *Daughters of Sarah:* 2716 West Cortland, Chicago, Illinois 60647. Bimonthly.

25. "Survey Results," *Daughters of Sarah* (March-April 1981): 20.

26. Jewett, *Man as Male and Female,* n. 17.

27. See Donald W. Dayton, *Discovering an Evangelical Heritage* (New York: Harper & Row, 1976). It is interesting to note that Frances Willard, as president of the World's Woman's Christian Temperance Union, was one of the official speakers at the World's Parliament of Religions (Chicago 1893) where she gave an address titled "A White Life for Two."

28. Quebedeaux, *The Worldly Evangelicals*, 120–26. A fine history of evangelical feminism until 1977 is Ina Kau's "Feminists in the American Evangelical Movement" (M.A. thesis, Pacific School of Religion, Berkeley, Calif., 1977). Available from the Graduate Theological Union Library, 2400 Ridge Road, Berkeley, Calif. 94709. Another recent evangelical feminist publication not considered in this paper is Kari Torjesen Malcolm, *Women at the Crossroads: A Path beyond Feminism and Traditionalism* (Downers Grove, Ill.: Inter-Varsity Press, 1982).

29. Edwards Shils, "Intellectuals," *International Encyclopedia of the Social Sciences* (New York and London: Macmillan, 1968).

30. Evangelical Christianity and modernity is the central theme of my book *By What Authority: The Rise of Personality Cults in American Christianity* (San Francisco: Harper & Row, 1982).

# 9

# The Ordination of Women, Natural Symbols, and What Even God Cannot Do

## HARRIET E. BABER

In 1976, the General Convention of the Episcopal Church voted to allow women to be ordained as priests. The move was opposed—and continues to be opposed—by a substantial, active minority within the church, as well as elsewhere on pragmatic, biblical and, what might be styled, metaphysical grounds.

Opponents of women's ordination frequently argue not that women ought not to be ordained as priests but rather that, given the nature of the priesthood, they *cannot* be ordained as priests:

The bishop or priest, in the exercise of his ministry, does not act in his own name, in *persona propria:* he represents Christ, who acts through him. . . . [T]he supreme expression of this representation is found in the altogether special form it assumes in the celebration of the Eucharist. . . . [T]he priest, who alone has the power to perform it, then acts not only through the effective power conferred on him by Christ, but *in persona Christi,* taking the role of Christ, to the point of being his very image, when he pronounces the words of consecration. . . .

The Christian priesthood is therefore of a sacramental nature: the priest is a sign, the supernatural effectiveness of which comes from the ordination received, but a sign that must be perceptible and which the faithful must be able to recognize with ease. The whole supernatural economy is in fact based upon natural signs, on symbols imprinted upon the human psychology: "Sacramental signs," says Saint Thomas, "represent what they signify by natural resemblance." The same natural resemblance is required for persons as for things: when Christ's role in the Eucharist is to be expressed sacramentally, there would not be this "natural resemblance" which must exist between Christ and his minister if the role of Christ were not taken by a man. In such a case it would be difficult to see in the minister the image of Christ. For Christ himself was and remains a man.[1]

The claim is then that women cannot be priests in virtue of their inability to function as "natural symbols" of Christ, because they are not male.

## Christ, Women and Natural Symbols

Why, one wonders, should a difference of sex disqualify one as a "natural symbol" of Christ in a way that a difference of race, height, or blood type does not? The reason, the document continues, is that the relation between Christ and his church is typically, and appropriately, represented in the biblical literature as a relation analogous to that between a husband and wife. The metaphor occurs in both the Old and New Testament and appears to be rooted in tradition and, indeed, in nature.

Though earlier writers were inclined to argue for the exclusion of women from the priesthood on the grounds of their alleged inferiority, contemporary writers are inclined to stress the alledgedly profound differentness and complementarity between men and women:

There is no question of "worthiness," but only appropriateness: man is a natural symbol of Christ (as woman is of the Church) in the same sense that wine is a natural symbol of the Eucharist.[2]

Wherein lies this appropriateness? It is not easy to discover since at this stage of the argument opponents of women's ordination are inclined either to wax Jungian and mythopoetic or to allude to mysteries whereof we cannot speak and thereof they, of necessity, remain silent. No doubt there is some dissension in the ranks concerning the precise nature of the allegedly profound differences between men and women which they invoke. Nevertheless, the burden of the arguments and effusions of many appear to be as follows:

There is a cluster of properties, let us call them "f-properties," which are constitutive of what might be called "the eternally feminine": these include receptivity, patience, nurturing, intuitiveness, and compliance with the natural order. There is another cluster of properties, let us call them "m-properties," which we may regard as constitutive of "the eternally masculine": these include initiative-taking, mastery, rationality, detachment, and a sort of transcendence of the natural order. (Neither cluster of properties, it is alleged, is in any sense inferior to the other.) The argument may then be reconstructed as follows:

(1) All women are in some unspecified way connected to f-properties in a way that no men are; all men are in the same unspecified way connected to m-properties in a way that no women are.

(2) Now though God transcends all human categories so that much of what we have to say about him is, at best, true only analogically, it is more appropriate to ascribe m-properties to him than f-properties. In this respect the God of the ancient Hebrews, the true God, differs from the deities of surrounding goddess cults.

The true God, revealed in scripture and in the experience of the church, is a God who takes the initiative. In effecting the salvation of mankind he freely chose Israel to be his people and, in the fullness of time, became incarnate for us and for our salvation. We did not choose God; it was he who sought us out.

Furthermore, our God, the true God, transcends nature. He is not an embodiment of the natural order nor is nature an emanation of him. He freely created it from nothing, sustains it, and acts within it though he himself is eternal and beyond time and space.

To this extent God embodies m-properties while all nature including us, his people, are, ideally receptive, responsive, and compliant to him.
(3) Only someone who is connected in the appropriate way to m-properties can be a "natural symbol" of Christ.
(4) Only someone who is a "natural symbol" of Christ can be a priest.
(5) Since only men and not women are connected in the apprropriate way to m-properties, only a man can be a priest.

Now the argument may be attacked on several points. Many suggest, for example, that the God depicted in (2) is too small. If, after all, we take seriously the claim that f-properties are in no sense inferior to m-properties, then it would seem that a being who was exclusively m-ish would be lacking in something—and God lacks nothing.

Along these lines it is often noted that while God is most frequently depicted in m-ish terms in the Bible, he occasionally shows his f-ish side. He is, for example, represented as the nurturer of his people Israel, patient in the face of his people's many sins and apostasies. In the New Testament especially, in the person of Christ, God appears in an f-ish light. Opponents of women's ordination frequently point out that Mary, a symbol of the church and presumably the model for all womankind, is f-ish vis-à-vis God: she responds obediently to his call ("behold the handmaid of the Lord") and, as his mother, nurtures him from the beginning of his earthly life. What should be even more obvious is that Jesus is distinctly f-ish vis-à-vis the father: He responds with perfect obedience to his father ("Not my will, but Thine be done"). He is represented not as the master of his people but the servant who washes the very feet of his disciples. He represents himself as the good shepherd who nurtures his sheep even unto laying down his life for them. In short, even if we can make sense of the notion of an all-perfect God who is exclusively or predominantly m-ish, it is hard to see how such a deity could become incarnate as Jesus Christ our Lord.

With God, however, all things are possible so we can only regard the argument sketched above as inconclusive. The m-ishness of God in the teeth of Christ's life and work may just be another theological mystery that is part and parcel of the incarnation which is itself a mystery. Thus I shall not press this objection to the anti-ordination argument.

## Unpacking the Notion of "Natural Symbol"

A second family of objections to the argument concerns the notion of a "natural symbol" invoked in (3) and (4). One might ask what reason there is for holding that resemblance, and then only resemblance with respect to a certain range of properties, is a necessary condition on something being a natural symbol of Christ. More radically, one might wonder what, if anything, can be meant by a "natural symbol," which might be considered a contradiction in terms.

All but extreme nominalists and Wittgensteinian nihilists recognize that there are resemblances "in nature" as it were, similarities among objects that are neither linguistic fictions nor the results of conceptual decisions on our part. That is to say, we regard certain ways of classifying things, e.g., as red things, or featherless bipeds, or things that go bump in the night, as a reflection of similarities in extralinguistic reality. But the relation of similarity which, we assume, obtains to this extent in the order of nature is not the same as the symbolizing relation. The relation of *similarity is reflexive* and symmetric, that is to say, every thing is similar to itself (in every respect) and for any objects you choose, *a* and *b,* if *a* is similar to *b* (in some respect) then *b* is similar to *a* (in that respect).

The symbolizing relation is quite different with regard to its formal features. First, it would seem that nothing symbolizes itself. An object may symbolize or represent a class of objects to which it belongs: one member of the philosophy department may represent the department at commencement and thus be a symbol of himself and his colleagues. It would, however, be queer to suggest that an object symbolizes itself. If I appear at commencement on my own behalf, I only represent myself in the Pickwickian sense that I do not represent anyone else. Strictly speaking, I do not represent or symbolize anything. Thus, it seems the symbolizing relation is irreflexive: a thing cannot symbolize itself.

More importantly, the symbolizing relation appears to be asymmetric: in general, where *a* symbolizes *b*, it follows that *b* does not symbolize *a*. The USD logo symbolizes the University of San Diego, but not vice versa. Arguably this directionality of the symbolizing relation is the result of human intent. In general, *a* symbolizes *b* because people use *a* to do a certain job, namely to pick out *b*. When people use *a* to represent *b*, they do not at the same time use *b* to pick out *a*. If this is correct, then it would seem that, while such similarities as exist between *a* and *b* are "in nature" as it were, *a's symbolizing b* is the fruit of human contrivance and hence that, in general, the notion of a "natural symbol" is simply incoherent. But this presupposes that natural symbols *resemble* what they symbolize.

Nevertheless, it does seem that some pairs of objects are, by their nature, related in ways that are especially conducive to symbolizing and being symbolized, so that where certain symbols are purely conventional or arbitrary others seem, somehow, appropriate. The words "curve ahead" on a road sign indicate a curve in the road in virtue of the conventions of English; a picture of a curvy line is often used to do the same job more naturally, as it were. Our understanding of what is meant by the picture does not presuppose any prior knowledge of linguistic conventions. Thus we might want to say that even if there is no symbolizing or being symbolized in nature, some ways of symbolizing things are more natural or intuitive than others. This is indeed all that those who speak of "natural symbols" appear to want. Thus it is not quite to the point to suggest that symbolizing is necessarily a human enterprise.

What is, however, very much to the point is the question raised by the previous discussion, namely, given that some objects are especially appropriate for use as symbols of other objects, what makes them so? The answer to this question appears to be, no one thing. Sometimes resemblance with respect to observable qualities makes one thing a "natural symbol" of another. The shape of the mark on the road sign symbolizes a curve in the road. Sometimes, particularly when the objects symbolized are abstract, there is no such observable similarity. Students of logic, for example, find '→' a much more natural symbol of the relation of entailment than '⊃.'

Certainly some things naturally put people in mind of others. In some cases this may be the result of cultural conditioning; in other cases, it may simply be a function of the way we are wired up—that is, there may be some symbols which are, in the terminology of the declaration, "imprinted upon the human psyche." It would seem to be an empirical matter, a job for social scientists rather than theologians or philosophers to discover which these are, if any. Without such investigations it is hard to see what reasons might be adduced for holding that man, but not woman, is a "natural symbol" of Christ or that woman, but not man, is a "natural symbol" of the church. Indeed, one may wonder how "natural" any of the symbolism which figures in the "sacramental economy" of the church is. It seems highly doubtful that a naive observer from a Protestant tradition would, without prompting, perceive a priest dressed in vestments as a natural symbol of Christ, or High Mass in the high style as a representation of Christ's sacrifice. It is also doubtful whether one who is accustomed to the church's symbolism would find insurmountable difficulties in perceiving a woman who acted and dressed appropriately as a natural symbol of Christ. If this is correct, there seems no plausible reason to hold that men are natural symbols of Christ, and hence can function as priests while women are not and therefore cannot.

## The Argument about "Natural Symbols"

The opponent of women's ordination may however argue that the question of whether a woman can be a natural symbol of Christ is not an empirical question at all and cannot be settled by any philosophical or sociological survey. The vague suggestion that one thing naturally symbolizes another, just in case it is the sort of thing that tends to put people in mind of things of the other sort, is not a theory of natural symbols at all but rather a refusal to theorize. Without such a theory, there is, indeed, no conclusive reason to accept (3) or (4), but there is not conclusive reason to reject them either.

The most questionable premise of the argument, however, appears to be (1). In what way are men, but not women, "connected to" m-properties? We might take (1) as a straightforward empirical claim about what men and women are like, the claim, in particular, that all men actually have m-properties and that no women do, or perhaps that every man is more m-ish than most women. Understood in this way the claim is plainly false. Even if we grant that there are innate differences between men and women with regard to aggression, rationality, patience, docility and the like, such differences are on-the-average differences: even if most men are more m-ish than most women, some women are more m-ish than most men. If, indeed, it is the actual possession of m-properties that qualifies a person as a "natural symbol" of Christ and, hence, as a potential priest, then it would seem that some women would qualify and that some men would not.

The connection to m-properties most opponents of women's ordination have in mind, however, appears to be somewhat more complicated. Perhaps it is this: even if in fact men are not the sole exemplars of m-properties, we have a deeply rooted inclination to think of m-properties as "masculine," just as we are by nature inclined to think of f-properties as "feminine." Actual flesh and blood women may be within ourselves, among the archetypes imprinted upon our psyches, the image of the woman, the embodiment of receptivity, patience, and intuition, the symbol of nature itself. This is shown not through sociology but through poetry and myth. The fact that without any knowledge of literary conventions we respond immediately and pre-rationally to certain imagery, for example, the imagery of color, of the seasons, of man and woman, shows that such images are deeply entrenched.

Moreover, the least "realistic" art paradoxically may reveal the deepest realities. Sophisticated artists may ignore the archetypes or stand them on their heads. Though Rembrandt may paint an old man's face as beautiful and Eliot may portray April as the cruelest month, this is possible only through artifice and contrivance. As sophisticated readers we are *persuaded* that April is the cruelest month, quite against our natural inclinations. The naive artist does not need to persuade us of anything to elicit the desired effect: he merely evokes the archetypal images already in us. When Chaucer tells us that it is April, the effect is immediate: we naturally think of spring as a symbol of sweetness and rebirth. Similarly, it may be suggested, even though a sophisticated artist may portray a woman as masterful, detached, and rational, he does so only through contrivance; he must *persuade* us that she has these properties. To depict a woman as "feminine" the artist does not need to persuade us; by merely portraying her as a woman, he elicits the archetype of woman and induces the reader to make the desired assumptions about her character. Nothing more need be said.

Now, the argument continues, the church's system of sacraments and symbols is mythopoetic. Through it God touches us at the depths of our being, not through artifice or by rational persuasion but by invoking the archetypal images which are embedded in our very souls. God does not merely tell us that we are radically changed for the better by becoming members of the church; he makes water, the archetypal symbol of cleansing, of death and rebirth, the outward and visible sign of the inward and spiritual grace conferred in baptism. Similarly, we are not merely told that Christ sacrificed himself for us; rather Christ repeats his sacrificial act as priest and victim in the Eucharist. In choosing men to act as his representatives, God is invoking our archetypal image of man, to make us understand in the deepest sense what he did in becoming incarnate. Whatever any individual woman is like, no woman can evoke in us that archetype; hence, no woman can be a priest.

In response to such thrashings-about in the mythopoetic quagmire, it might be pointed out that the suggestion that there are archetypal images of man and woman embedded in the human psyche is controversial. But even if there are certain images and symbols which are universal and deeply entrenched, among them the archetypes of man and woman, it does not follow that the church is bound, or even permitted, to exploit them. Even if the church makes use of some natural symbols, the message seems clear that all symbols are non-ultimate and that some are to be rejected or transcended.

One of the most deeply entrenched symbols of moral goodness is physical beauty: Spenser's heroines and Milton's angels are beautiful. Conversely, ugliness and deformity are symbols of wickedness; thus Shakespeare confers a hump on Richard III. But Christ was not beautiful and he died an ugly death. "His face was so marred, more than man's. . . . there was no beauty in him that we should desire him." He was an offense to the Greeks. By mythopoetic standards he was a wholly inappropriate candidate for the role of incarnate deity. He was not a king or a military hero. In worldly terms he was a failure, but He is God.

Again, the most natural symbol of community is blood kinship. The family and the tribe are natural affinity groups. Christ, however, said that his true family were those who heard his message and obeyed, and he urged his hearers to leave their blood relatives and to follow him. His church, the ultimate community, is bound together not by race, blood, caste, culture or any other natural affinity, but by grace.

We may see David, king in Jerusalem, as a type of Christ and Israel as a type of church. We may respond religiously to the contemporary myths of C. S. Lewis and Charles Williams. We may platonize or remythologize the gospel to render it less offensive to "Greeks." But Christ is not Aslan or the corn-king, and the church is not the court of the Faerie Queene. Types and shadows have their ending for the newer rite is here. Even if women are not mythopoetically appropriate representatives of Christ, it does not follow the church is bound to exclude them from the priesthood.

## The Argument from Revelation

At this point it may be suggested that the impropriety of ordaining women to the priesthood is not merely discovered through reflection on the supposedly archetypal images of man and woman but by revelation. Jesus did not ordain women to be apostles in spite of ample opportunity to do so and, it is argued, this shows that he intended to exclude women from the priesthood. To repudiate his intent is to repudiate his authority and, by implication, his divinity.

You cannot introduce a Christian priesthood of women without accepting, at least by implication, the idea that the founder of Christianity, Christ Himself, could be wrong on a central point of His teaching in practice.

If He did not call them (women) either to the apostleship proper, or to any kind of apostolic ministry it must be a matter, not of chance, nor of a lack of practical and actual opportunity, but of principle.[3]

There have been a variety of responses to such arguments. It may be suggested that Jesus did not ordain anyone or that the number of apostles included a variety of persons who were not appointed by Jesus, among them women like "Junia . . . outstanding among the apostles" (Rom. 16:7). Again it may be suggested that even if there were no women among the apostles, the intent of Jesus was not to exclude them.

Even if we could, however, establish that Jesus and his early followers did intentionally exclude women from any kind of apostolic ministry, it does not follow that the church ought to exclude women from the priesthood. For one thing, Jesus and his earliest followers may simply have been wrong about women and their place in the church—as, for example, they appear to have been wrong about Gentiles:

The admission of Gentiles to baptism required a specific divine revelation (Acts 10:1–11:18). Evidently ethnic differences were more, not less, religiously significant in the early church than sexual ones. The amazement of Jesus at the faith of the Gentiles (e.g., Matt. 8:10–12; Mark 7:24–30), which has no parallel in regard to women, suggests that this might also have been true of Jesus.[4]

If we regard Jesus solely as a great religious teacher and moralist, then we shall certainly be shaken by the suggestion that he was mistaken on these points. If his significance for us depends on the originality or correctness of his teachings, then his significance is questionable. If, however, we regard Jesus as God incarnate, then we should not be worried if it turns out that he was unoriginal or mistaken on some points: to err is human and he is wholly human as well as wholly divine.

The opponent of women's ordination may at this point respond that even if Jesus could and did make mistakes about empirical matters, he did not err regarding moral matters. To suggest that Jesus was mistaken about the authorship of the Psalms is one thing; to suggest that his moral vision was obscured by the wrongheaded attitudes and conventions of his social milieu is quite another. If he regarded women as unsuitable for the apostolic ministry, as arguably he did, it could not be because he did not know any better, for that would mean he failed to recognize the injustice of sexism.

Nevertheless, we might respond as follows: God could have become incarnate as a woman if he chose. He could have chosen women to be apostles—or Greeks, or Abyssinians. But there are some things even God cannot do. He cannot (pace Descartes) make a mountain without any valley, and he cannot tell an English-speaking person that it is day and *mean* it is night. Such actions are logically impossible. The latter is impossible because "meaning" is not an inner action that one does while he speaks which is separable from his overt utterances and from the linguistic conventions with which he and his hearer operate. When a person utters the sentence "It is day" in the appropriate social context, he *means* it is day, regardless of what mental imagery he conjures up or fails to conjure up at the time of the utterance. Of course, he may modify the linguistic conventions by fiat by stipulating to his hearers, perhaps, "Let 'day' mean night." He cannot, however, perform an inner act which, unbeknownst to anyone but himself, changes his meaning, for "meaning" is a public, social enterprise.

Now Christ *meant* something by appointing twelve Jewish males as his inner circle. He meant that the church was to be the new Israel, the successor of the twelve tribes. Given the symbolic conventions of his social milieu he could not have chosen Gentiles or women and *meant* the same thing. He could of course have *stipulated* that the church was to be the new Israel but, for some reason we do not entirely understand, God prefers to use and transform existing symbolic conventions in communicating with us. He speaks to us in our own languages, as it were.

Similarly, it might be argued that in excluding women from the priesthood of the church until recently God *meant* something: He meant that He was a God who takes the initiative, a God who transcends nature. Given the character of local goddess cults and the view of women which prevailed in the Mediterranean world during the first century C. E., it is arguable that God could not have meant that about himself had he admitted women to the priesthood.

## Women and the Priesthood

As long as women occupy a radically different position in society from men and are commonly assumed to be different from men in some profound and metaphysically interesting way, the exclusion of women from the priesthood *means* something: it makes a theological statement, perhaps a correct one. Where such assumptions are not current, the restriction of the priesthood to males means nothing and will only be perceived as a pleasant anachronism or a gross injustice.

Arguably, in light of prevailing cultural assumptions, there were compelling theological reasons to exclude women from the priesthood in the past. But with the erosion of these assumptions the theological rationale for an all-male priesthood no longer exists. External verities do not change but their symbols and images do:

Like living beings they grow and they die. They grow when the situation is ripe for them, and they die when the situation changes. . . . They die because they can no longer produce response in the group where they originally found expression.[5]

As many opponents of women's ordination have themselves noted, we no longer perceive gender as deep or metaphysically interesting. Consequently the all-male priesthood meant nothing to us, and thus there was no compelling theological reason to retain it. For the same reason there was no compelling theological reason to *admit* women to the priesthood. In spite of the rather peculiar arguments of some advocates of women's ordination to the effect that by excluding women from the priesthood the church was distorting the image of God by representing him as wholly "masculine," the ordination of women meant nothing to us.

It seems neither unorthodox nor unreasonable to suggest that in the past God spoke to us in a manner accommodated to the then current conventions and cultural assumptions, using symbolism and imagery to which people responded, not in order to tell us that those assumptions were true or that those images were shadows of some deep and ineffable realities, but in order to make himself understood. If this is correct and if, as I suggest, gender has lost its symbolic import for us, then there is currently no reason to exclude women from the priesthood. Note that I am not claiming that the church's refusal to ordain women in the past was an injustice or even an excusable error due to ignorance. I am suggesting rather that it was in the past proper, indeed *obligatory* to exclude women from the priesthood, but that it no longer is.

To say that there are currently no compelling theological reasons to exclude women from the priesthood is not, however, to say that there are compelling reasons of any kind to admit them, or, in particular, that it was proper for the Anglican Church in the past decade to become the only branch of the Catholic church to ordain women priests. Opponents of women's ordination frequently charged that those of us who favored women's ordination were responding to theological arguments with pragmatic or political ones as a consequence of their ignorance or refusal to take theology seriously. Ironically, it appears that the worst arguments against women's ordination are theological and those that come closest to being convincing are of a thoroughly pragmatic nature.

The decision to ordain women in the Episcopal Church in 1976 had a great many undesirable consequences. It generated much dissension and bitterness, it polarized opinion within the church, and as a result it produced an unholy alliance of conservative Catholics and evangelicals. Nevertheless, even if such pragmatic considerations did show that women *should* not have been, they do not show that women *cannot* be ordained. And the argument that they cannot be ordained in virtue of their inability to function as "natural symbols" of Christ is, I have suggested, unsuccessful.

# NOTES

1. "Declaration on the Question of the Admission of Women to the Ministerial Priesthood" in Leonard Swidler and Arlene Swidler, eds., *Women Priests: A Catholic Commentary on the Vatican Declaration* (New York: Paulist Press, 1977), 43–44.

2. John Paul Boyer, "The 'Open Mind' and the Mind of Christ," in H. Karl Lutge, ed., *Sexuality—Theology—Priesthood: Reflections on the Ordination of Women to the Priesthood* (San Gabriel, Calif.: Concerned Fellow Episcopalians, n.d.), 55.

3. Louis Bouyer in *Sexuality, Theology, Priesthood,* 17–18.

4. Sandra M. Schneider, "Did Jesus Exclude Women from Priesthood" in Swidler and Swidler, *Women Priests,* 232n.

5. Paul Tillich, "Symbols of Faith" in Ronald E. Santoni, ed., *Religious Language and the Problem of Religious Meaning* (Bloomington: Indiana University Press, 1968), 137–38.

# 10

# Unification: Liberation
# for the Femininity of God?
## SARAH PETERSEN

The Unification Church, formally known as the Holy Spirit Association for the Unification of World Christianity, considers itself a development of the Judeo-Christian religious tradition.[1] Women's spirituality and the view of femininity in the movement include dimensions familiar to traditional Christian experience and newer aspects.

I shall explore creative and problematic aspects of the Unification perspective in several parts: images of the feminine, images of women, spiritual practice, ritual, mysticism, Unification doctrine, and problems of substance and relationality. A final section provides some conclusions from a survey by the author on "The Image of Woman in the Unification Church."

### Images of the Feminine

So God created man in his own image, in the image of God he created him; male and female he created them.          (Gen. 1:27)

Unification theology emphasizes the role of God as parent that is found in Christianity. The model of this on earth is the family. Thus, it would appear that Unification theology is an affirmation of traditional values. There are, however, significant transformations of this model in the doctrine of God.

In the Bible and the spirituality of Christians there are images of God which are both masculine and feminine. God as father is dominant, but there are also feminine images.[2] Despite these, the description of God as trinity is usually all male—Father, Son and Holy Spirit.[3] Unification theology breaks with the trend of both Protestant and Catholic spirituality in describing the aspects of God as formed of two fundamental polarities. One polarity is that of inner character and outer form; the other polarity is that of femininity and masculinity. These polarities are non–dualistic, complementary, equal, and reciprocal. Because God's innermost nature is that of heart, God is described as a parent, the unity of the masculine and feminine forms of parenthood.

This holistic image is reflected in Unification theology in the description of the trinity. The Holy Spirit is thought to function as a female spirit.[4] Through belief in Jesus and the Holy Spirit, Christians can be reborn as spiritual children. The representation of both the masculine and feminine aspects of God as parent are necessary for spiritual rebirth; thus, the first Christians did not experience rebirth after Jesus' death until the coming of the Holy Spirit. The interaction of both the Holy Spirit and Jesus with the believer makes spiritual rebirth possible.

Similarly, Unification theology describes the primary model for God's dwelling on earth as the holy family, sometimes referred to as the second four-position foundation. Husband and wife represent God's image on earth, while God's full presence is confirmed when there is a completion of reciprocal relationships within the family between God, husband, wife, and offspring. Thus, the feminine is an equal and fundamental part of the image of God and God's work and dwelling on earth.

The image of God as masculine and feminine is affirmed in the pastors and sacraments of the Unification Church. Reverend and Mrs. Moon are considered spiritual parents of the religious community. Pictures of the mass wedding in New York on 1 July 1982, for example, show Mrs. Moon blessing the wedding participants with her husband. The sacramental couple, parents of the family, represent God on earth. Neither man nor woman alone can fully reflect God. Thus, God's feminine aspect is an object of worship for Unificationists and is represented in church ritual.

## Images for Women

Providential history begins with father–daughter cooperation. But it must be succeeded by husband–wife cooperation, which in turn must be followed by mother–son cooperation. And ultimately, in winning over the Communists, women must lead the way.[5]

The *Divine Principle,* the scripture of the Unification Church, teaches that providential history informs and influences our relationship with God. The quality of heart or offering which made possible the victories of religious people is an example for one's individual life of faith. For instance, Sarah, the wife of Abraham, the father of faith, is herself a model of faith. Rebecca fulfilled the role of a mother who guides her son to do the will of God when she taught Jacob how to receive the blessing from his father. Moses' mother, sister, and wife all contributed significantly to his work for God.[6]

Women have been prominent in the development of the Unification movement, even though the established Unification churches are dominated by male leadership. As a young girl Mrs. Moon received the blessing of a female spiritualist whom Reverend Moon tried to contact during his mission to North Korea in the late 1940s.[7] Two grandmothers became members of his church at that time, and remained faithful through the trials that followed,[8] along with a male disciple, Won Pil Kim. Several professors and students at Ewha Women's University sacrificed their academic careers when the university forced them to choose between church membership and their studies in 1955.

In 1959, Young Oon Kim came to the United States as the first missionary from Korea; trained in theology earlier, she now teaches at the Unification Theological Seminary. She sent missionaries, several of them women, to Europe in the 1960s, and that tradition is continued in the mission leaders worldwide today. Early leaders of the movement in America were women.[9] Women attend the Unification Theological Seminary, and there are a few women among the doctoral students in religion sponsored by the church.[10] In Korea, Japan, and America both married and single women have at various times gone out to witness in new territories, travelling with only "heavenly protection." In 1983, Unification sisters in America were asked to form and lead travelling mission teams, and thus began an evangelical trend which spread to the men as well.

Like Deborah of the Old Testament or Joan of Arc in Christian history, Unification women sally forth to pioneer spiritual activities, often leaving a husband and family. Yet the other female image relevant to sisters is that of the mother of Jesus, or the picture of Tamar waiting for Judah at the roadside, giving their lives to their children. Motherhood is an essential part of Unification theology (as is fatherhood). Thus, Unificationists live between two poles—that of physical parenthood, seeking to fulfill the second blessing of Gen. 1:28, in which one establishes a marital relationship and bears children in a godly relationship, and that of spiritual parenthood, taking on the suffering of the world and striving to alleviate it. The common theme uniting these two poles is God's heart, a God who has shed many tears for Her children who are lost, who longs to dwell eternally in the hearts of all people. This dynamic role requires emotional flexibility.

Amplifying the sense of conflict between these two roles is the absence of a description of women's providential contributions in the written doctrine of the Unification Church. While the Old Testament era described in Unification theology includes an explanation of some significant actions of women, the teachings are silent on those of Christian history. Furthermore, religious leaders described as the "central figures" of an era are always male. Even so, the supportive contributions of women may be overlooked. St. Augustine, for example, is lauded for his vision of the city of God, but the spiritual contribution of his mother to his conversion, involving years of prayer and hope, is not mentioned. The Babylonian Captivity of the Pope (in France) is considered significant in Unification theology; St. Catherine of Siena was influential with two Popes, and sought to reform the church and heal the schism.[11] As is typical of much religious literature, the contributions of women are invisible in the church's present written account.

Consequently, Unificationists are sometimes uncertain of the proper role of women once restoration is accomplished and an ideal world established. Is women's contribution merely indemnity for Eve's failure? Is woman destined for domesticity? Asked what the role of woman will be in the ideal world, Reverend and Mrs. Moon both responded—completely flexible: a woman can stay at home or go out (to work, etc.).[12]

## Spiritual Practice

God's resentment consists of the fact that the standard of the number eight—of true father, husband, older brother, son, true mother, wife, older sister, and daughter—was not truly established.[13]

God always guides those who impress Him through their life of motherly heart. Then children of God are the pride of His heart.[14]

Spiritual discipline and practices in the Unification Church are diverse, and participation is open to male and female without discrimination. While members may practice individual disciplines, some drawn from other religions and worldviews (such as vegetarianism), there are also common practices. Among these are fasting, prayer conditions, witnessing, the offering of material objects, celibacy before marriage, separation of spouses after marriage, fidelity within marriage, the temporary separation of parent and child for mission work, obedience and humility toward church elders, and creating harmonious relationships among members of the movement as spiritual brothers and sisters. Hard work and challenging one's physical and spiritual limitations also constitute a basic spiritual attitude.

Women participate in all these practices without protection or regard for the "weaker sex." They may be out late at night witnessing or fundraising; they may learn a martial art; they may form an all-female boat crew to catch a thousand-pound giant tuna on the open ocean. Spirituality means an intense engagement with the world, transforming all activities and offering them to God.

While thus engaged in hectic activity, a member undergoes an internal odyssey. Each Unificationist seeks to develop the heart of a child toward God, and the heart of a parent and servant to the world. Members of the movement live as brothers and sisters within the same buildings and work closely together. Their celibacy, or marital fidelity, is not protected by walls or romantic interludes, but relies on a purity of heart and mind which must be developed. Before marriage, sisters seek to develop a mother's heart toward others and relate to men as brothers, an attitude comparable to that of a religious sister in the Christian tradition.

The period of celibacy is followed by an engagement and marriage called "The Blessing" in which women make the transition to a God-centered married state. Physical motherhood follows spiritual motherhood. Thus the celibate state is preparation and training to create Godly love within the family; the circle is completed when the bonds of family love extend to the community.

However, marriage and children are often delayed until the woman is past thirty years of age. This delay causes a suppression and subsequent expression of physical desires within a spiritual framework, and requires discipline and patience. More importantly, the delay of childbearing can be difficult when there is a limited period for a woman to conceive. Still, separations between husband and wife immediately after marriage are a minimum of forty days, and can exceed three years.[15]

There may also occur times when the blessed wife leaves her family to do work elsewhere in the movement.[16] In a more modified form, sisters may work during the day as a means of serving the church or as a way of meeting financial need. The challenges of this spiritual path can stimulate flexibility, faith, and an inner certainty of one's value as a person, regardless of one's external circumstances.

## Ritual

Would you pledge to observe heavenly law as an original man and woman, and, should you fail, pledge to take responsibility for that?

Would you, as an ideal husband and wife, pledge to establish an eternal family with which God can be happy?

Would you pledge to inherit heavenly tradition and, as the eternal parents of goodness, raise up your children to be examples of this standard before the family and the world?

Would you pledge to be the center of love before the society, nation, world and universe based upon the ideal family?

Wedding Vows
July 1, 1982

Unification teaching considers the "blessed" marriage, that is marriage within the Unification Church with the blessing of Reverend and Mrs. Moon, a more holy state than the celibate or vowed life.[17] This contrasts with the Roman Catholic scholastic tradition, which associates the figure of Eve (woman) with the body and the lower state of marriage: "Eve's being fashioned separately by God is a symbol that man should have a preference for contemplation, a nobler way to spend his time."[18] "Marriage, then, is seen as intrinsically inferior to virginity."[19]

The Hebrew tradition contains various curses regarding childbirth and conception, as in Genesis 3:16 and Psalm 51:5, ". . . in sin did my mother conceive me." As woman is the childbearer of humanity, belief in original sin and the fallenness of people often associates woman and her body more closely with evil.[20] Woman is thus often seen as the temptress, symbolized by Eve in the garden. The other image, that of the virgin Mary, is physically impossible to imitate.

In some traditions woman is conditionally redeemed from her lower status by marriage, which requires obedience and fidelity to the husband (who does not have to reciprocate), or in the Christian tradition by celibacy in the vowed life as a religious sister or nun.[21] However, even the relatively greater freedom of the religious life is tempered by the supervision of church leadership, necessarily male because woman could not represent Jesus (man) at the altar. Within the Protestant tradition, married women were considered the property of the husband under United States law until the mid-nineteenth century; female ministers are a relatively new arrival on the pastoral scene as well.

Against this tradition, Unification theology asserts that the blessed state of marriage is necessary for complete salvation. One enters the kingdom of heaven as a couple, not individually. The Unification sacraments of blessed marriage affirm the sanctity of childbirth and married life, thus blessing fundamental processes which women embody.

Blessed marriage is important not only eschatologically, but in the ideal of creation is the fulfillment of the second blessing of Genesis 1:28 (to be fruitful), in which a couple seeks to inherit the parenthood of God. It is believed that a couple blessed in the church tradition who live a holy life are forgiven of original sin; their children receive the benefit of that absolution, and thus do not need baptism or redemption at birth. This view redeems the body as well.

The role of woman in a blessed marriage is vital. As restored Eve the sister offers the wine (symbol of redemption) to her prospective husband, after receiving it from the pastors of the ceremony. This holy wine ceremony occurs once, at the time of engagement. It is the woman who initiates a God-centered relationship within the couple; for a period of time, her prayer may focus on being a "mother" to her husband. Later her husband will reciprocate. Eventually there should be a smooth exchange of positions in which the husband may be father, brother, or son to his wife, and the wife may be mother, sister, or daughter to her husband as they encourage each other in a holy life. The couple are saved together as male and female.

At the time of childbirth seven candles are lit shortly before delivery. They invoke God's grace, protection, and blessing on the birth; this author found the flickering candles a symbol of comfort and assurance during her first child's birth. At an appropriate time later, the family dedicates the child to God in a prayer ceremony. The parents act as the sacramental couple; both pray, and then the father offers the dedicatory prayer.

The marriage and childbirth ceremonies are the primary rituals of the church. There are also daily and Sunday prayers; all members pray together, usually led by a brother but sometimes by a sister. Sunday services and Wednesday night prayer meetings may be conducted by either a brother or sister. However, male leadership often prevails.

## Mysticism

When you pray, your heart should be as earnest as a baby who cries for his mother's milk.[22]

Unification Church life is not a vocation of silent contemplation but one of activity. Prayer, nevertheless, is important. Prayer can be undertaken anywhere, at any time, although there is usually an area set aside for prayer in each center or home. The purpose of all activity is restoration, to move it out of the secular dimension and offer it to God, so that it becomes a God-centered activity. In the process, one discovers that God inspires in the most mundane activity: office work, for example, or the purchase of a family vehicle. Naturally, prayer is the essential foundation for all spiritual activities.

Forms of mystic experience may come through dreams, visions, and spiritual gifts. Members often report dreams of either Reverend or Mrs. Moon. One member had a corrective operation after joining the church. Out of gratitude for the surgery he determined not to take any pain medication afterwards. However, a nose operation can be very painful. Lying awake in pain in the early morning at the hospital, firmly resolved not to use drugs, but with tears running down his face, he saw a vision of Mrs. Moon smiling at him. After she appeared to him, the pain vanished.[23]

Early Korean members report many spiritual experiences. One woman, a fervent Christian who prayed in the Korean mountains for several years, had a vision which led her directly to the small church headquarters. Early members testify that the period of the 1950s in the Korean church was a time of intense spiritual activity; these experiences comforted and encouraged the members during a period of extreme persecution and suffering.

While the gifts of healing and speaking in tongues do occur in the church, they are not usually cultivated deliberately. Church practice emphasizes the importance of devoting one's energy and spiritual strength to restoration of this world; spiritual gifts, while useful and valid, are not an end in themselves. Members are, however, encouraged to spend long hours in prayer and to cultivate a sense of immediate relationship with God's heart and guidance.

There is a certain custom of prayer by trinities of sisters in the church. In several cases, three elderly women, long-time church members, have been asked to pray as a trinity for their country. On a smaller scale, the older sisters in a church center may form a trinity to pray for the leadership and members in their community. Among the blessed families the network of support is still in the embryonic stage, but recently prayer trinities of sisters focusing on problems ranging from missions to family have met near Washington, D.C. Also in this area a women's prayer group has begun to meet regularly. These structures may be more developed in Japan, where blessed sisters may assist each other with childcare, etc. so that mothers can help the family economically.

Korea, for over 500 years the land of the male Confucian scholar, was also the home of the shaman, usually a woman. It would be interesting to explore resemblances between prayer tradition and shamanistic practices. In any event, it is the experience and confidence of sisters that prayer by women is powerful.

Finally, some sisters report having encounters in prayer with Heavenly Mother, God's feminine aspect. A graduate student received a moving response to her prayer one day; she felt God's presence as Mother, and was told that God's feminine nature had been waiting so long to be expressed.[24]

## Unification Doctrine

Everyone, without exception, is struggling to gain happiness.

(*Divine Principle,* 1)

The *Divine Principle* explains that within God there is a reciprocal relationship of dual characteristics of positivity (masculinity) and negativity (femininity), as well as a reciprocal relationship between God's essential character and God's essential form.[25] The relationship between the polarities is that of "subject" and "object." Give-and-take action between subject and object creates a unified base which then stands as a third object to God. This establishes the "four-position-foundation."[26] ". . .[W]hen the subject and object unite in circular movement, the subject is able to stand in the position of the object, and the object in that of the subject."[27] This is true harmony of relationship.

The husband/wife relationship is the primary example of a four-position-foundation on earth. Reverend Moon explained recently in a speech that the husband is the subject and the wife is in the object position; the person who gives the most love, however, is the true subject, because God is a subject of love.[28] This view protects the mutuality, equality, and reciprocity of the marriage relationship, paradigm for all social relationships. It confirms in the ideal of creation an interrelationship of soteriology.

Unfortunately, the written doctrine currently describing masculine and feminine attributes tempers this relational sense of equality, mutuality, and freedom in expressing God's femininity. Positivity (masculinity) and negativity (femininity) cannot be directly equated with male and female in Unification theology because male and female contain both positivity and negativity within their character and form. Theoretically, however, the male has more positive characteristics, and the female more negative characteristics.[29] Furthermore, *Unification Thought* asserts:

Man is the encapsulation of all the positive and subjective things in the cosmos; he corresponds to totality of the positive parts in the cosmos and is their representative. On the other hand, woman is the encapsulation of all the negative and objective things in the cosmos and represents them.[30]

The *Divine Principle* suggests similarly that if Adam and Eve had been perfected, they would have been respectively the "substantial embodiment" of all the subject and object elements in the cosmos.[31] These views imply that the attributes of negativity might influence the view of femininity, the view of woman, and the attitude toward the object.

Descriptions of the positive and negative aspects vary in church teaching materials. Positive characteristics have been listed as:

Positive emotion, which is bright or lively . . . positive intellect which is active . . . positive will, which initiates and takes charge.[32]

Positive, active and creative will; bright, delightful and joyful feeling; and bright, clear and abundant concepts and good memory within the intellect, all belong to the positive aspect of the Sung Sang (inner character).[33]

Perspicacity, keen perceptiveness, imaginativeness, good memory, pleasantness, cheerfulness, brightness, activeness, decisiveness, creativeness.[34]

The characteristics described as negative are:

Negative emotion, which is sentimental or placid . . . negative intellect, which is passive . . . there is negative will, which is passive, or responsive.[35]

Negative, passive, and conservative will; melancholy, unpleasant and sad feelings; and stupid, ambiguous, bewildered and absent-minded intellect belong to the negative aspect of Sung Sang (internal character).[36]

Obtuseness, dullness, unimaginativeness, poor memory, unpleasantness, melancholy, gloominess, passiveness, indecisiveness, conservativeness.[37]

The characteristics described as positive are generally thought to be more desirable for a human being to encapsulate, represent, and embody. It seems unlikely that a stupid and unpleasant character pleases God and embodies Her femininity.

The belief that male and female differ emotionally and otherwise is often found in religious and secular thought. Feminists draw on that tradition when they claim that men are more eager to wage war, and thus that women should govern.[38] An early father of the church, Clement of Alexandria, believed that men and women are equal in Christ, but that woman is created by God for domesticity and serving her husband. *The Feminine Character* outlines a wide variety of descriptions by scholars, and indicates that the view of the feminine may be shaped by the scholastic discipline, personal life history, and social and historical milieu.[39] Some observers conclude that description of masculinity and femininity is inherently oppressive and can only lead to rigid role tracking and the unhealthy repression of an individual's unique character.

It may be useful, however, to attribute broad qualities to masculinity and femininity. Male and female are physically different, and there may also be spiritual differences. Otherwise it would not be necessary in Unification theology for one male and one female to represent God's image together. The danger is that description can stifle growth as well as promote it.

Historically, male philosophers, theologians, and psychologists have shaped the dominant cultural myths about woman, the "Other." Simone de Beauvoir suggests that women learn an unhealthy, alienated value system in which they are valued through male eyes and definitions.[40] Theologically, this implies that women might learn to value themselves because of male approval, not because of God's creation and approval of their personhood.

In fact, it may only be human nature that makes it difficult to imagine the needs, wants, desires, qualities, and virtues of a person different from ourselves. Men have dominated most human activities outside the home, but women participate increasingly in our modern age. The *Divine Principle* clearly states that "equality between the sexes" is a sign of the last days and of God's effort to build the kingdom of heaven on earth. According to Unification teaching, this is evidence of the restoration of the first blessing, the reversal of the fall in which people lost their original value.[41] Thus, it may be that the present Unification descriptions of negativity are transitional. When humanity finally understands the original value and character of male and female, God's femininity will be expressed with joy and beauty.

## Problems of Substance and Relationality

There is evidence that Unification theology inherits both the problems and the benefits of having philosophical roots in the western and eastern traditions. A major area of restoration for women and for male/female relationships originates in platonic thought, which promotes a hierarchical order of mind over body, male over female. Rosemary Ruether states:

In *Timaeus* Plato says that when the incarnate soul loses its struggle against the passions and appetites, it is incarnated into a woman and then into "some brute which resembled him in the evil nature which he had acquired," The hierarchy of spirit to physical nature as male to female is made explicit. The chain of being, God-spirits-male-female-non-human-nature-matter, is at the same time the chain of command. . . .[42]

In Christian tradition, woman often became a symbol of earthly desire, temptation, and mortal decay. Although woman could be saved, some even thought that women were resurrected as male.[43]

Fundamental Unification theory clearly repudiates the more obvious errors of the earlier Christian traditions. Women are necessary to represent God's image on earth and in heaven. However, the tension between relationality and substance-promoting-hierarchy with its implications of a superior nature is unresolved in current written doctrine. Two theologians comment:

I make a big distinction between the Principle and the book *Divine Principle*. In this book I notice on one level a relational language, a language of give-and-take, and on another level a language of entity, of substance, of hierarchy of superordination and subordination. . . . I feel the relational language is closer to the Principle but at the same time I see in *Divine Principle* an ambiguity about this. . . . This . . . pertains . . . directly to the male-female question.[44]

[T]he Unification community is under a kind of double-bind. . . . There is the inheritance of biblical patriarchalism. . . . In addition to that . . . there is the Confucian-Oriental tradition. . . . One is the Confucian concept of relationality. . . . In Confucianism relationality is hierarchical. . . . [T]here is historically a subordination of the wife to the husband.[45]

The tension between a static order of substance and the mutuality of relational exchange in the written church teachings complicates the understanding of "negativity" and "object" in church doctrine. Consequently the written descriptions may be clarified or repudiated in the oral teachings, or in Reverend Moon's speeches.

The use of the word "negative," for example, and its description requires repeated explanations by church teachers that this is not a misogynous doctrine. Young Oon Kim explains that the positive/negative concept originates with yin/yang theory, and that it is a complementary, dipolar concept:

Nor is one necessarily superior to the other in value. Hardness and softness are equally desirable. Wetness and dryness possess similar merit, depending upon the circumstances. So it is with masculinity and femininity or activity and receptiveness.[46]

Similarly, Nora Spurgin suggests a fluid, mutual image:

Masculinity is the kind of energy that is very focused, very pointed and very initiating energy. Femininity is the name given to energy that is more encompassing, more nurturing . . . [W]ithin each man and woman there are both . . . different people have different amounts of different qualities. And then I feel that as a couple within the church we work this out and there isn't a specific image imposed upon us.[47]

These views contrast sharply with the more static view inferred from the *Divine Principle* and *Unification Thought*. However, as Young Oon Kim pointed out at a conference in the Bahamas in February, 1983, until now all teaching materials in the church have been written by men.

Ambiguity regarding the nature of femininity is aggravated by an unfortunate vocabulary. There are problems with translation from Korean into English, and thus the assurances of Korean members that the terms in Korean do not imply derogation must be taken in good faith, apart from the problem of the actual descriptions. However, "negative" and "object" at best do not abet the image of femininity. Some sisters also find the use of male language, e.g., man to represent people, and the exclusive use of father to refer to God to be confusing or excluding.[48]

The view of the subject/object relationship also suffers from a lack of clarification or distinction between mutuality and subordination. The *Divine Principle* describes the relationships between God and "man" (people), senior and junior males, parents and children, and husband and wife as subject/object; there is no distinction between relationships in which the subject has greater authority, power, and respect, and the mutuality of marriage.[49] *The Outline of the Principle: Level Four* uses diagrams with the same effect.[50] This suggests that a Confucian view influences the description. Gene James outlines the traditional Confucian virtues and view of woman, asking, "Are women to be equal partners in marriage or are they to be under the dominion of their husbands? *Divine Principle* does not speak with an unequivocal voice."[51] It is appropriate to note that the one female author of the church teachings emphasizes the mutuality of the marriage, "subject/object" relationship: "A husband and wife will enjoy mutual concern and affection. Both will be united in bonds of fidelity and loyalty."[52]

To clarify and liberate the image of femininity Unification scholars must reexamine not only the influence of Confucian tradition but that of Christian biblical patriarchy. Eleanor McLaughlin describes the trend of theology, suggesting that "complementarity" may disguise a hierarchical order:

It is easy to find recent literature within the Christian theological tradition that insists on a nondualist anthropology and on an unambiguous moral equivalence of sexes, but dwells at the same time upon the differences between women and men that imply not only separate function but also an unambiguous superordination and subordination, grounded paradigmatically in the relationship of God to his creatures. Thus Karl Barth has spoken of man and woman as an A and a B; in respect of order woman is B . . . and therefore behind and subordinate to man. . . . There is indeed implied an inadequate definition of human nature: static, ahistorical, hierarchical, Platonizing in its assumption of ontologically fixed relationships between the sexes . . . difference becomes rationalized subordination.[53]

Given the strength of the hierarchical tradition, one must assume that the use and description of "object" and "negativity" distorts the relational nature of Unification theology.

Centuries ago the early Christian church permitted an equality of participation for male and female, but as authority became more established, the contributions of women became subordinate to the male structure. At present the oral tradition repudiates the bias of the written doctrine in the young Unification movement.

## Survey Results

There is some ambivalence in the Unification Church about the role of women. On the one hand, women are active and hold leadership and sacramental positions. On the other hand, aspects of the doctrine display a familiar religious bias. There are sisters in the movement who have been told, on occasion, "You can't be the leader; you're a woman," or "You can't be the lecturer; you're a woman," even though women do lecture and do lead.

Results of a small survey conducted by this writer in December 1982 show that church members tend to reject undesirable descriptions of positive, negative, subject, and object.[54] While there was acceptance of some difference between men and women, there was a basic attitude of flexibility in roles. Self-images expressed by sisters in the survey show confidence and assertiveness.

There were some significant response differences between male and female church members on statements concerning the role of the mother in the home. Men were more eager to ascribe nurturing qualities to women, while the women were more careful about assuming the entire burden of responsibility for family care and harmony. One might conclude, with respect to the view of femininity, that the tradition of relationality and mutuality is at this time more influential to members' faith than that of substance and hierarchy.

## Conclusion

In Unification thought and practice one can see the face of femininity in divinity, in activity, in tradition, in history, and in the home. Sometimes the image is blurred, unclear or tentative, but its presence is acknowledged perhaps more powerfully than in the Judeo-Christian tradition out of which the Unification Church arises. Whether the Unification approach will finally liberate the face of femininity for both male and female will not be decided now—salvation is both an event and a process.

Woman's fate and role has often been determined by the destiny of the family. In Unification theology the family is the model for society. If a true family model reflecting the ideal of creation can be established and emulated, it may be that God's femininity will finally be liberated in Her children.

# NOTES

1. For a discussion of different aspects of Unification theology, see H. Richardson, ed., *Ten Theologians Respond to the Unification Church* (Barrytown, N.Y. Unification Theological Seminary, 1981), especially F. Sontag, "The God of Principle: A Critical Evaluation" (107–39) and F. Clark, "The Fall of Man in *Divine Principle*" (143–65); also Dagfinn Aslid, "Spiritual Discipline as the Actualization of the Heart of God" in J. Duerlinger, ed., *Ultimate Reality and Spiritual Discipline* (New York: Paragon House, 1984), 139–53.

2. Young Oon Kim, *Unification Theology* (New York: Holy Spirit Association for the Unification of World Christianity [hereafter HSA-UWC], 1980), 57–60.

3. The exception to this is Greek Orthodox Christianity, which sees the Holy Spirit as feminine. This is not the dominant strand of Christianity in the West or in Korea.

4. See Warren Lewis, *Witnesses to the Holy Spirit: An Anthology* (Valley Forge, Pa. Judson, 1978) for material suggesting a subordinate view of the Holy Spirit as feminine in traditional Christianity.

5. Young Whi Kim, ed., *The Way of God's Will* (New York; HSA-UWC, 1980), 40–41. This is a collection of excerpts from speeches by Reverend Moon in Japan and Korea.

6. See *Divine Principle*, 5th ed. (New York: HSA-UWC, 1973), re: Sarah, 264–65; re: Rebecca and Moses' mother, 290. These brief written references are greatly expanded in oral teaching.

7. Mrs. Moon's mother was a member of the spiritualist movement called the "Inside Belly Church."

8. The earliest picture of Reverend Moon doing his mission shows Won Pil Kim at Reverend Moon's feet, with two elderly women on either side of Reverend Moon. In July, 1975, in Korea, this writer heard one of them testify that she visited Reverend Moon during his imprisonment in the Hungnam communist labor camp. She cut off her hair to make him warm socks; consequently, she says, her hair never turned gray. She was about eighty at the time of the testimony, and her hair was black. Her name is Se Hyun Ok. See the testimony in *Today's World* 5, no. 3 (1984); 14–16: "Mrs. Se Hyun Ok came [to visit Reverend Moon in Hungnam prison camp] almost every two months. . . . When she came she brought socks, underwear and misukaru (rice powder)."

9. Statement by Hugh Spurgin in R. Quebedeaux, ed., *Lifestyle, Conversations with Members of the Unification Church* (Barrytown, N.Y.: Unification Theological Seminary, 1982), 25.

10. Ibid., 113–15, regarding church leaders' attitudes toward female participation in conferences, and social influence and church process toward male/female roles.

11. Eleanor McLaughlin, "Women, Power and the Pursuit of Holiness in Medieval Christianity," in Rosemary Ruether and Eleanor McLaughlin, eds., *Women of Spirit, Female Leadership in the Jewish and Christian Traditions* (New York: Simon & Schuster, 1979), 115–19.

12. Response to a question by a doctoral student over a breakfast attended by this writer in late October, 1981. Reverend and Mrs. Moon both said something in Korean, and there was one English translation.

13. Young Whi Kim, *The Way of God's Will*, 57.

14. Ibid., 229.

15. See the testimony of Mrs. Nora Spurgin in Quebedeaux, *Lifestyle*, 12.

16. Ibid., 12–16. See also the testimony of Mrs. Betsy Jones in Susan Hodges and M. Darrol Bryant, eds., *Exploring Unification Theology* (New York: Edwin Mellen, 1978), 167: "In my own case, my family and I have gone through periods of separation from each other. That's partly because it's an emergency time. But I also know that it's been a liberating experience of finding myself, finding my own value, having a freer attitude towards my children. I hope I will see it not just as an emergency measure, but as an internal training experience so that I can live together with and also live freely within my family."

17. However, Unification thought would agree that the vowed life of a celibate in most religious traditions is higher than that of marriage in that tradition and that, historically, virginity is a holier state than most marriages.

18. Joseph E. Kearns, S.J., *The Theology of Marriage: The Historical Development of Christian Attitudes toward Sex and Sanctity in Marriage* (New York: Sheed & Ward, 1964), 163.

19. Rosemary Radford Ruether, "Misogynism and Virginal Feminism in the Fathers of the Church," in R. Ruether, ed., *Religion and Sexism: Images of Woman in the Jewish and Christian Traditions* (New York: Simon & Schuster, 1974), 164.

20. This point is developed by Ruether in her article while discussing St. Augustine. She states: "This definition of femaleness as body decrees a natural subordination of female to male, as flesh must be subject to spirit in the right ordering of nature. It also makes her peculiarly the symbol of the Fall and sin. . . ." Ibid., 157.

21. Ruether states: "Virginity, then, is interpreted as the resurrected life of the gospel whereby woman is freed from this twofold curse on Eve of the sorrows of childbearing and male domination." Ibid., 159. She adds that both Augustine and Jerome believe that while humanity will resurrect as male and female (some ascetics thought all females would be changed into males at the

Resurrection), the female bodily characteristics would be transformed so that they are no longer suited to intercourse and childbearing, thus losing their shameful aspects. Ibid., 160.

22. Young Whi Kim, *The Way of God's Will*, 359.

23. Testimony heard by this writer at an International One World Crusade church meeting in Japan in February, 1975.

24. Testimony of Diana Muxworthy Feige in 1979. She also received the feeling that it is very important not to have resentment.

25. *Divine Principle,* 24. According to Korean church leaders, "negative" does not have derogatory connotations in this usage.

26. Ibid., 32.

27. Ibid., 49.

28. Speech heard by the author given by Reverend Moon, 25 September 1983 in the Washington, D.C. church.

29. *Explaining Unification Thought* (New York: Unification Thought Institute, 1981), 52.

30. *Unification Thought* (New York: Unification Thought Institute, 1973), 156.

31. *Divine Principle,* 38.

32. *Outline of the Principle: Level 4* (New York: HSA-UWC, 1980), 12.

33. *Unification Thought,* 40.

34. *Explaining Unification Thought,* 52.

35. *Outline of the Principle: Level 4,* 12.

36. *Unification Thought,* 40.

37. *Explaining Unification Thought,* 52.

38. See "Statement to the Press" from the Sonia Johnson - Citizen for President Committee, 3318 Second St. S., Arlington, VA 22204: "Women's voices, particularly feminist voices—the least co-opted women's voices—must be heard over the gunfire. . . . My second day in the oval office would be spent sitting in a circle of non-patriarchal women from every country, planning how to bring arms immediately and globally under female control. Men have never made weapons they have not used, and there is every indication that this trend will continue until women intervene. . . . The human family is therefore much safer with weapons in the hands of the average woman than of the average man," 1–4.

39. Viola Klein, *The Feminine Character, History of an Ideology* (Chicago: University of Illinois Press, 1971), xix–xx.

40. Simone de Beauvoir, *The Second Sex,* trans. H. M. Parshley (New York: Vintage Books, 1974), 54, 58, 87.

41. *Divine Principle,* 121.

42. Rosemary Radford Ruether, *Sexism and God-Talk: Toward a Feminist Theology* (Boston: Beacon, 1983), 79.

43. Ibid., 80–81.

44. Comment by Frank Flinn in Quebedeaux, *Lifestyle,* 117.

45. Comment by Durwood Foster in Quebedeaux, *Lifestyle,* 118.

46. Young Oon Kim, *Unification Theology,* 56.

47. Quebedeaux, *Lifestyle,* 119.

48. See the statements of Patricia Zulkosky in Quebedeaux, *Lifestyle,* 117; and in Patricia Zulkosky, "Women: Guilt, Spirituality, and Family," in Gene James, ed., *The Family and the Unification Church* (New York: Unification Theological Seminary, 1983), 181–91. Other sisters express similar concerns. At the time of this writing there is a possibility that the new teaching volume on the *Divine Principle* will use non-gender-specific language when referring to all people or male and female persons generally.

49. *Divine Principle,* 49.

50. *Outline of the Principle: Level 4,* 16–17.

51. Gene James, "Family, Spiritual Values and World Government," in James, *Family,* 263.

52. Young Oon Kim, *Unification Theology,* 72.

53. Eleanor Commo McLaughlin, "Equality of Souls, Inequality of Sexes: Woman in Medieval Theology," in *Religion and Sexism,* 259–60.

54. Unpublished survey by Sarah E. Petersen, "The Image of Woman in the Unification Church," December, 1982. The survey was answered by twenty-four respondents. Long but unofficial, this survey is inconclusive due to the small pool of respondents. A copy is available on request.

# 11

# Women and Religious Experience Among the Anlo of West Africa
## CHRISTIAN R. GABA

This paper studies the nature of spirituality open to women in a particular African religious experience. It also discusses how this spirituality shapes and is shaped by womanhood. The particular African society chosen is the Anlo, a section of the Ewe-speaking peoples of West Africa, not only because this is the African ethnic group best known to me but, more importantly, because it gives a practical direction how contemporary studies on African life and thought should best be conducted to yield scholarly dividends. Subjects like the present one have not yet received sufficient scholarly attention to make possible studies across ethnic boundaries which will not lead to facile and inadequately substantiated generalizations on behalf of the whole of traditional Africa.

The material for this study shall be mainly, but not exclusively, the ritual of worship since this is, at present, the principal source which constitutes the people's own account of their experience, non-literate as they largely are. In fact, we need not labor the point that in any study that considers religion as something that exists in its own right and should be regarded as such, this source is indispensably needed if a scholarly investigation is intended. Our concern is the indigenous, autochthonous conception of the religious experience of the Anlo as it exists at present in contradistinction to the Christian and Islamic conceptions which predominate any African society today.

## Anlo Religious Experience and Ritual Specialists

Anlo religious experience, in the language of Ninian Smart, is numinous rather than mystical, with worship rather than contemplation as its central mode of expression. The conception of the sacred, which is the central pivot of this experience, is theistic with divine beings both positive and negative populating this nonempirical dimension of life. The worshipful among the spirit beings are hierarchically conceived. First comes *Mawu*, God, who is the creator directly or indirectly of all that is, including the lower spirit beings. He is regarded as male. Then come the non-human spirit beings, *trowo*, followed by the human spirit beings, *togbeawo*.

The non-human spirit beings are both male and female; so also are the human ones. Out of 105 recitals that form part of the ritual of worship collected from this African society,[1] four have female spirit beings as objects of cultic attention apart from reference made to them in ritual sayings addressed specifically to the male spirit beings.[2] Anlo religious experience also makes mention of the earth, *Anyigba*, as a deity, as the following passage suggests:

> O Heaven, your attention please.
> I also invoke the presence of your spouse, Earth.
>
> (LXXVII, 7–8)

For an effective communion, Anlo spirituality interposes human ritual specialists[3] between humankind and the sacred. These sacred specialists are both male and female. Usually a female spirit being has a male principal ritual specialist dedicated to her service. But it is not a common practice to have female principal ritual specialists serving male spirit beings. The principal sacred specialists, *tsifodilawo*, who lead in ancestral rituals, are all male. But in the cultic attention paid to the non-human spirits, the ritual specialists may be either male or female. In the hierarchy of the priesthood come first *kukutawo*, that is, priests and priestesses who wear a special raffia hat. They are followed by *tagbasiawo*, priests and priestesses who wear headgear in the form of a turban.[4]

Other sacred specialists are diviners, *nukulawo*, and are from both sexes. *Bokowo* are a special category of male sacred specialists who practice *Afa* (Yoruba Ifa) divination. *Amegasiwo* are female diviners and are predominantly necromancers. The "medium's" grade of ritual specialists also exists among the Anlo. These are called *agbasiwo* and are only women. The messages they receive in a state of trance from the divine for the benefit of worshippers are meaningless unless interpreted by the principal ritual specialist in charge of the deity who may be male or female. Another category of human beings who are in the special service of non-human spirit beings are *fiasidewo*, wives of a deity. They are vestal virgins dedicated to the service of both male and female deities as sacrifice to atone for the breach of some interdictions imposed by these spirit beings. The breach could be by man. It is a lass, not a lad, who should be offered as sacrifice.

Sorcerers *(dzoduametowo)*, magicians *(dzotowo),* and witches *(adzetowo)* are a class of human beings who possess a special knowledge of the sacred and are therefore able to use its powers effectively. *Adzetowo* are women and *dzoduametowo* are men. Both employ the supernatural to harm their neighbors. Witches operate on the psychic plane in dreams, which in this society are a matter-of-fact affair. The material plane provides the field for sorcery activities. *Dzotowo,* magicians, are male. They employ the supernatural to protect members of society against the harmful activities of the sorcerers and the witches.

Anlo spirituality demands that any worshipper who wishes to maximally appropriate the blessings corporately conferred on society by worship should avoid any form of contact with a menstruating woman at least 24 hours before worship. Both sexes must allow a full day to pass after having sex before they join in organized worship. Menstruating women cannot participate in any formal expression of the religious experience. These ritual demands, however, are waived in situations of stress requiring immediate divine assistance. In such cases, the worshipper is the ritual specialist.

During the ritual of sacrifice the preparation of the communal meal, especially that which is to serve the purpose of holy communion, is the responsibility of men and women who have reached menopause. One at times finds young women taking part in preparing some ritual meals. But care is taken that these women should not have their period during that time. Moreover, such ritual meals, usually shared by the worshippers rather than the deity, are generally for festive and not sacramental purpose. The principal festival rites of bathing, anointing, feeding and clothing the deity are performed by "hat" priests and priestesses. A female deity is attended to by a priestess and a male deity by a priest. Here again since it is a "hat" priestess who qualifies, the implication is that a woman should cease from her female habit of menstruation before she could quaify to perform this sacred obligation. In case of the ancestors these rites are discharged only by men.

During the performance of some festival rites when the symbolic representations of the sacred are exposed to the full view of worshippers, an inspired worshipper, male or female, can address the deity directly without priestly assistance.[5] Such personal communion with the sacred is also permitted to worshippers who participate in the major pilgrimage rites or join in the ritual of promenading a deity.

## Anlo Symbolism and Religious Rites

Symbolism in Anlo religious experience is both masculine and feminine. Phallicism provides a dominant symbolism for fertility, plenty and abundance. The functions of ritual specialists are spoken of in feminine terms. Ritual specialists are "wives," *asiwo,* of deities they serve and also their "cooks," *dzonuviwo.* This human activity is a feminine responsibility.

Femininity also finds expression in the common symbolic language of proverbs which are freely used to portray religious ideas in African societies. A deity may be referred to as "Red substance which is always present in a woman's bathroom" (XLIX, 2). "Red substance" may be a reference to the menstrual flow in women or the piece of red cloth which women in Anlo society use to cover their private parts. Every woman has at least two which are alternately dried in the bathroom, a simple unroofed enclosure. Since bathrooms are attached to compound type of houses and are shared by all the women inmates, who are usually many, a "red substance" in the form of menstrual flow or a piece of red cloth will "always be present in a woman's bathroom."

This feminine symbolic language is intended to convey the common religious idea of omnipresence with an implicit omniscience attributed to the sacred. As menstrual flow, "red substance" also symbolises fertility, plenty, abundance, in fact life not death, expressed by the word *dagbe* which constitutes the goal of all religious activities in Anloland.

Reference must also be made to the "rites of passage." These are ceremonies of the life cycle—rituals involving birth, puberty, marriage and death. Even though rituals attending birth are centered on the child, they also involve all those who may have something to do with the well-being of the child, parents and mid-wives who for instance, assist with delivery. But the degree of involvement is determined by the closeness of the connection between an individual and the child. This implies that parents will be more extensively involved with mothers' participation than with fathers'. There is no differentiation on sex grounds in the rite of "outdooring."[6] The child, whether male or female, is "out-doored" on the eighth day after birth. But the individual who takes the child out of the room of confinement into the open air must be of the same sex as the child.

*Megbekpokpo,* the rite of reincarnation, is also a pertinent birth ritual of note. Divination to ascertain whether a child is a rein-carnated ancestor is permissible to male diviners. But the difficult and important task of identifying the particular reincarnated ancestor is a female diviner's prerogative. Moreover, the principal functionary in *dzonusasa,* the ritual of tying reincarnation beads around the wrist of a child, is a woman, a father's sister. Other rituals of note connected with birth are *doflefle,* a ritual in which a childless couple petitions a female non-human spirit being to become biological parents, and *evewowo,* a ritual involving twins and their parents in which women are the principal functionaries.

The male puberty rite among the Anlo people is circumcision. It takes place on the eighth day after birth. There is no female puberty rite. Even menarche is not of any real significance except that a mother uses it as an occasion to give her daughter prelimi-nary instructions in womanhood, especially those that will help her cope with the new phase of life. Most important here are instructions in the disabilities, especially their religious dimen-sions, that go with menstruation in order to ensure life-affirming experience.

Women may at times be offered in marriage to men even before menarche, and parental as well as extended family consent may be the deciding factor. All the same, women have a voice in choosing their husbands.[7] Not only a man, but also a woman can initiate a divorce, and the custody of the children may be granted to either parent. Usually a mother readily opts for this responsibility, often without assistance from a father, for fear of ill-treatment from her former husband's wives. Levirate is practiced but a widow is not bound by it; she is free to remain single or marry anyone of her choice. A woman who marries for the first time is expected to be a virgin. Premarital sex is not prohibited to a man before he mar-ries for the first time. Even though both sexes can commit adul-tery in Anlo society, a more serious view is taken of female than male adultery.

Women, as wives, are expected to undergo a ritual to establish their innocence in the death of their husbands. This is *yodzog-bonono,* drinking the funeral pap. A common spontaneous practice in this respect is for a wife to swallow her tears which she must allow to flow into her mouth during her husband's funeral. A husband is not expected to demonstrate this innocence.

It is the duty of women to prepare the corpses of both men and women for burial. But the surgical ritual performed on the corpses of those who suffer some forms of abnormal death is the work of men.[8] Spouses must observe a ritual period of mourning for a deceased partner. A man observes only the seven-day confinement ritual. But in addition to this a woman must subject herself to eighteen months of ceremonial mourning. Sex is not permitted to her during this period at the close of which she observes a ceremony, *zameyiyi,* to prove her chastity. A surviving husband pays for his ceremonial mourning ritual. A wife's ceremonial ritual mourning is paid for by the deceased husband's family. It is required of a widow to perform the ceremonial mourning ritual before remarrying. But a widower, as a polygamist, is not bound to do this but, when he does it, it is for a comparatively short period. Both men and women who die natural deaths are subjected to practically the same ritual to launch them safely into the appropriate society beyond the grave. So also are those who suffer unnatural deaths. Any difference of note in these postmortem personal rites relates to the form of death and status in life rather than differences of sex.

## Femininity and Spirituality

The above account of Anlo indigenous religious experience, symbolism and rites reveals that femininity forms part of it. There is also femaleness in the sacred. The earth is a feminine deity and "is the spouse of heaven," God. There are females among the non-human spirit beings. Fair examples are *mamawo* (an honorific female title meaning grandmother), *Asife, Tomi, Sui,* and *Zio.* In fact, chapters I, LIX-LXII of my book *Scriptures of an African People* are prayers addressed to female deities. The human spirit beings too are not all males, as the following verse affirms:

I invoke the presence of all our
Grandmothers. (XXXIV, 12)

Human intermediaries between humankind and the sacred can be women. They are not restricted to the lowest ranks only but occupy all grades up to the highest offices of "hat" priesthood. Chapters LIX–LXII and LXXVII are prayers led by a member of this class of priestesses, as LIX, 31 reveals:

*We* the women pray
for success in trade.

As diviners, women can practice necromancy, one of the highest and most complicated forms of divination in Anlo society. We have also noted that women can prepare some ritual meals. They may also have a personal communion with the sacred even during formal worship when emphasis is on priestly intermediaries.

Reference should be made in Chapter LVI and the prayers by any worshippers who join in the major pilgrimage rites or in promenading their objects of worship. It is in informal worship that the personal spirituality of women finds the deepest expression. When all hope is gone and immediate divine assistance is most needed, they can personally call upon their objects of worship and expect help to come.

Anlo religious language also draws freely upon femininity. Priests and priestesses are all "wives" and "cooks" of the deities whom they serve and all members of any cultic group could be referred to as "wives" of their deity. "Red substance" (XLIX, 2), we have noted, is a feminine symbolism expressing the common religious idea of omnipresence and depicting fertility which, as *Dagbe,* abundant life, is the ultimate goal of worship, indeed of religion among the Anlo.

Some of the manifestations of femininity in the expression of Anlo indigenous religious experience portray womanhood in favorable light even to the point of placing it above manhood. Femininity directs the spirituality of both men and women. Female spirit beings, clan deities and ancestresses, for example, claim allegiance from both sexes. Female ritual functionaries, be they as low as mediums or as high as "hat" priestesses, serve as a link between the sacred and all members of the worshipping community, men or women, regardless of their status in society. Femininity is also employed in the expression of the highest conception of spirituality. The earth is "the spouse of heaven," God, who occupies the highest level of the supernatural hierarchy. Moreover, feminine symbolism is used to signify the highest watermark of spiritual development, namely the ultimate goal of religion in this society.

Anlo religious experience extends the highest form of spirituality to women. Women can participate in any form of organized expression of the religious experience and realize the ultimate goal of worship. The highest grade of ritual functionaries is also open to them. Women too can "see" and "converse" directly with their objects of worship when they join in the rites of pilgrimage and promenading the deity during the annual festivals. Then, the important religious duty of bathing, anointing, feeding and clothing the deity is also done by women. Other religious duties performed by women elevate womanhood above manhood. One recalls the reincarnation rite, the rite that is believed to make a childless couple biological parents, and some mortuary rites involving surviving spouses. Only women perform the most important part of some of these rites.

However, other feminine elements in the Anlo religious expression seem to suggest a less positive attitude. That a childless couple must "buy a womb" (a feminine symbolism) from a deity to become parents seems to imply that it is womanhood that is responsible for the unfortunate situation of childlessness. In fact, when a marriage is not blessed with children, a husband takes another wife. This also happens when a couple has no male child, known in Anlo society as *Afeti,* the main pillar of the house, that is, the one in whom survival of the family is assured.

When an offense committed against the sacred demands a "human sacrifice," it is women, vestal virgins, who pay this price regardless of the sex of the offender. In referring to ritual functionaries, indeed the entire worshipping community, as "wives" of the sacred, one sees an inferior social status assigned to womanhood, for the role of ritual functionaries and worshippers vis-à-vis the sacred is that of servants. In fact, members of the worshipping community are explicitly called slaves, *kluwo* (male) and *kosiwo* (female).

## Ambivalence towards Womanhood

Above all, it is quite true that the highest spirituality is within the reach of women since they can occupy the highest office as ritual functionaries and personally realize the ultimate goal of personal communion with the sacred, if only they so desire and strive for it.

However, the smooth flow of feminine spirituality in Anlo indigenous life and thought is disturbed by a distinctive characteristic of womanhood, namely menstruation. A woman in her period cannot appear in the sacred presence through participation in any organized expression of the religious experience. Hence a menstruating ritual functionary cannot discharge her sacred obligations, even if she so desires.

Even though it is permissible for women to ascend to the highest priestly office of "hat" priesthood, this sacred status is open only to those women who have completely ceased from the distinguishing characteristic of menstruation. In fact, they dress exactly like their male counterparts. In the figurative language of the Anlo people, women qualify for the "hat" priesthood when they become men, that is, reach the age of menopause. But this highest priestly rank is open to male ritual functionaries of any age. Womanhood in Anlo life and thought, therefore, is extolled and at the same time despised; it is noble and at the same time ignoble; it is superior yet at the same time inferior.

Thus there exists ambivalence towards womanhood through its connection with blood visible in menstruation. In Anlo thought blood signifies life because its appearance in a woman's menstrual flow heralds a new life—a good omen that the goal of life, survival, is in full view and assured. But when blood is separated from whatever contains it, life ceases at once—survival, the goal of life, is seriously threatened. Since sacrifice is the dramatization of the Anlo desire for the realization of the goal of existence, that is, the perpetuation of life, and since the sacred is believed to reciprocate at least what is offered it in sacrifice, animal sacrifice, because it contains blood, constitutes the sacrifice par excellence in Anlo thought. The entire blood is offered to the sacred in any given animal sacrifice so that, in reciprocating, it may release life in its fullest expression in human affairs.

Until menstruating women offer their entire blood, so to speak, to the sacred, that is, until their menses ceases, life cannot be fully expected. But where the retention of blood is permitted by the sacred through participation in the sacrament of holy communion, this retention manifests itself not in life-negating but life-promoting experiences. Because the menstrual cycle cannot be accurately predicted, feminine ritual functionaries who have not ceased completely from menstruation are debarred from an unrestricted performance of their duties so that the ritual's goal of assuring survival may be realized. Blood then is a symbol of ambivalence in Anlo life and thought because it can make or mar anyone who comes in contact with it.

However, those elements in Anlo life and thought which portray womanhood in an unfavorable light do not on the whole evidence sexism, a downright prejudice towards womanhood. The highest manifestation of the sacred in the thinking of this people, God, may be male, but he has a spouse, earth, who as much as possible is made to reflect the wifely status befitting her as consort. There is no God cult in Anloland; it is likewise, with the earth as the spouse of God. It should be noted that all other female deities, as a sign of their inferior status to God, receive cultic attention like their male counterparts in Anloland.

Witches may be women, but there are sorcerers in Anlo society, the male counterpart of witches, who also use sacred power to engage in anti-social activities. Men may be magicians protecting society against the wicked deeds of both witches and sorcerers. All the same Anlo women, as *amegasiwo,* perform similar functions. But men and women, through the sex act, may disqualify themselves from an effective participation in any organized ritual. This provides an instance when manhood, like womanhood, shares in numinous unworthiness.

The ambivalence towards womanhood, due to womanhood's connection with blood, does not seem to offer a sufficient explanation, since manhood is also a victim of this ambivalence yet unconnected with blood. A more exhaustive explanation perhaps, is the sense that it takes the entire Anlo situation into account, sees this ambivalence as a human rather than specifically feminine or masculine phenomenon in Anlo society. In other words, it constitutes an expression of the people's world-view which it reinforces, and it is, in turn, reinforced by it. In fact, the ambivalence towards blood is itself an expression of this fundamental understanding of existence.

## Fundamental Dualities of Human Existence

The Anlo world-view posits a number of two-dimension concepts which characterize human existence. First is the sacred/profane dimension. Life, in the Anlo view, has a sacred and invisible aspect as well as a profane, visible, material dimension. The sacred is the real and the profane is the unreal. Life exists only if these two dimensions are in union with the sacred dictating the pace for existence. In isolation from the sacred, the profane is dead. But the sacred, the real, cannot be known except when it makes use of the profane as its vehicle. This means that the sacred and the profane are indispensable to the other other.

The second two-dimension concept is the male/female dimension into which all existence, including the sacred, is divided. In Anlo thought there are both male and female sacred beings. God, *Mawu,* and earth, *anyigba,* indeed *togbe* for grandfather, and *mama* for grandmother, which are honorific titles prefixed to the personal names of Anlo spirit beings, supply suitable illustrations. Again, the union of these two, maleness and femaleness, results in life, existence. God is male in Anlo thought because maleness, as it is conceived in this society, is characteristic of God's activities. Likewise, Anlo society perceives the earth revealing femaleness in her functions.

God's abode is the sky *above* and he sends down rain, water (*tsi* is the Anlo word for both water and semen), into the earth *below;* at once fertility, life, results and the goal of existence, survival, is assured.[9] Without God, in the sense of water from above, the earth is completely infertile, dead. On the other hand, if God, as water from above, does not enter the earth, creation attributed to him is not possible. In fact, God is pictured in one Anlo creation myth as making use of clay, *anyi* (earth is *anyigba*), to create life, man.

Third, there is the good/evil dimension. The Anlo people realize that existence is characterized by both good and evil. Human experiences bring either joy or suffering. It is the union of good and evil that constitutes human existence. Within the sacred and the profane dimensions, one finds both good and evil. There are good and evil spirit beings, and there are both good and evil human beings. Even that which is regarded as good in Anlo thought is not completely free from evil; *Mawu,* God, is good, but punishes. And punishment is not a happy experience even if it is deserved.

Similarly evil has good in it. Death is evil, but when it ends the life of a "chronic" sufferer, whose illness does not seem to respond to treatment, it is considered good. *Kunyowu* may be a personal name which means death is better (than life).

Fourth, we may note the superior/inferior dimension of existence. The sacred, that in which life inheres, is regarded as superior to the profane which, by itself alone, is perceived as dead. But if the sacred must by all means make use of the profane, as the profane must make use of the sacred to be active, then the sacred too must bow at times to the profane. The good may be superior, but evil also can be.

The sacred, God, as male reveals maleness as superior to the profane, earth, matter. But maleness bows to femaleness when God takes the initiative to go to earth in the form of rain to perform his task of creation. It is pertinent to mention that in the Anlo situation a woman does not invite a man for sex. It is a man who invites, goes in to a woman. And it is for the man to plead with the woman before he achieves his goal.

In Anlo life and thought, then, one perceives running through all human existence a principle of duality which gives rise to ambivalence at once extolling and despising one and the same thing. Anything that forms part of human existence is governed by this principle of ambivalence. In terms of our study, womanhood and manhood are both subject to this principle. Hence, even though in one sense the ambivalence towards womanhood may seem to derive from its connection with blood, yet it is ultimately so simple because womanhood is essentially part of existence. This is why we noted earlier that blood itself is an expression of this fundamental conception of existence because blood too belongs to existence.

## Women in Anlo Society and Contemporary Industrialized Societies

Thus far we have argued that a study of Anlo religious experience reveals an attitude of ambivalence towards womanhood, that this ambivalence originates from and is nurtured by womanhood's connection with blood, but that the ultimate origin and nurture of this ambivalence is the human condition itself, implying that any phenomenon, once it is part of the human condition, cannot refuse to exhibit this ambivalence. In other words, there inheres in the human condition an attitude that simultaneously accepts and rejects a phenomenon resulting in a feeling of both superiority and inferiority towards this phenomenon.

However, this does not in any sense imply that this natural attitude of ambivalence cannot manifest itself in an exploitative manner. One such manifestation is sexism, a downright prejudice against womanhood which condemns it to a state of inferiority and oppression from manhood jealously guarding its own self-allocated preserves which womanhood should not, under any circumstances, be allowed to invade. Otherwise stated, it is argued that inequality is endemic to the human condition, that any phenomenon that forms part of the human condition is an heir to it, that inequality can become a tool for oppression, and that sex roles in society provide an instance of this inequality and its abuse.

A study of female spirituality in Anlo indigenous religious experience reveals inequality between the sexes, but this inequality does not appear unnecessarily oppressive of one sex by the other, namely womanhood by manhood. We have noted that femininity occupies quite a central place in Anlo spirituality in the sense that it is employed in the expression of even the highest watermark of Anlo spirituality and that womanhood can also reach the highest level in personal spiritual development.

Of course there is a restriction imposed on womanhood, namely, it should shed the habit of menstruation before it can reach the highest level of the *formal* expression of religious experience. However, as far as the realization of the ultimate goal of spirituality in terms of personal communion with the sacred, blood restrictions and all other ritual proscriptions imposed not only on womanhood but on manhood as well are ultimately of no consequence, for the individual can achieve the ultimate goal of religion, personal communion with the sacred, in the very midst of a breach of any of these ritual proscriptions. This implies that the constitutive parts of the profane, including inequalities, are unreal and all require self-transcendence, symbolically expressed as female becoming male, that is, the profane becoming the sacred in a union of the two in which the sacred, the real, renders insignificant the profane, the unreal.

It is also pertinent to note that Anlo religious thought affirms that the sacred in turn must make use of the unreal, the profane, implying self-transcendence for the real, the sacred, as well. In other words, not only femaleness but also maleness must transcend itself for the ultimate goal of existence, life not death, to be realized. Both maleness and femaleness in Anlo thought must have mutual respect for each other if religion's goal of survival is to be achieved. We have also noted that the earth, like God, her spouse, receives no organized cultic attention to make her reflect the same status as her spouse.

189

Granting that religion epitomizes a people's world-view and that religion, as world-view, employs the known human condition for self-expression, one is not surprised by the sort of inequality deriving from sex roles which one finds in Anlo society. Quite apposite here is an observation by Denise Carmody on women's spirituality in archaic societies to which the Anlo people belong:

In fact there is evidence that archaic cultures did, indeed, treat women more equitably than most later societies did.[10]

One of her earlier statements, namely that religions are irredeemably sexist,[11] which makes uneasy anyone who is acquainted with life in contemporary "archaic" societies, should be understood as applicable to religions in modern industrialized societies and to the uncompromisingly male monotheistic faiths like Judaism, Christianity and Islam. One is, therefore, inclined to opine that this whole "woman question" is at present a burning issue in the industrialized societies and the "developed" religions of the world. One is confirmed in this view because feminist works are overwhelmingly studies dealing with conditions in and by people from such societies and religions. Janet Sayers' recent work,[12] which surveys quite extensive material produced over the years on feminism and anti-feminism vis-à-vis biology, comes readily to mind as an example of a secular treatment of the issue, in contradiction to Denise Carmody's, which is a religious analysis.

That desacralized, industrialized, societies provide a fertile ground for feminism to take root may be traced to a religious factor though one is fully aware, as Sayers for example has copiously demonstrated, that non-religious factors, namely economic, social, psychological and biological, also play quite a significant role. Whether they like it or not, these desacralized societies—desacralized because they either reduce religion into just an optional societal institution or officially base their world-views on non-religion—are, without choice, heirs to a religious world-view (the Judeo-Christian tradition) which is an uncompromising male monotheism, that is, a religion which upholds the highest value for society as only one and personified as male. This doubtless, as Eliade[13] for instance is at pains to demonstrate, shaped the world-views of contemporary industrialized societies in the past when these societies ordered their lives mainly by a world-view dominated by this individualistic male-controlled conception of the religious experience.

Hence the world-views of contemporary industrialized societies, highly individualistic and male-dominated as they are, are vestiges of a male-dominated society which, like its jealous male ultimate value, God, brooks no competition. This lends some credence to the position that polytheism has an advantage of inculcating a tolerant world-view which recognizes pluralism as a fact of the human condition, and therefore does not object to an equal right of others to existence. This pluralism also renders societal inequalities, which are inevitable anyway, of no significance even where this pluralism derives from a society like the Anlo where an over-arching male deity (but remember he *has* a spouse) features in this polytheism.

Granted that a people's religion is also shaped by their world-view (which does happen), it is not surprising that the forms of Judeo-Christian tradition in the industrialized societies today are nurtured by secular conditions in these societies and have thus, on the whole, remained male-dominated institutions jealously guarding their own male preserves.

Nevertheless, that archaic cultures "treat women *more equitably*" (emphasis is the writer's) doubtlessly implies that a kind of unencouraging image of womanhood vis-à-vis manhood deriving from societal roles based on sex does exist in Anlo society as an example of archaic culture. In fact, this study has all along implied this but has attempted an *understanding* of it within its own historic and cultural context.

Two glaring areas of inequality may be noted. First, women are excluded from politics because in the past its essential function was to defend the society against external aggression for which womanhood was considered lacking the requisite physical strength. Then the society being patrilineal, clan heads and elders who participated in the decision-making processes were all males. One should remember that religiously a "person with blood" is a "holy thing," that is, has become a breeding ground especially for the evil manifestation of the sacred—and this means trouble for the entire society. It is understandable, therefore, to exclude women from political activities, since the menses, like external aggression, the main concern of Anlo politics in the past, are unpredictable. It is on medical record, I am told, that a woman under stress (for instance, at the battle front) could menstruate.

Secondly, a woman can have only one spouse at a time, while a man can have more than one. Thus there is polygyny (monogyny is also practiced), but not polyandry in the Anlo society. The religious explanation for this is that even though God is a monogynist; the non-human spirit beings are polygynists. The sacred dimension of life, which should order the life of humans, knows no polyandry but polygyny and monogyny—polygyny for the majority (the many non-human spirit beings) and monogyny for the minority (God alone).

The social reason advanced is that Anlo society is patrilineal and polygyny ensures paternity, which is of immense importance in such a social system. Economically many children provide the needed labor force which benefits both the father and the mother, who are equal economic partners. One could argue that polyandry can produce many children and that a woman who has sex with only one man after a given menstrual period can ensure paternity, different though the fathers of the children will be.

This argument would be sound if there were no societal "givens" and society itself was not a *system*. What feminism is questioning, however, is the validity in the contemporary situation of these societal "givens," some of which are religious or corresponding world-views, all of which determine the societal image of womanhood. In any case, politics and marriage furnish fair examples of factors that promote an unencouraging image of womanhood deriving from inequality between the sexes in Anloland.

Be that as it may, the Anlo religious world-view reveals a built-in mechanism to prevent an exploitative use, at least consciously, of inevitable societal inequalities between the sexes in this case. Every phenomenon, in the Anlo world-view, requires self-transcendence before it can be what it ought to be. This self-transcendence generates a strong corporate outlook on life, but not to the disadvantage of the individual.[14]

One does not foresee a sexual inequality which favors manhood assuming the dimension we find in today's industrialized societies, should the Anlo society become industrialized one day. We have noted that such societies, given certain conditions, provide a breeding ground for feminism. One main condition is an uncompromising, male monotheism or the inheritance of it in the form of a secular world-view. But this is not a condition that is likely to characterize any probable industrialized Anlo society.

Ghana, the larger society to which the Anlo society belongs, is pursuing a vigorous industrialization. Though she takes advantage of the experiences of contemporary industrialized societies, she does not accept everything implicitly. The Christian faith today, in both its orthodox and African originated forms, adopts elements from the Anlo indigenous religious expression for its self-expression, notably in our case giving prominent recognition to women leadership-roles, in some cases up to the highest level of Christian spirituality. Whatever Islam does has no real impact on the Anlo society as this religion, because it is mainly practiced within the Anlo society by non-Anlo Africans of low social status, has no attraction for the Anlo people. In any case, the Ahmadiyyah expression of Islam, which could impact favourably on the Anlo people in this connection because of its attitude towards women, is little known in the area.

## Concluding Remarks

Independence from political domination has given rise to a concept of returning to our indigenous values. Educational requirements now demand that indigenes who profess religions other than the Anlo indigenous religion study their indigenous ways of life.[15] Some of the formally educated have started to declare themselves professing believers in the Anlo indigenous religious experience though they may not as yet, because the faith is largely non-literate, know exactly what they believe and why they believe it, and thus remain unable at present to evolve a sound theology for this faith.

The characteristic pluralism of Anlo faith, through polytheism and its good/evil dimension, has a strong hold on the larger majority of the Anlo people, including those who do not order their lives by the Anlo traditional religion itself. This difficulty that one has in extricating oneself from a world-view when the corresponding religion is abandoned means that a world-view (be it religious or non-religious) nurtured by an uncompromising male monotheism cannot succeed in Anlo society. Moreover, independent Ghana has given equal rights to both sexes in politics, education and job placements, as well as encouragement to organizations overseeing women's affairs. Within the Anlo society itself the creation of the political office of queen-mother, regardless of blood restrictions, is one significant way to open the door to feminine participation in politics.

Above all, education, communication and travel have introduced Anlo women to remarkable feminine achievements in other societies hitherto unknown in their society. All these factors have exposed both sexes to new roles, some of which were permitted in the past to either men or women only. With all these devastating factors of social change invading Anlo society, patrilineal and patriarchal as it is, one cannot but expect the eruption of feminism one day.

However, because of the kind of image of womanhood one finds in Anlo society, when the inevitable feminism erupts, it will take a much milder form than is known at present, especially in the desacralized modern and industrialized societies. The people could even eventually give up religion altogether and adopt a religion-free world-view. (Non-religious world-views have already entered the Ghanaian milieu.) But taking the cue from the world-views of the non-religious industrialized societies today, as world-views that reflect the abandoned religions, the non-religious Anlo world-view will also carry vestiges of the abandoned religion and will not worsen the present position of women in this society.

The central surviving element in this probably secular world-view is self-transcendence. This self-transcendence, which nourishes a strong sense of corporate responsibility but not at the expense of the individual, will continue to order the lives of all regardless of social status, even as God, who has the highest status in the people's once religious world-view, also should. This mutual self-transcendence is the solution—a holistic solution—that the Anlo indigenous religious experience, as it exists now, offers as an answer not only to the "woman question" but also to all others like it which inhere in the human condition.

Indeed this is also the answer of *religion,* not necessarily of religions, to the vexing and perennial problem of creating a just and equitable society for all and not just for one section of a society in isolation from the others. This indeed must be the preoccupation of feminism if its goal is a lasting solution of the problem that confronts it.

# NOTES

1. Christian R. Gaba, *Scriptures of an African People* (New York: NOK, 1973).

2. Ibid., chap. 49–51; see also chaps. 34, 77.

3. Ritual specialist, sacred specialist and ritual fuctionary are used interchangeably in this study.

4. See Gaba, *Scriptures,* verses 1–2 of chaps. 59, 61, 62.

5. Ibid., chap. 56.

6. Outdooring is a socializing ceremony in which a baby is ritually taken out of confinement for the first time on the eighth day after birth. On this day, the baby is also named (cf. Luke 2:2–10) even though there does not appear to be any Christian influence here as this ritual was long practiced before the dawn of Christianity.

7. See Gaba, *Scriptures,* chap. 78: 8–16; in fact, the whole chapter is illuminating.

8. Abnormal death in this case is the death of the following people, for instance: pregnant women, the hunchbacked, and people with enlarged scrotums. The unborn baby and the deformities are removed through ritual surgery from the respective corpses before burial so the unborn baby can reincarnate and the deformed can reincarnate undeformed.

9. The Gā people of West Africa, for instance, use the same word *Nyonmo* for both God and rain. See e.g., Margaret J. Field, *Religion and Medicine of the Gā People* (Oxford: Oxford University Press, 1937), passim, but specifically 211, "*Nyonmo* (rain) supreme god."

10. Denise L. Carmody, *Women and World Religions* (Nashville: Abingdon, 1979), 31.

11. Ibid., 14.

12. Janet Sayers, *Biological Politics: Feminist and Antifeminist Perspectives* (London and New York: Tavistock Publications, 1982).

13. See e.g., Mircea Eliade, *The Sacred and the Profane* (New York: Harper & Row, 1957), esp. 201–213.

14. Ritual provides clear evidence. Formal worship opens and may close with corporate prayers for the entire school group. Practically all other prayers are for individuals even though they always end on the communal note. See Gaba, *Scriptures.*

15. Ibid., 50: 5–14.

# III.

# FEMINIST REFLECTIONS

# Introduction by the editor
## URSULA KING

Feminism is closely intertwined with consciousness raising, a new sense of self, a new identity, a new independence and newly experienced freedom. All these experiences, and the concepts derived from them, traditionally have strong religious connotations, for they integrally belong to the human spiritual quest. Several of these are explored from different perspectives in the following three chapters.

The first examines the connection between contemporary feminism and the changing nature of religious consciousness. Ursula King's chapter is less concerned with the important insights and achievements of feminist theology, only briefly mentioned, than with the newly developing forms of spirituality which relate directly to the experience of women today. An important phenomenon is the new goddess worship among certain groups of western women who draw freely on the mythology and symbols of different goddesses of the past. The goddess is celebrated as Mother Goddess and Great Goddess, but these two aspects are often insufficiently distinguished. New rituals have been created or old ones revived by the free spirituality movement, madrian and matriarchy groups, and also by the modern witchcraft movement. For many members of these movements woman's own experience, especially as rooted in her biology and physiology, has acquired a normative character which can be questioned on several grounds, some of which are explored here. A considerable number of women want to go beyond the dichotomy of patriarchy/matriarchy by seeking an androgynous model of self and ultimate reality. While the latter appears to be more integral and holistic, critics have suggested that the ideal of androgyny is itself rooted in the dichotomy of male/female it wants to overcome. To achieve true integration and the transcendence of opposites requires going beyond the dualistic presuppositions on which much of religious thought and practice are based.

The second contribution considers human dependency needs in relation to sexuality and religion. Kendra Smith writes from the perspective of a clinical psychologist. She illustrates how dependency conflicts may be related to the religious quest and shows how dependence is differently experienced by women and men. Her examples are mainly drawn from Buddhism, and their discussion is related to some current debates among western psychologists. At the psychological level there is always the tension between self and other, between fusion and separateness, and yet, as many a story from Buddhist scriptures illustrates, at the ultimate level of liberation or enlightenment there is neither male nor female.

The notion of the self is central to the last chapter of this section. The philosophical reflections of Catherine Keller draw widely on examples from contemporary literature, especially on Doris Lessing's *Four-Gated City*. The self may be seen as a walled city, but making connections is also part of the sense of self or "selving." This idea of making connections is a central focus of contemporary feminist experience. The author imaginatively explores the mutual interconnections between the experience of self, the overcoming of a divided self in finding a new wholeness, and the contemporary experience of feminism which raises our consciousness of sexual injustice and seeks a new paradigm for self and society. Keller also discusses another interconnection, that of feminism and the new physics, already celebrated by Robin Morgan. Here a new revisioning is taking place through the perception of connections not seen before. Some important methodological issues are raised by feminism which may have overstepped its claims and which may be unable to maintain its utopian vision. The writer underlines that love in particular is an activity of conscious interconnections, and concludes with the observation that feminism has the "capacity to make the very concept of self interesting again, a source of disclosure and relation rather than the strange, alternately shrinking and imperialistic entity which is the ghost of the substantial soul."

These reflections provide some examples of the ways feminism opens new paradigms for contemporary life and thought which can enhance the capacity of being more fully human for both women and men in our age. Feminist reflections are an ongoing process, not a settled result. Thus we have to continue to explore feminist perspectives in both the past and the present. The reader is invited to take part in this process by reflecting further on the ideas expressed in this book and by sharing in the rich experience of women found in the religious heritage of humankind.

# 12

# Goddesses, Witches, Androgyny and Beyond? Feminism and the Transformation of Religious Consciousness

## URSULA KING

Certain themes in contemporary feminist literature point to some quite remarkable religious developments in small segments of western society. If religious consciousness concerns the perceptions, ideas, beliefs and symbols regarding Ultimate Reality which help to shape religious experience and other aspects of religious life, then the discussions about goddesses and witches or the search for androgynous ideals and their transcendence in certain feminist circles may well be full of meaning for both the present and future theory and practice of religion.

Contemporary feminist movements are multidimensional and far from unitary in character. It has been shown that feminists are generally less religious than the average population but that those feminists who are religiously inclined often seek new forms of religious experience and expression, and experiment with new conceptual models of Ultimate Reality which include and enhance female experience rather than negate and exclude it.

### Contemporary Feminism

Much of contemporary feminism is explicitly secular and devoted to a radical change of social and political structures and cultural norms. In fact, at one level the feminist movement can itself be seen as part of the secularizing process, but, at another level, there are also within the feminist movement elements of a new religious quest which, in some cases, may give or have given birth to new religious movements little studied up to now.

So far modern feminism is perhaps better known for its critique of religion than for its attempts at religious reconstruction or for the creation of new religious movements. At present, the feminist movement is for the most part still a western, urban, middle-class phenomenon where women have the necessary education and leisure to articulate a powerful protest against the deeply rooted hierarchical and patriarchal structures of oppression embedded in our male-dominated culture. But it is a movement which addresses itself to women in all cultures, and ripples of its influence can now be felt around the entire globe.

Some thinkers have heralded contemporary feminism as perhaps the most significant movement for which the twentieth century will be remembered in the future, that is, if it is really successful in creating a "new woman" and a "new earth," to use the powerful title words of one of the works by the feminist theologian Rosemary Radford Ruether.[1]

In what sense can one speak about a transformation of religious consciousness under the influence of the feminist movement? The complex process of the transformation of modern consciousness in general and of religious consciousness in particular is deeply embedded in and closely interdependent with other processes of transformation in modern society, whether we quote as example the dominance of technology in our life- and work-world; the developments in global communication, especially in the field of satellites and electronics; the exponential world population growth with its accompanying competition for decreasing energy resources; the democratization of human aspirations, desires and hopes; or the experience of a growing social, racial and religious pluralism at a regional, national and global level. There is also the extraordinary paradox of the increased growth of enhanced identities and the separateness of ever more groups in the contemporary world, while at the same time there is the growing ideal of greater unification as well as the vision of a planetary civilization.

The processes of transformation in modern society and consciousness are often examined in sociological literature. But how far contemporary religious consciousness is being affected and perhaps being transformed by feminist thinking and praxis has barely been analyzed. One of the reasons for this may be that most sociologists of religion are men; the more imporant reason, not unconnected to the first, is that feminism wants to get away from much traditional overrational-objectifying thinking divorced from feeling which has often led to a reification rather than a humanization of people and events. Some writers claim that the understanding of the feminist movement requires its own specific methodology, namely a kind of "participatory hermeneutics."

More than in the experience of individual femaleness or womanhood, feminism as a movement is grounded in the experience of *sisterhood,* of women's *togetherness* which has forged a new solidarity expressing itself in new ways of thinking and in the search for new forms of community which are non-hierarchical and non-elitist. The experience of sisterhood is understood as a new way of being which may include implicit religious elements: elements of faith and hope, of a vision, even of a dream, which has strong prophetic, eschatological and utopian as well as liberating and salvific features. More than anything else the feminist movement is characterized by the challenge of all dualisms and by its desire to develop a new holistic approach to structures, institutions, ways of thought and experience.

## The Feminist Challenge to Religion

The feminist challenge addresses itself especially to the dualistic thought patterns which were the matrix of and became enshrined in the great historical religions, whether one looks at their scriptures, their theologies and doctrines, their rites, or their institutions. So far, most of the feminist critique of religion has been based on data drawn from the Judeo-Christian rather than from other religious traditions, and much further work is needed in this area. The essential challenge at the level of religious thought rather than practice can be summed up in two questions:

1. How far has women's experience been taken into account in the articulations and theological reflections of the world's religions?
2. How far can traditional religious teachings and theologies still speak to women today and remain credible?

The loss of the plausibility of religion for most contemporary feminists has so far largely escaped the notice of male religious authorities who are mostly ignorant of the wider feminist issues and often do not wish to take the feminist critique of religion seriously. In the Christian churches a number of feminist theologians, mostly female but also some male, have taken up the tasks of feminist theology, i.e., the critical examination of theological premises to uncover the hidden structures, and especially the sexist assumptions, in theological thought and practical church life, as well as the positive construction of a new theology which draws on feminine symbols and experiences in scripture and tradition and wishes to give women's experience and participation full expression in church life. There exists a considerable debate among women theologians whether Christian symbols can be simply reformed or must be radically *transformed*. To do justice to this debate, a far more detailed analysis would be required than is possible here. But let it be said that feminist theology, however recent and however little developed so far, is *theology* in its truest sense in that it is centrally concerned with the meaning of the images and symbols used for God, that is to say, with the conceptualization and expression of the experience of Ultimate Reality or the dimension of transcendence. It tries to balance the male images of God which have been predominant in the Judeo-Christian tradition and contrasts these with the rich images of God as mother and other female expressions referring to God's activity of which the Hebrew language of the Old Testament is particularly rich. These are not missing in the New Testament and other Christian writings although they have been marginalized in the past.[2]

Feminist theology is of particular theological interest as *a new way of doing theology,* but from a sociological point of view it is of greater interest and significance to consider the expressions of a new spirituality and religiosity found among certain feminists today. Again, we do not deal with *one movement* but with *different currents* which in some cases may be incipient cults or even nascent religious movements. What is common to them is the radical rejection of the Judeo-Christian tradition and of all theology. They do not seek female symbols and imagery *for* God but worship the female *as* God or rather as Goddess, the great Mother Goddess, and seek to create a new tradition, a thea*logy*, often said to be based on earlier traditions, especially on postulated matriarchies predating both Judaism and Christianity. I can only briefly describe some facets of these cults, largely based on the self-descriptions of members found in pamphlets, tracts, articles or books. Little analytical and critical literature on these developments has been produced so far.

## New Spirituality and Goddess Worship

The new and sometimes so-called free spirituality movements which center on the worship of the goddess are largely found in the United States but are not absent in England. Much of their thinking is inspired by what one might call a rather indiscriminate use of goddess figures and symbols found in a wide variety of the religious histories of the world. Merlin Stone's classic *When God Was A Woman* (New York, 1976) draws on the veneration of the goddess in the ancient Near East while other writers quote North European, African, Indian, or Far Eastern goddesses without any attention to the wide-ranging historical and cultural varieties or ambiguity of some of these figures, or to the distinction between the Great Mother figure and the Great Goddess in ancient cultures.

One study describes the radical transformation arising out of feminist consciousness as "Changing the Gods"[3] and carries subtitles such as "Feminists are cooking up a 'Götterdämmerung,'" "New Gods are coming," "No Feminist can save God," "In Search of Living Religion," and "Androgyne."

An articulate group of goddess worshippers is represented by the contemporary witchcraft movement which blends mediaeval witchcraft beliefs and practices with modern views of the power of the goddess. It is thus characterized by a retraditionalization on one hand and religious innovation on the other, for the formation of contemporary witches' covens occurs in a way in which these covens did not exist in the Middle Ages. They are a new creative blend specifically linked to the contemporary feminist movement.[4]

The covens are small and varied; entrance is gained through initiation, and the ritual is always celebrated in a circle to allow for the flow of spiritual and other energy. According to Starhawk, alias Miriam Simos, one of the high priestesses of the American witchcraft movement and first national president of the "Covenant of the Goddess," witchcraft is "the craft of the wise" and remains the last survival in the West of the time of women's strength and power. According to her, through the dark ages of persecution the covens of Europe preserved what was left of the mythology, rituals and knowledge of the ancient matricentric (mother-centered) times. The old religion of witchcraft before the advent of Christianity is said to have been an earth-centered, nature-oriented worship that venerated the goddess, the source of all life, as well as her son-lover-consort, who was seen as the "Horned God" of the hunt and animal life.

Contemporary covens are extremely diverse. Some are of hereditary witches who are said to practice rites unchanged for hundreds of years while others prefer to create their own ritual. There are covens of so-called "perfect couples" with an even number of women and men permanently paired, but there are also covens of lesbian feminists or of gay men, or covens of only women, who prefer to explore women's spirituality in a space removed from men. The latter are sometimes referred to as the Dianic, women-only tradition. The witches use the goddess concept to give women positive self-images in all stages of life. They teach that the goddess appears in three forms: *maiden, mother,* and *crone.* To quote the words of Starhawk:

Our great symbol for the Goddess is the moon, whose three aspects reflect the three stages in women's lives and whose cycles of waxing and waning coincide with women's menstrual cycles. As the new moon or crescent, she is the Maid, the Virgin—not chaste, but belonging to herself alone, not bound to any man. She is the wild child, lady of the woods, the huntress, free and untamed—Artemis, Kore, Aradia, Nimue. White is her color. As the full moon, she is the mature woman, the sexual being, the mother and nurturer, giver of life, fertility, grain, offspring, potency, joy—Tana, Demeter, Diana, Ceres, Mari. Her colors are the red of blood and the green of growth. As waning or dark moon, she is the old woman, past menopause, the hag or crone that is ripe with wisdom, patroness of secrets, prophecy, divination, inspiration, power—Hecate, Geridwen, Kali, Anna. Her color is the black of night.

The Goddess is also earth—Mother Earth, who sustains all growing things, who is the body, our bones and cells. She is air—the winds that move in the trees and over the waves, breath. She is the fire of the hearth, or the blazing bonfire and the fuming volcano; the power of transformation and change. And she is water—the sea, original source of life; the rivers, streams, lakes and wells; the blood that flows in the rivers of our veins. She is mare, cow, cat, owl, crane, flower, tree, apple, seed, lion, sow, stone, woman. She is found in the world around us, in the cycles and seasons of nature, and in mind, body, spirit, and emotions within each of us. Thou art Goddess. I am Goddess. All that lives (and all that is, lives), all that serves life, is Goddess.[5]

The same author claims that the patriarchal religions are all death cults, and only a goddess-oriented spirituality can bring about the necessary transformation of our culture and give it new life. The cult values independence, personal strength, and the self, but it has no set of doctrines other than the only law of "love unto all beings."

I have no information on the strength of the goddess-worshipping witchcraft movement in England but among the religious statistics listed in the *World Christian Encyclopedia* it is stated that there are currently "about 30,000 practising self-styled witches who practise occultism and black magic in England."[6] Unfortunately there is no indication how many of these center their cult on the goddess.

The movement of goddess worship, inside and outside the witchcraft movement, has gained considerable momentum in the United States. Since 1974 there has existed *Woman Spirit,* a magazine which expresses the grass-roots nature of the women's spirituality movement, and since 1976, another regular publication, entitled *Lady Unique,* which is more explicitly devoted to the goddess. In 1975, the first women's spirituality conference was organized in Boston and was attended by 1800 women, while another gathering in 1978 at Santa Cruz, devoted to a course on the goddess, drew over 500 people. They would be from diverse backgrounds as, not surprisingly, the understanding of what the goddess means varies considerably. It is claimed that thealogy is fundamentally different from theology in that it gives primacy to the symbol rather than to rational explanations which figure so dominantly in theology. The most basic meaning of the goddess symbol is the acknowledgement of the legitimacy of female power as a beneficent and independent power in contrast to the patriarchal view that women's power is inferior and dangerous.

## Different Meanings of the Goddess

The goddess has different meanings for different people. Carol Christ has distinguished three major views:
1. The goddess as a personification, a divine female who can be invoked in prayer and ritual and who is believed to really exist.
2. The goddess as a symbol of life, death, and rebirth energy in nature and culture, in personal and communal life.
3. The goddess as a symbol who affirms the legitimacy and beauty of female power, made possible by the new "becoming" of women in the women's liberation movement.[7]

Thus the concept of the goddess often seems to be internalized and psychologized without being linked to any metaphysical claims about an absolute godhead. Religion and ritual are then primarily used in some parts of the feminist movement as psychological tools to develop individual strength. Historical traditions about the goddess are drawn upon selectively and eclectically. Starhawk, the president of the American "Covenant of the

Goddess," admits with candor that her own considerations about the goddess are limited to the history of traditions from northern Europe. Although she affirms at the same time that southern and eastern Europe, Asia, India, Africa, and the Americas all have rich traditions of goddess religions and matricentric cultures, she seems to be little attentive to their individual differences. Her history of the goddess is said to be the "inner" or "mythic" history that provides the touchstone for modern witches: "Like the histories of all peoples, its truth is intuited in the meaning it gives to life, even though it may be recognized that scholars might dispute some facets of the story."[8] It is precisely here that a more detailed scholarly investigation is called for, but in the opinion of one woman writer scholars of religion seem to be scared of witches! But the modern witchcraft movement's claim to articulate a new perception of the Ultimate certainly requires closer critical analysis and more research.

Feminists appeal to the goddess for quite different reasons and in different contexts; they attribute to the concept of the divine female, of which there are numerous examples in the history of religions, quite different and sometimes contradictory meanings. Many see the ancient mother goddess figures as a proof of female power and status or even of matriarchy, but the historical data are often tenuous here, by no means conclusive and certainly not unambiguous.

What is certainly not sufficiently analyzed is the question how far ancient goddesses are symbols of fertility and sexuality projected by men rather than signs of women's independent power. A Norwegian author, Monica Sjoo, published in 1981 *The Ancient Religion of the Great Cosmic Mother of All*[9] whose theme is claimed to be "no less than a reclamation of the early cultures of mankind where the deities were held to be female and society reflected such female leadership." A contemporary woman reviewer of this book (who described herself as a member of the "Matriarchy Research and Reclaim Network" in London) disagrees with the interpretation put forward here for the mother goddess and her link with human motherhood. She writes:

. . . I must call in question . . . that women's spirituality and creativity are linked to motherhood, to parturition itself. (The authoress) has explained how the natural birth of her second child opened up for her these previously blocked off areas, but for many there is no connection. On the contrary, in our society, Motherhood cuts women off from the time and the confidence to create anything personal, and motherhood is generally undervalued. Even if this were not so, I think that our creativity and our biological capacity are aspects of ourselves, no more specifically linked than other aspects. The goddess religions presented Isis as Mistress of Science, Nephtys as inventor of the arts of spinning and weaving, Demeter as bringing the art and science of agricultures to the world. Science, as this book actually shows, was part of the creativity associated with women's culture and religion and did not depend on reproduction.[10]

In other words, there is no consensus about the meaning of the mother goddess either in the feminist movement in general or among the witchcraft movement in particular, and different feminists may go as far as to reject each other's interpretation of the goddess as spurious. The Christian feminist theologian R. Radford Ruether describes the witchcraft movement as "pagan feminism"[11] whereas the British group *Lux Madriana*, entirely centered on the worship of the goddess, refers with contempt to the "self-styled witches" and other modern cultists whose "occult traditions" are nothing more than "modern fabrications."[12]

*Lux Madriana*, which claims to trace its ancestry back to primordial matriarchal tradition, possesses the most coherently formulated theology and developed community structure I have come across so far, though I have not as yet been able to gather data about its membership or origin. It started some years ago as a women's group in Oxford and moved eventually to Todmorden, Lancs. (England), and from there to Burtonport on the west coast of Ireland. It claims to have affiliated groups elsewhere in England.

It produces a regular monthly magazine called *The Coming Age*, first described as the "Magazine of the religion of the Goddess" and later as that "of the British matriarchal tradition." It has stated its beliefs clearly in several publications: *The Catechism of the Children of the Goddess* (= its beliefs); *The Creation and the Crystal Tablet* (= its scriptures); *The Mythos of the Divine Maid* (= its scripture of the nativity, life, death and resurrection of the daughter of the goddess). There could be no closer Christian theology in reverse from creation to redemption to the idea of a trinity, all expressed in female form. All souls are female too, while males embody the material principle; the spiritual principle is female and thus are men's souls!

These women have created a small, self-sufficent community far removed from modern life; they believe that we have fallen from a golden age to one of the worst possible materialism which has to be overcome by returning to a primordial tradition where all of life is governed by spiritual principles. There was traditional society, first matriarchal, then patriarchal, but the worst of all possible worlds is the modern patriarchal society. Thus they want to live a traditional way of life, wear traditional clothes, pursue traditional crafts (no electricity!), and create a new language (they have already created many new terms, for example, for the months of the year, their rites, etc.) and new rites, and thereby bring in a new age—the coming age. It is impossible to go into greater detail here but *Lux Madriana* has its own cosmology, theology, ecclesiology, salvation history, and a liturgy with domestic and public rites, sacraments of initiation, religious education.

The use of the mother goddess symbol raises questions of biology, history, and theology. Ken Wilber, in his transpersonal view of human evolution *Up From Eden,* makes a clear distinction between the *Great Mother* figure and that of the *Great Goddess.* The explanation of their respective genesis and function must not be confused. He gives a naturalistic explanation of the existence and function of the mother goddess whose image arose as a

correlate of bodily existence, with such biological impacts as womb birth, breast feeding, separation anxieties, and so on—all of which necessarily centre on the *biological* mother. That simple biological dependence, amplified by the notion of the earth as the mother of farmed crops, accounted for the prevalence of the Mother Image in the Basic mythologies. . . . All manifestation was seen to be *mother, maya, measure, menses, menstrual, metered*—which are all words stemming from the same Sanskrit root *ma* (or *matr*), which means essentially "production."[13]

In his view the Great Mother reflects the mythic-membership level of reality when human beings were still close to the body, to instincts, to nature, whereas the Great Goddess reflects a metaphysical truth, namely, that all is One and a truly higher level of reality. Different anthropologists and, one might add, many a feminist writer make the mistake of either *reducing* the Great Goddess to the biological Great Mother (an image of bodily dependence and seduction) or they *elevate* the Great Mother to the status of the Great Goddess and then are forced to read deeply metaphysical insights into every Great Mother ritual when in fact they were mostly nothing more than primitive, crude, and magical attempts to coerce the fertility of the earth. According to Wilber the Great Mother religion dominated during the matriarchal period, but there were also glimpses of the Great Goddess. The two figures could often exist side by side in the same place, using the same symbols.

I consider this distinction a helpful heuristic tool to differentiate, for the purpose of clearer analysis, between diverse historical data about the goddess, so as to distinguish a mythic layer of thought from a more critical-reflective theological layer and to separate a *biologically dependent* symbol of the goddess (dependent on fertility, birth, and motherhood) from another biologically independent or, perhaps better, *biology-transcendent* symbol where the beauty, the power, and the independence of the goddess are celebrated in their own right. This distinction can also help to remove some of the inherent paradoxes of different feminist reactions to the goddess and clarifies some of the contradictions within contemporary feminist thinking.

The figure of the independent Great Goddess can be a powerful symbol of inspiration for feminists, but it remains far more anthropomorphic than the traditional symbol of the classic conception of the Judeo-Christian God; that is to say, its power as a symbol of transcendence is considerably restricted and does not encompass the wholeness many are looking for.

## Women's Experience and Androgyny

At a more empirical level there is the question how far women's experience has acquired a new *normative* character in radical feminist thought to the exclusion of all other human experience. Here the relationship between biology and thought does seem in need of some detailed analysis. How can it be on one hand maintained by women that biology is not destiny, and on the other hand women's experience is often understood by feminist writers to be particularly patterned by female bodily existence, from menstruation over coition and conception to parturition? The emphasis on the birthing process can be romanticizing to the extreme and comes at a moment, in the development of critical reflection, when most women in the western world give birth far more rarely than any of their female ancestors, while some women are alienated from the biological birthing process altogether. Why then should *women's experience*—which surely must be explored in all its joyful, painful, and occasionally tragic dimensions—be so exclusively linked to its biological roots? Why not at least an equal emphasis on different spheres of women's experience, the experience of work and creativity in particular, to include all the dimensions of the self-creating, self-defining, and self-transcending activity of women? But perhaps these are questions for the future when the feminist movement will have come of age.

Another question concerns women's understanding of the nature of reality. Some feminists are aware that the replacement of the patriarchal god-symbol by the counter-symbol of the goddess does not overcome the fundamental dualism underlying patriarchy but merely replaces it by its opposite. In contrast to these dualistic models of either father-god or mother-goddess they seek for another, holistic model and thus have chosen the *androgyne*—the integration of *male and female* into one unity—as the conceptual model of divine reality and especially of mystical experience.

This androgyne—known to the religions of antiquity, found in Indian thought, and used by early Christian writers[14]—is understood first of all psychologically in the sense that both sexes are said to possess feminine and masculine characteristics. This integrative psychological model is then transferred to the concept of the divine where the fullness of divine reality encompasses all differences in unity. In a recent encyclopedia on feminist literature, *The Nature of Woman*,[15] androgyny is defined in such psychological terms:

Many feminists have been attracted by androgyny as an ideal of human development: the view that it is possible and desirable, if not morally mandatory, for *both* males and females to possess *both* what are traditionally known as masculine virtues and feminine virtues. . . . On the prevailing feminist definition . . . an androgyne is a person who combines both "masculine" and "feminine" virtues, someone capable of both rationality and intuitiveness, humility and self-assertion. Unisex styles of dress or manner are not entirely irrelevant to androgyny in this sense—which we may call *psychological androgyny*. . . . There are two importantly distinct versions of the androgynist ideal. Some androgynists argue that *everyone* should strive to become androgynous; they view androgyny as a state of being which is clearly superior to all others, as a norm to which all should aspire. Others see androgyny as merely one of a wide range of equally valid options, and argue for a complete freedom of choice, for a tolerant attitude which permits each person to develop whatever so-called masculine and feminine traits she or he may happen to value or to be naturally disposed towards. . . . [16]

Though modern protagonists of the ideal of androgyne draw a great deal on Jungian psychology, feminist critics have pointed out that despite its long history the androgynist ideal has generally been presumed to apply primarily to men. Jung, for example, is much more explicit about the integration of "feminine" traits into the masculine psyche than about the integration of "masculine" ones into the feminine, in spite of the apparent symmetry of his theory of the feminine *anima* in men and the masculine *animus* in women. In the words of one male writer, "men have rarely had the imagination sufficiently capacious to envisage a female androgyny, i.e., a woman entitled to the same self-completion that men require for themselves."[17]

Philip E. Lampe, an American sociologist, recently examined the correlation between androgyny and religiosity.[18] He speaks of the growing advocates of "a genderless or androgynous lifestyle" and says if this ideal would be realized the result would be an androgynous society defined by the *Encyclopedia of Sociology* as a society

whose members would have the social and personality characteristics of both sexes. In such a society, roles, behaviours and personality traits would no longer be defined as either male or female, but each individual would incorporate characteristics of both, regardless of biological sex.[19]

While feminists have been shown to be less religious than non-feminists, some feminists can identify more easily with androgynous thinking that extends to the understanding of Ultimate Reality. Lampe's empirical study of religiosity is based on the premise that the ideological or belief dimension of religiosity is most highly correlated with all other dimensions of an individual's religiosity. His preliminary conclusions are therefore that

any move toward androgyny may be expected to be accompanied by some change in religiosity. This change will not necessarily be a general decline in religiosity. Neither will the probable reduction in sex role differences result solely from a spread of characteristics and experiences currently defined as masculine. Characteristics and experiences now looked upon as feminine will also become more widespread. Therefore, whether a change will result in an overall increase or decrease in religiosity within the total population will ultimately depend on the specific characteristics which are selected and encouraged.[20]

It is interesting to see the androgynous ideal taken up in socio-logical literature while perceptive critics have pointed to the inherent paradox that it is an ideal formulated in terms of the discredited conceptions of masculinity and femininity which it ultimately wishes to reject; it almost reifies them and thus perpetuates the assumption that there are innate and nearly universal differences between the sexes above and beyond physiological ones.

## The Search for Integration

The debates in feminist literature range from the rejection of a patriarchal god-image and its replacement by the mother-goddess symbol to the integrating model of the androgyny and, in turn, its repudiation in the search for a symbol that goes beyond patriarchal, matriarchal, and androgynous models. The American feminist Carol Ochs considers the phase of contemporary androgynous thinking as a transitional one in the process towards more unitary thinking about Ultimate Reality. In her book *Behind the Sex of God: Towards a New Consciousness—Transcending Matriarchy and Patriarchy* she argues for a monistic position which sees "reality in one, undivided, with no unrelated aspects." In her view this monism may be theistic or atheistic, but she opts to map out what she calls a position of "theistic monism" where "God is not father, nor mother, nor even parent, because God is not other than, distinct from, or opposed to creation."[21]

This is an inadequately expressed search for a more unitary or monistic way of thinking, but it is not a new alternative, as the author claims, nor does she discuss how far this view can be translated into new religious and social structures. Many feminists do not seem to realize either that such an integral concept of God is already available in the discussions about the transcendence and immanence of God or the description of the Absolute found in the classical theologies of many religions. It is also experimentally available in the witness to the God-experience of the mystics, both female and male. The substantial contribution of women mystics to the life of all religious traditions requires further investigation here.[22] It is well known that the language of the mystics is deeply rooted in experience and thus generally much less rationalistic than formal theology. It is especially in this field of religion that feminism, or what is sometimes called "spiritual feminism," can find many models for inspiration.

When discussing the relationship between women and world religions from a contemporary perspective, it seems imperative to reconsider the central issue of religious experience which so far has been largely described without attention to gender differences. Scholars have examined different variables affecting religious experience but sexual differentiation has not been one of them.[23] One certainly needs to inquire how far the nature, expression, and interpretation of female religious experience has been or is similar to or different from male religious experience. However, some works in this area, for example the symposium *Women's Religious Experience: Cross-cultural Perspectives,*[24] remain too descriptive without sufficiently analyzing the anthropological and ethnographic data on women in different religious traditions. In my view it is not enough to pay attention "to the everyday religious experience of ordinary women" while deliberately eschewing the experiences of "exceptional women," such as "nuns, mystics and charismatic leaders."[25] One must certainly inquire how the "ordinary" may relate to the "exceptional experience" and how far the latter often embodies a more advanced mode of consciousness which may provide a breakthrough or ideal for others to follow. For some women in the western world only new forms of religious experience, different from or opposed to those from the past, may answer their religious quest while in other parts of the globe women in other religious traditions may well aspire, through their newly gained autonomy and the influence of feminist thinking, to gain access to traditional forms of religious experience and practice. This is, for example, the case of contemporary women ascetics in Hinduism who seek and gain access to traditional forms of *sannyasa,* not open to them until recently.[26]

The topics of this article need further elaboration, but they indicate the close interrelationship between religion and society. In his famous paper on "Religious Evolution" Robert Bellah[27] provided a typology of the interdependent development of religious and social evolution which moves from the monistic orientation of archaic religion to the dualistic thinking of the historical religions over several stages to new unitary ways of thinking and being in what he calls the "modern religion" of the contemporary period. Although his schematic typology may be criticized for being too simplified and lacking dynamism and complexity, one could transfer some of its aspects to the contemporary reflection on the meaning of sexual differentiation (again, at the level of symbol, the level of religious and social action, and the level of religious and social organization). Instead of the simplistic matriarchy/patriarchy opposition, which is historically difficult to maintain, one could say that throughout most of human history sexual differentiation was taken for granted without being critically reflected upon. We now have reached a stage of critical reflection which divisively highlights these differences, and yet eventually it also intends to overcome these differences in a new, more meaningful unity which requires a more integral symbol-system, religious action and organization,[28] to mention the three areas where Bellah applied his analysis.

If one shares this perspective of integration through differentiation, then the current feminist practices of goddess worship or the adoption of an androgynous ideal for the conceptualization of Ultimate Reality does require a "beyond," a transcendence of the oppositions on which they are based. Thus I can see an interdependence of religious, social, and sexual evolution which will affect the notion of God or the Ultimate, our understanding of human persons, as well as the understanding and practice of the autonomy of the acting subject. All three bear the seeds of a new religion, a new spirituality, and a new mysticism.

# NOTES

1. See Rosemary Radford Ruether, *New Woman, New Earth: Sexist Ideologies and Human Liberation* (New York: Winston, Seabury, 1975).

2. Jean Marie Aubert, *La Femme: Antiféminisme et Christianisme* (Paris: Cerf/Descleé, 1975) speaks of "une exegèse marginalisante"; see also the studies by Catharine J. M. Halkes, *Gott hat nicht nur starke Söhne: Grundzüge einer feministischen Theologie* (Gütersloh: Gerd Mohn, 1980); Susan Dowell and Linda Hurcombe, *Dispossessed Daughters of Eve: Faith and Feminism* (London: SCM Press, 1981); Sara Maitland, *A Map of the New Country: Women and Christianity* (London: Routledge, Kegan and Paul, 1983).

3. See Naomi R. Goldenberg, *Changing the Gods: Feminism and the End of Traditional Religions* (Boston: Beacon, 1973).

4. This is forcefully argued by Rosemary R. Ruether; see her articles "The Female Nature of God: A Problem in Contemporary Religious Life," *Concilium* 3 (1981): 61–66; "Goddesses and Witches," *Christian Action Journal* (Spring 1982): 7–9; "Witches and Jews: The Demonic Alien in Christian Culture" in her book *New Woman, New Earth*, 89–114.

5. Starhawk, "Witchcraft and Women's Culture" in Carol P. Christ and Judith Plaskow, eds., *Womanspirit Rising: A Feminist Reader in Religion* (New York: Harper & Row, 1979), 259–68. Another account of the modern witchcraft movement is "Feminist Witchcraft—The Goddess is Alive!" in Goldenberg, *Changing the Gods,* chap. 7.

6. See David Barrett, ed., *World Christian Encyclopedia* (Oxford: Oxford University Press, 1982), 700.

7. See Carol P. Christ, "Why Women Need the Goddess: Phenomenological, Psychological and Political Reflections" in Christ and Plaskow, *Womanspirit Rising,* 273–87.

8. Starhawk, "Witchcraft," 268.

9. Monica Sjöö and Barbara Moor, *The Ancient Religion of the Great Cosmic Mother of All* (Trondheim: Rainbow Press, 1981). This work was reviewed by Asphodel (described as "a member of the Matriarchy Research and Reclaim Network") in *Women Speaking* (July-December 1981): 17–18.

10. Ibid., 18.

11. In Ruether, "The Female Nature of God."

12. In their own journal *The Coming Age* 14 (n.d.): 21.

13. Ken Wilber, *Up from Eden* (London: Routledge, Kegan and Paul, 1983), 146–47. For ample historical documentation on the goddess see M. Gimbutas, *The Goddesses and Gods of Old Europe: Myths and Cult Images* (Berkeley and Los Angeles: University of California, 1982).

14. Wayne A. Meeks, "The Image of the Androgyne: Some Uses of a Symbol in Earliest Christianity," *History of Religions* 13 (1973–74): 165–208.

15. See Mary Anne Warren, *The Nature of Woman: An Encyclopedia and Guide to the Literature* (Inverness, Calif.: Edgepress, 1980).

16. Ibid., 16, 18, 21.

17. Daniel Harris, "Androgyny, the Sexist Myth in Disguise" quoted in Warren, *The Nature of Woman,* 22.

18. See Philip E. Lampe, "Androgyny and Religiosity," *International Journal of Women's Studies* 4, no. 1 (1981): 27–34.

19. Ibid., 30, quoted from the *Encyclopedia of Sociology* (Guildford, Conn.: Dushkin Publishing Group, 1974), 11.

20. Lampe, "Androgyny and Religiosity," 32.

21. Carol Ochs, *Behind the Sex of God* (Boston: Beacon, 1977), 137.

22. I have discussed this further in my article "Mysticism and Feminism— Why look at Women Mystics?" *World Faiths—Insight,* New Series 5 (1982): 13–19.

23. But see the perceptive article by Lucy Bregman, "Women and Ecstatic Experience," *Encounter* 38 (1977): 43–53. The need to give special attention to women's religious experience and to develop a specific methodology for doing this is emphasized by Rita M. Gross, "Women's Studies in Religion: The State of the Art, 1980" in P. Slater and D. Wiebe, eds., *Traditions and Change,* Selected Proceedings of the XIVth Congress of the International Association for the History of Religions (Waterloo, Ontario: Wilfrid Laurier Press, 1983), 579–91.

24. Pat Holden, ed., *Women's Religious Experience: Cross-Cultural Perspectives* (London: Croom Helm, 1983).

25. Ibid., 2.

26. I have dealt with this development at length in "The Effects of Social Change on Religious Self-Understanding: Women Ascetics in Modern Hinduism" in K. Ballhatchet and D. Taylor, eds., *Changing South Asia: Religion and Society* (Hong Kong: Asian Research Service, 1984), 69–83.

27. In Robert N. Bellah, *Beyond Belief: Essays on Religion in a Post-Traditional World* (New York and London: Harper & Row, 1976), 20–50. Bellah defines evolution as " a process of increasing differentiation and complexity of organisation that endows the organism, social system, etc. . . . with greater capacity to adapt to its environment, so that it is in some sense more autonomous relative to its environment than were its less complex ancestors," 21.

28. I have explored this in "Towards an Integral Spirituality: Sexual Differences and the Christian Doctrine of Man," *Vidyajyoti* 45 (September 1981): 358–71.

# 13

# Sex, Dependency, and Religion— Reflections from a Buddhist Perspective

## KENDRA SMITH

Ever since the snake appeared in the Garden of Eden, it has been commonly supposed that, of all our innate drives, sexual tempta- tion has been the biggest obstacle in the spiritual path. (Perhaps spiritual pride shares pride of place as an impediment to spiritual progress, but it is less fundamental.) The hypothesis proposed here is that the sex drive, formidable though it is, takes second place to dependency needs as a problem for the religious aspirant.

By dependency needs, I refer to the human yearning for a special relationship with someone who is reliably there to care for us—interested, responsive, and reassuring. This longing is universal for persons who have developed normally, and, as we shall see, it is a religious problem. A second conjecture is that the ambivalence expressed toward woman in religious literature, most of it authored by men, has its deepest roots in dependency conflicts. In support of my hypothesis I will draw on psychiatric theory and on some experimental data. Although I believe that this issue may be relevant to all traditions, I will refer most fre- quently to Buddhism.

## Ambivalence toward Woman

Ambivalence toward woman scarcely needs documentation. From time immemorial she has been pictured as an unholy mantrap of sexuality: succubus, witch, hag, or dark Kali with her girdle of severed hands. It was the *daughter* of Mara who tempted Sakyamuni under his bodhi tree. "Woman brings death, man overcomes it through spirit" (Bachofen, *Das Muttermecht*).[1] Even when sex is used as a vehicle for self-transcendence, as in esoteric Taoism, Tantrism, and some Sufi sects, woman is means, an alien object, without possibility of mutuality or real communication.

Women who are mothers are considered to be unsuitable as partners for Taoist or Tantric practices. The *Yu-fang cheu-yao* states, "Even if she is young, she *cannot be used* [italics mine] if she has had a child."[2] The foregoing is the negative side of ambivalence.

On the positive side is woman as the epitome of purity and unselfish devotion; or as the symbol of *prajna,* discerning wisdom, that is the essence of enlightenment. In Buddhist stories it is often women who act as midwives for the enlightenment of male saints and sages. The great scholar, Naropa, is an example: He was twitted by an old woman, who compared his accumulation of knowledge that was empty of insight to someone who knows all the recipes but has never tasted cake. Struck by the truth of her words, Naropa repaired to the forest until he realized the Dharma in his own experience. A Tibetan story indicates that even a non-human female may be the catalyst for enlightenment. A murderous brigand, seeing a bitch whose belly was swollen with unborn pups, callously thrust his lance into the animal, whereupon her pups were convulsively delivered. In her death throes the she-dog licked her pups into life. The outlaw, on seeing this act of selflessness that transcended mortal agony, was instantly enlightened.

The conflicting symbols of woman as witch (or bewitcher) and madonna are obvious. That the ambivalence these symbols mirror is deeply rooted in dependency conflicts requires some demonstration. The conflict is our longing to merge with an Other, while at the same time fearing the extinction of our separate selves in such fusion. The basic problem of human relations, Schopenhauer wrote,

resembles that of hedgehogs on a cold night. They creep closer to each other for warmth, are pricked by quills and move away, but then get cold and again try to come nearer. This movement to and fro is repeated until an optimum position is reached in which the body temperature is above the freezing point and yet the pain inflicted by the quills (the nearness of the other) is still bearable.[3]

Dependency conflict has its origin in the initial experience of fusion with one's mother and subsequent separation from her. A contemporary psychologist, Louise Kaplan, puts it this way:

In his first partnership outside the womb, the infant is filled up with the bliss of unconditional love—the bliss of oneness with his mother. . . . All later love and dialogue is a striving to reconcile our longings to restore the lost bliss of oneness with our equally intense need for separateness and individual self-hood.[4]

Woman becomes, for a male, symbol of the dilemma: it was a woman who first gave comfort, or withheld it; it was she whose countenance shone upon him like a beacon of security, and who later curbed his expansive striving for autonomy. The child, in a psychological "splitting," alternately knew Good Mother and Bad Mother. The splitting continues to color a man's relationships with women in adulthood. At first he sees his wife as the adored/adoring one of his archaic bliss. But not infrequently she becomes in his eyes the tyrannizing Bad Mother who robs him of his self-hood; and he may then project his image of feminine perfection onto some other woman.

Let me emphasize, parenthetically, that women too are ambivalent toward the opposite sex,[5] but their ambivalence has different roots. Nor are women free of dependency conflicts; but having identified with the mother and internalized her nurturing aspect, they develop a different conflict, with different symbols and defense mechanisms.

## Pervasiveness of Human Dependency-Needs

An Indian psychiatrist, Sudhir Kakar, looks at the problem of dependency from a cross-cultural perspective:

Our lifelong dependence on other human beings forces us to live as if on edge. On one side, should we stumble and fall, is a state of complete dependence and defencelessness which snuffs out individuality; on the other, is a state of utter independence and the loneliness that comes with it.[6]

Different cultures, like different individuals, find varying compromises between the two poles of fusion and separation. Asia has, by and large, opted for the fusion end of the pole, providing the individual with a secure sense of belonging to family, caste, or other group, at the cost of autonomy.[7] In Japan the depth and pervasiveness of human dependency-needs, more simply understood as the need for a reliable, nurturing, fear-dispelling Other, is conceptualized as *amae*.[8] It is there perceived to be the key to understanding human nature. *"Amatus ergo sum"* (Having been loved, I am) perhaps better expresses the Asian attitude than Descartes' *"Cogito, ergo sum"* (I think, therefore I am). The former one emphasizes our dependence on others, the latter our separateness.

The West, by contrast, has honored separation as the nobler choice. A typically western stand is articulated in the works of Ernest Becker,[9] who advocated a radical assertion of one's separateness and self-sufficiency; anything less he regarded as neurosis or regression, and a denial of one's freedom. A hero figure in the West is the "lone wolf," he who stands alone, responsible to no one but himself, "owing nothing to nobody." From a western point of view, with its Faustian model of development, Asian institutions hinder the growth of such traits as independence, initiative, and motivation for achievement. The western value choice of independence over security, separation over fusion, appears in the practice of isolating an infant in its *own* room, in its *own* bed, with its *own* toys. The price of such isolation, from an eastern perspective, is a weakened mother–child bond on which future socialization and family cohesiveness depends.

Western psychology has been slow to recognize the critical importance of a child's experience of fusion and separation in its first social relationship. Freud paid scant attention to the vicissitudes of the mother–child dyad. Believing the sexual instinct to be primary, he regarded the father's role and the fate of the oedipal conflict as decisive in personality formation (a view that echoed an earlier belief that babies grow from the seed of the father, the mother furnishing only the incubation vessel). Only in recent decades has the instinctual-drive theory of early psychoanalysis been largely replaced by "object relations theory"—that is, a primary need for attachment to an Other takes precedence over need satisfaction.

The change has come about through studies[10] that have traced a variety of severe pathologies to deficits in the earliest human relationship, with the mother or mothering person. "Failure to thrive"—even death—were found to be the consequences for institutionalized infants who missed out on the stage that Kaplan calls "blissful oneness" with an Other. Those for whom separation was too soon or too abrupt do not develop impulse control, a capacity to reflect on the consequences of their actions, nor a capacity for affection marked by empathic understanding of another. While such persons seem to be free of dependency-needs, they are not infrequently drug-dependent; and they do not have those traits which are part of "the fully human endowment" that is essential for enlightenment. When the separation phase is less traumatic, the child's persistent longing for the lost relationship "is often suffused with intense generalized hostility."[11]

No one has made the fundamental point so clearly as a neglected figure, Ian Suttie.[12] Suttie believed that the infant, before it can differentiate self from other, is not narcissistic as Freud theorized but solipsistic. He asserted that the infant is not so much motivated for pan-sexual gratification as by an innate thrust toward a social interplay that Suttie named love. "Love" he defined as a harmonious interplay, a social give-and-take in which neither partner feels "taken." Suckling is a prototype of such interplay, with both baby and mother giving and sharing physical pleasure as well as a sociable sharing, the mother gazing at the baby who fixes its eyes on her face and soon learns to initiate interaction by dropping the nipple from time to time to gurgle and smile.

As self-consciousness emerges, the child has a growing sense of being a separate self. This separation, or psychological second birth, is an unavoidable seedbed of neurosis in Suttie's view. (One is reminded of the Buddha's "All worldlings are deranged" because of the ubiquitous illusion of a separate, unchanging core self and self-consciousness that is fundamentally anxious.) The pain of separation leads to a "repression of tenderness," self-doubt, and a nameless longing that resembles the "thirsting desire" of Buddhist literature. When the original desire for love (in the sense of mutuality) is repressed or conflicted, a quest for power, direct or indirect, is likely to take its place. Repression of tenderness turns sexuality into "venery" in its archaic sense, meaning both sexual pursuit and the hunting of wild game. The female breast becomes an object of arousal and sort of a trophy, disconnected from its earliest association with a mutual fusion. A contemporary psychiatrist, Rollo May, supports the view that sex becomes obsessive and aggressive when there is a fear of closeness and tenderness is repressed.[13]

## Dependency and the Religious Quest

The forces that shape and re-shape a person are infinitely complex; but if we are persuaded that a legacy of infancy is a striving to reconcile our longings to restore the lost bliss of oneness with an equally intense need for separateness and individual fulfillment, then we must ask what bearing this has on religious understanding.

My answer has two parts. First, with regard to negative passions such as anger and lust, which religions regularly abjure and seek to conquer, Suttie's theory suggests that those passions (a) derive from dependency conflicts and the repression of affection, and (b) are more easily dealt with than the dependency conflicts that give rise to them.

Second, virtues such as openness and compassion which religions seek to foster are, for their part, also complicated by the basic fusion/autonomy conflict. Repression of tenderness, a guarded distance springing from a fear of closeness, clinging dependency, or ambivalence—these obviously affect and confine our aspirations to love our neighbors as ourselves.

Let me return to the first answer. Some research by a pair of ingenious psychologists, Daniel P. Brown and Jack Engler,[14] appears to confirm that longings for a reassuring special relationship are more of an obstacle in the spiritual path than anger or lust. The researchers' purpose was to test by independent means the claims set forth in Buddhist literature that specific changes in mental experience are associated with each level of progress in meditation. Brown and Engler conducted tests with four different groups of meditators distinguished by different levels of proficiency, and then compared the test results to see if each group could be discerned by the type of responses given. The subjects were assigned to specific proficiency-levels by consensual agreement among Buddhist meditation teachers. The four groups were Beginners; Access, persons who had mastered the mind's tendency to flit about rather than remain "one-pointed" on a chosen object; Beginning Insight, persons who were no longer caught up with the emotional content of their mental experience like the Beginners but able instead to observe microscopically their mental processes; and an Advanced Insight group. The chief instrument used was the Rorschach "inkblot" test.

When the subjects' responses to the Rorschachs were analyzed, it was found that the qualitative features (i.e., the type of content) shared in common by persons who were at the same level of meditative practice were far more striking than differences related to individual personalities. Responses that exposed sexual and aggressive themes came from those in the Beginning Insight group, although recognizing these as mere "mind states," they had no impulse to act on them. There were also a striking number of responses that the research team called life-affirming, creative, and empathic.

In contrast to the Beginning Insight group, aggressive and sexual themes were not generated by the Advanced Insight group. The conflictual themes that appeared in this group's Rorschach responses were all related to intimacy: fear of rejection, struggles with dependency and the wish for a close relationship, fear and doubt in heterosexual relationships, and fear of their potential destructiveness. Thus the fears and desires associated with dependency-needs were found in this study to be a greater problem than anger and lust for those subjects who were seeking freedom from emotional turmoil. (Significant perceptual-cognitive changes were also found in the four groups of subjects, confirming Buddhist accounts, but these are not pertinent here.)

The persistency of dependency-needs has also been confirmed in my clinical counseling practice. Priests and members of religious communities, who were struggling with decisions to rescind their vows and return to lay life, have confided that their most compelling reason was an aching loneliness for a special relationship.

There is a second answer to the question how dependency conflicts are related to the religious quest. All religions seek a profound change in the way we relate to one another. Compassion, Buddhist teachers say, is the beginning, middle, and end of spiritual practice. What is sought is selflessness, altruism, and loving-kindness. Alienation from others must be replaced by a capacity to glimpse one's self, with empathy and forgiveness, in every other sinner. For males, it seems that there is no one more alien, more incomprehensible, than woman. This is the import of Freud's well-known complaint that he would never understand what women want. D. H. Lawrence, with eloquence and insight, wrote:

Man is willing to accept woman as an equal, as a man in skirts, as an angel, a devil, a baby-face, a machine, an instrument, a bosom, a womb, a pair of legs, a servant, an encyclopedia, an ideal or an obscenity; the only thing he won't accept her as is a real human being of the female sex.[15]

Woman is alien until man reclaims, as a part of himself, the "feminine" part of himself that has been repressed as a defense against the pain of his original separation from his mother, and against both his fear and his longing to merge with another. In other words, he must resolve the conflict that has been projected onto woman, that is, the riddle posed by his contradictory desires for oneness and for separateness. This can be accomplished, according to Buddhists, only through a "turning at the deepest seat of consciousness"[16] that spells the end of a grasping for identity that is either masculine or feminine.

## Buddhism and Western Psychologists

This "turning" also spells the end of dual awareness in which we perceive polarities of I and Other and a conflict between autonomous selfhood and subordination of self. And it spells the end, as well, of egocentric perception in which we seem to be divided from ourselves and our experience. Dual awareness begins with the first seed of self-consciousness in early infancy, and with it a dependency on others to solidify and affirm our self-portraits. Buddhists claim that this narcissistic preoccupation can be overcome, although such attainment is rare. An American, Ernest Becker,[17] believed this Buddhist claim to be based on subtle self-deception.

Becker, like Suttie and myself, names the dependence/independence conflict as "the problem of life," but Becker's solution is different. Because the popularity of his books in the United States suggests widespread agreement with his alternative solution, I shall briefly summarize his thought.

Becker saw the human situation as one of freedom, albeit limited, but a freedom mocked by death. He believed that sex and childbirth remind men of their dependence on nature, and therefore of their death. As woman is intimately connected with these physical functions, she symbolizes "death-terror" and is therefore an object of male ambivalence.

A major motive in all human endeavors is a need to repress and deny our death-terror; otherwise, our will to freedom is paralyzed, in Becker's view. All human beings, therefore, spend their lives striving to maintain the illusion that they are god-like heroes, in some way immortal and free of nature. Thus we spend our lives cultivating an illusion of self-sufficiency through the "self-project" or "hero system" (an illusion that one is self-begotten and self-made, what Buddhism calls I-grasping). In the face of nature's indifference there "throbs the ache for cosmic specialness. . . . He must stand out, be a hero, show that he counts more than anyone else."[18] Man is ever dependent on others "for crumbs of self-worth" to fortify his illusion of having some special importance, yet he must persuade himself that he is wholly independent and self-sufficient.

Thus far Becker's diagnosis of the human situation is the same as the Buddhist understanding of *dukkha*. But in Buddhist belief it is possible to open fully to pain, death, and loneliness—and to let go of the self-project which only perpetuates anxiety and suffering. Becker, in his refutation of this claim, insists that "Even holy men who withdraw for years of spiritual development, come back into the fold of society to earn recognition for their powers."[19]

In his book on Zen Buddhism, Becker also dismissed Buddhist meditation practice as leading to self-deception rather than to a more valid (non-dual) perception. He described Zen as "brainwashing" and a "coercion process" that "breaks people down mentally" until "the dependent person takes on the reality of the stronger person"[20] (i.e., that reality of the Zen master). From Becker's perspective, the Zen aspirant has chosen to resolve the dependency conflict by surrendering the insecurity of freedom and autonomy for the security of slavish dependence on another.

Oddly enough, despite Becker's rejection of Zen as self-deception, he named religion as "the most life enhancing illusion": one that puts

self-esteem firmly under one's control so that one is freed of any need for affirmation from others. The value of deriving one's power and meaning from the highest level of generality [religion] is that it makes this task for the self-esteem easier. One can feel that he has ultimate value deep down inside just by serving in the cosmic hero-system; he has a sense of duty to the very powers of creation and not principally or only to the social world. Ideally this would give him the liberation of the saint, who couldn't care less about the jeerings and opinions of the mob, or even of his nearest loved ones. . . . If God is hidden and intangible, all the better; that allows man to expand and develop himself.[21]

Thus Becker and Buddhism come to opposite conclusions. To be free of all fear, the Buddhist believes one must rid oneself of the illusion that one has a separate core of undying being. Becker, on the other hand, regards such illusion as the "indispensable illusion" provided by religion. It is indispensable because, in his view, *only* when one is convinced of having some indestructible, individual core can one exercise one's will freely, unhampered by dependency-needs.

## In Search of True Freedom from Dependency

Rollo May takes a different view of the will, one that is closer to Buddhist understanding: we *will* according to what we care about. In our ordinary experience the autonomous will, identified with our sense of a separate self, tends to be set against love. The roots of this opposition lie early in childhood, when we first experienced separate identity as a "No!" Love, May writes, is often a mask for the self-project; but when love is a profound caring and acceptance of another demanding nothing, expecting nothing, it is the opposite of alienation and fear. It "is the *will made free*" [italics mine]. The highest form of caring, the most freeing, is a disinterested and impersonal caring for all being. But for May this is not a reachable star but a star to guide us. Like Becker, he assumes that no human beings are wholly free of self-interest, and he is inclined to see such perfection as a diminution of being:

The serious problems of life are never solved, and if it seems that they have been solved something [the central importance of Self?] has been lost.[22]

Perhaps it is the West's strong attachment to the separation end of the pole that prevents May, and many lesser thinkers, from conceiving of the Buddhist goal of no-self as anything but loss. This attachment may also account for the fact that few westerners, though they diligently sit like so many stone Buddhas, progress beyond the beginner's level in meditation. But there is another possible explanation: Human beings tend to dismiss as unreal anything totally foreign to their experience. We are like Columbus, who called the lands he discovered the Indies because he had no inkling that the world was so wide and that there were continents unknown.

In similar fashion, western psychology[23] has tended to assume that the experience of *anatta* (no-self) or *sunyata* (no-thingness) must be the fusion state that existed before Self and Other were differentiated. Some physicists appear to find it easier to entertain the notion that our everyday perceptions of reality may not be ultimately "real." Einstein was such a one. In a letter written to a friend of his, who had asked Einstein to console a young woman whose sister had died, Einstein indicated that without a profound change in perspective there can be no consolation:

A human being is part of the whole, called by us 'universe,' a part limited in time and space. He experiences himself, his thoughts and feelings, as something separate from the rest, a kind of optical delusion of his consciousness. This delusion is a kind of prison for us, restricting us to our personal decisions and to affection for a few persons nearest to us. Our task must be to free ourselves from this prison by widening our circle of compassion to embrace all living creatures and the whole of nature in its beauty.[24]

The "kind of optical delusion" that Einstein referred to is dual awareness. Non-dual awareness, Buddhists say, is not the undifferentiated oneness such as we knew as infants; rather, it is not-twoness. From the perspective of not-twoness, dependence and independence are not seen as polar opposites but as different angles of the same reality. "Mother" depends on "child," because without a child there is no mother; and if there were no mother, there would be no child. The conception of one implies the other. Mother and child are not the same, but neither exists as an independent entity. Intellectual understanding of this point does not cure dual awareness—our *avidya* or ignorance. The lived experience of not-twoness requires a radical reorganization of our perceptual/cognitive apparatus according to Buddhists.

St. Paul stated that in Christ there is neither Jew nor Gentile. Another Buddhist story illustrates that in the Dharma there is neither male nor female: Sariputra, a famous sage, went to a great female saint and said, "If you are really enlightened, why have you not transformed into a male body?" The saint changed Sariputra into a woman. "Why," she then asked him, "are not *you* in male form?" She then explained that with enlightenment one is no longer concerned with such conventional designations as "female" and "male."

Whether the tension between Self and Other, fusion and separateness, can ever be fully resolved, and whether narcissism can be overcome, is not likely to be settled by either psychological studies or theorizing. The Buddha repeatedly advised us not to rely on authority nor on abstract speculation, but to test out the truth of the Eightfold Path through our own experience:

I invite you now to Buddhahood
And, by the way, to happiness.

Santideva

# NOTES

1. Quoted by Julius Evola, *The Metaphysics of Sex* (1969; reprint, New York: Inner Traditions International, 1983).

2. Ibid., 248.

3. Paraphrased by Sudhir Kakar, *The Inner World: A Psychoanalytic Study of Childhood and Society in India* (Oxford: Oxford University Press, 1978), 87.

4. Louise J. Kaplan, *Oneness and Separateness: From Infant to Individual* (New York: Simon and Schuster, 1978), 27.

5. For a discussion of female ambivalence toward men, see Philip Slater, *The Glory of Hera* (Boston: Beacon, 1966). The most comprehensive theory of ambivalence toward the opposite sex, for both males and females, is found in Carl G. Jung, *Analytical Psychology: Its Theory and Practice* (New York: Vintage Press, 1968). Each, according to Jung, projects onto the other sex aspects of the self that one has rejected or denied.

6. Sudhir Kakar, 35.

7. Ibid., 10.

8. L. T. Doi, "Amae: A key concept for understanding Japanese personality structure," *Psychologia* 5 (1962): 1–7.

9. Ernest Becker, *The Birth and Death of Meaning* (New York: Macmillan, 1962) and *The Denial of Death* (New York: Macmillan, 1973). The reader is also referred to Philip Slater's *The Pursuit of Loneliness: American Culture at the Breaking Point* (Boston: Beacon, 1970).

10. See John Bowlby, *Attachment and Loss,* 3 vols. (New York: Basic Books, 1969, 1973, 1980); René Spitz, *The First Year of Life* (New York: International Universities, 1965); Donald W. Winnicott, *The Maturational Process and the Facilitating Environment* (New York: International Universities, 1965); Margaret Mahler, Fred Pine & Anni Bergman, *The Psychological Birth of the Human Infant* (New York: Basic Books, 1975).

11. Althea J. Horner, *Object Relations and the Developing Ego in Therapy* (New York: Jason Aronson, 1979), 49.

12. Ian Suttie, *The Origins of Love and Hate* (1952; reprint, New York: Julian Press, 1966). Erik Erikson, like Suttie, went beyond those who studied the effects of mothering deficits in his thinking about the importance of the first year of life. He postulated that a wholesome transit through the fusion-separation stages of early childhood provides a basis for trust in one's world and trust in one's self. The basic trust established in the first years he linked to a faith at the end of one's life cycle that life has been meaningful and death can be accepted without despair. *Childhood and Society* (New York: W. W. Norton, 1950).

13. Rollo May, *Love and Will* (New York: W. W. Norton, 1969).

14. Daniel P. Brown and Jack Engler, "The stages of mindfulness meditation: a validation study," *The Journal of Transpersonal Psychology* 12, no. 2 (1980): 143–200. The form of meditation practiced by the experimental subjects was Theravada *vipassana* meditation in the Mahasi Sayadaw tradition. Some variant of this form, right mindfulness (the eighth step of the Buddhist Eightfold Path), is used in all Buddhist schools of meditation.

15. Quoted in Robin Morgan, ed., *Sisterhood Is Powerful: An Anthology of Writings from the Women's Liberation Movement* (New York: Random House, 1970), 564.

16. Irmgard Schloegl, *The Zen Way* (London: Sheldon Press, 1977).

17. Becker, *Birth and Death of Meaning*.

18. Becker, *Denial of Death*, 4.

19. Becker, *Birth and Death of Meaning*, 70.

20. Ernest Becker, "Zen Buddhism, 'Thought Reform' (Brainwashing) and Various Psychotherapies" (Ph.D. diss., dept. of anthropology, Syracuse University, 1960).

21. Becker, *Denial of Death*, 191–92.

22. May, *Love and Will*, 175.

23. "Mysticism: Spiritual quest or psychic disorder?" *Group for the Advancement of Psychiatry, Committee on Psychiatry and Religion*, Washington, D.C., 1976.

24. Albert Einstein, as reported in the *New York Times*, 29 March 1972.

# 14

# Walls, Women and Intimations of Interconnection

## CATHERINE KELLER

For the part of the mind that is dark to us in this culture, that is sleeping in us, that we name 'unconscious', is the knowledge that we are inseparable from all other beings in the universe. Intimations of this have reached us.

Susan Griffin, *Pornography and Silence*[1]

Thus the continuum is present in each actual entity, and each actual entity pervades the continuum.

A. N. Whitehead, *Process and Reality*[2]

## The Self as Walled City

What is then the connection between the self, severed from its relational field, variously called individualistic, atomistic, isolated, separate, or simply selfish, and that common denominator of world-society called sexism? Or to put the question positively, anticipating the negation of the negation: what pattern of self crystallizes in response at once to the crisis of the separate subject, and to the crisis of feminism? The hypothesis hiding in the questions is that there is a radical connection between the crises, one that neither those interested in the concept of self for its own sake nor those interested in feminism for the sake of women alone can afford to ignore. But suddenly the hypothesis turns into a koan: it is emptied before it is filled. For the answer to be tested grins like a flowering plum tree at the question: the connection is connectivity itself.

When we think about connection, or establishing connection, or "connecting with" something or someone, we tend to think from the vantage point of separation. That to which I connect is, first of all, outside of myself. Connection is something which must be established, made—the ultimate parody of this movement from the outside in is coveyed by the phrase, "making connections." The point of thinking of connectivity in intimate conjunction with the notion of self is to reverse the movement: to render self, or better, in Hopkins' idiom "selving," a single process with its connecting. In the words of the comic heroine and lesbian mother Arden Benbow:

Things are connected, you know. Human events are all linked by a brilliant network of feelings, beliefs, ideas that wink on and off like Christmas tree lights. And time is the Christmas tree.[3]

Once we can experience selves as events, processes of selving and acts of connection, rather than discrete and enduring things, we will find the question of time already present. But for now let us dwell upon and within the *space* of self opened when its conventional system of walls and boundaries begins to fall away.

Do we in fact "know" that things are connected? Is not this precisely the knowledge which is "dark to us in this culture"? Yet, in two opposing senses of knowledge I suspect Arden speaks the truth. There seems to be a barely conscious knowing, knowledge enough to suggest our unknowing, felt as a "heavy, primitive experience"[4] or as lightening poetic fancy. This is the preconscious sensing, the a-rational feel for the raw textures of things, before consciousness can pick the threads apart. It is, perhaps, the knowing that reveals itself to Doris Lessing's Martha in the depths of her confrontation with at once her self and the inner figure of the "self-hater": "You've got to be alert enough to catch a thought as it is born."[5] If we simply *know* that things are connected, we experience the togetherness of knower and known suggested by the carnal undertones of "biblical knowledge," or an intellectual ecstasy akin to the Platonic Eros. In such proximate knowing, we sense filaments that run between all things because they run through us, like our very nerves, leaping our synapses and swimming our blood, and finally, simply, shaping our selves as knower, our selves' content as the known. This sort of connectivity, though, suggests a wider and deeper network than the "society" of "generalized other" suggested by George Herbert Mead of social behaviorism.

Knowledge in the conventional sense, the knowledge controlled by the cognitive cultural repertoire and based upon the subject's epistemic control of object, aiming always at the knower's mastery of the known, at data-control, at dominion, at the "phallogocentric subjectivity" or "deconstructionism," appears indeed precisely to oppose the previous sense. It seems involved in a conspiracy to suppress the primal knowing, where we might know ourselves as connecting links rather than severed lumps. Theory has gone the way of Plato's *diairesis,* the butcher's skill of "chopping at the joints" *(Phaedrus)*, leaving synthesis to reconnect—from the perspective of the disjoined. We can then hardly speak of catching a thought as it is born, as though to follow it from there, when there is an epistemological abortion performed by the cultural structure of consciousness on precisely such inchoate sensibility. But must the knowledge of our inseparability be put to sleep?

If culture claims as its prime commodity not only knowledge but the means of knowledge, its power depends upon epistemological dominion, inasmuch as it seeks to maintain coercive regulation of its subjects. The well-regulated subject of culture is then, ironically, the subject seeking to control its own finite domain of objects, its property. In most cases this will boil down to the master of the household—the *oikos* Aristotle knows to be the fundamental political-economic unit and model—lording it over his own subjects, his properties, the most important of which is his wife.

The most pervasive image for organized cultural life is the city, and the image of the city very quickly became that of the Walled City. We, however, are interested in the shape of selves, grown as they are within the protection of these civic walls. In fact, our civilization has advanced well beyond stone walls and is attempting for our protection to close the final "windows of vulnerability." Gilgamesh, epic hero, ruled in Uruk, archetypal fortified city—the strength and grandeur of whose walls frame, as beginning and end of the hero's quest, the epic itself.[6] And from the land of biblical knowledge we hear a strange metamorphosis of the collective, civic image into an individual psychological structure. This is YHWH speaking to his chosen mouthpiece: "I, for my part, today will make you into a fortified city, a pillar of iron, and a wall of bronze" (Jer. 1:18).

Self as walled city, abode of the hero: a master metaphor of the disconnected ego, which gradually rarifies its walls into unassailable presuppositions fortified by philosophical theory and theological doctrine. Yet this invulnerable city of an ego-ideal, foisted upon the male by his overpowering vocation, his articulate

Superego, crumbles. "You raped me, O Lord, and I was raped" (Heschel's translation of Jeremiah 20:7). The lone prophet, silhouetted darkly in his solitary antagonism against the advent of the new epoch of "axial individuals,"[7] now knows himself violated, victim of the ultimate patriarchal humiliation, male rape of male. Reduced to the woman's role, the prophet suffers the helplessness of his bronzed ego to protect him against the very One, the inner voice, who erected its walls in the first place. So he concludes by cursing the day of his birth—an act of verbal suicide. His career ends with an ironic inversion of images; he laments that he did not die in the womb: "Then my mother would have been my grave, her womb confining me forever." The "identity crisis," in the overused parlance of the ego-psychologist, brought on by the invasion from within and without of the boundaries of the severed self, gives utterance to a *regressio ad oppositorum* by which one extreme reverts to its opposite. The bronze-walled self becomes the enwombed, entombed infant: two opposing yet profoundly parallel structures of enclosed existence. The symbol of the splendid citadel of the One over against the many shatters as the heroic individual yearns backward from the Living Lord to a Death Mother. But the deathly darkness of womb, whether comfort or horror, is but the shape of the shadow of self-annihilation, the anti-world of an ego which poses the world as his opposite. Here we have an example of the first paradox of divided selfhood, casting its feminine shadow. "Mother" is the ambivalent residue of its alterity within himself—the coveted, dreaded place of origin and exhausted collapse.

Let us set in counterpoint the image of mad Lynda in her basement abode in the appositely named novel, *The Four-Gated City*. Lynda's life-history, inverting that of Jeremiah, begins in madness (a victim of mental institutions since adolescence) and ends in prophecy. Both hear "voices." Both function as "world-historical individuals" (Hegel's term), suffering cataclysmic social crisis as individual pathos, their gifts of special "hearing" burdening them with unimaginably bad news. Moving furiously around walls smudged by a ring bloodstained by bitten nails, Lynda's wild banging motion is only exacerbated by Martha's first, rational attempts to reassure her: "Lynda, those are ordinary walls. This is where you live. You can walk out any-time you like."[8] Only through entering consciously and empathetically into Lynda's mental state does she discover the meaning of the particular madness. In her the second paradox, woman's self-negating subjectivity, is fierce. The diabolic "self-hater" serves to keep Lynda enwalled, corroding her talents of world-hearing—the extrasensory experience of connectivity turned nightmarish in a society which torments rather than teaches its seers, its prophets.

Yet these very gifts play an indispensable role in the apocalyptic finale of the novel. Lynda will finally learn the needed mental disciplines so as no longer to be inundated by the "sea of sound," but to sort and hear the objective world of a multitude of immanent others. If within the walls of our culture, the knowledge of interconnecting means madness, self-hate, self-loss, then how can the breakdown of those very walls become part of a "knowledge" which as conscious, linguistic theory is indistinguishable from culture?

## Feminism and the New Paradigm

Theory has a revolutionary potential along with its reactionary tendencies to shore up cultural norms. Thus it is of vital importance that some of the most abstract theorizing in this century has been moving toward a radical revisioning of the universe in terms of interconnection. It is as though the vague, primal eros is finally attracting to itself the very capacity, discursive reason, which has most successfully opposed it. Theory spun from the interplay of physics and metaphysics envisions an "implicate order" of reality as web of cosmic relations (Bohm), "a quantum interconnectedness of distant systems" (Bell), suggesting "that each happening is a factor in the nature of every other happening."[9]

But what does this theoretical rousing into consciousness of some fundamental connectedness have to do with the feminist attempt to raise our consciousness of sexual injustice? Everything, I would suggest—indeed, so much that it will be impossible for the emergent "paradigm" to embody itself in the *sensus communis,* to become the living world-sense from which we spin our norms, our actions, our discourse, until such time as the feminist revolution in life-forms and awareness has been realized. For in the relations dictated by sexism, the old paradigm is rehearsed into an abiding conciousness from earliest childhood. This claim stretches the boundaries both of the political and of the personal into the thinner atmospheres of theory. But such an ontological-comprehensive loom is needed. I am trying to say that insights into physical and personal fields of relation will remain merely "academic," or "popular" (in the sense of shallow, premature, ineffectual enthusiasms), unless the alliance between the metaphors of interconnectedness and of post-patriarchy are woven ever more tightly together. I do not construe my present task in terms of drawing parallels between the new physics and feminist sensibility but rather of seeking theoretical and empirical "conditions of the possibility" of the affinity between feminism and the "new paradigm." We must ask *why* the world-sense of the disconnected self parallels historically the ascendancy of patriarchy, in order to grasp, conversely, how its severed, wounded state can be healed only through an explicit embrace of the project of gender re-creation. This is happening within feminism:

The global feminist movement is bringing about the end of patriarchy, the eclipse of the politics of separation, and the beginning of a new era modeled on the dynamic, holistic paradigm. In working toward these goals, we have many allies among men. Radical feminists envision that era, and the long process leading toward it, as a *comprehensive transformation.*[10]

Yet this dependency works both ways: if it is true that the much-anticipated paradigm-shift cannot occur without a concurrent transformation of gender-role, it is also the case that the realization of the goals of feminism (inasmuch as they exceed what can be legislated) would require the global and practical actualization of the paradigm-shift. Feminism is beginning to explore its own extension beyond the psycho-politics of sex-role, into the domain of ontology and cosmology. The quantum leap from the century intuition of a cosmic web of vibrating energies, to the concrete concerns of women, has begun to occur in a vast range of writings (often those relating to the field of religion and myth, goddess, wicca, and spirituality). From a background of literacy and political creativity, Robin Morgan accomplishes a new and delightful correlation of themes from the new physics and feminism:

Gender, race, global politics, family structure, economics, the environment, childhood, ageing—all reveal their interconnectedness as we move around the holograph. . . . The internal workings of the human body or of an atomic particle . . . of spiritual faith and scientific fact, of aesthetics and astrophysics, disclose themselves as interwoven expressions of one dynamic whole. It's for this reason that I've chosen quantum physics and its themes of relativity and interrelationship as the central analogy for feminism and for freedom.[11]

Morgan (who bears as well as any woman today the current wave of feminist activism, reflection, and poetry) has discovered the cosmological connection through an encounter with the metaphysics of physics. Years earlier she had drawn the same fundamental intuition from her background in poetry:

It is the insistence on the *connections,* the demand to synthesis, the refusal to be narrowed into desiring less than everything—that is so much the form of metaphysical feminism. The unified sensibility.[12]

Her precedents here lie in the love-mysticism of the metaphysical poets, above all John Donne. Through the "metaphysical" frame of reference, as a huge liberation from the domestic constraints of traditional feminine relatedness, may be emerging a non-sentimental, post-sexist metaphor for love as an activity of conscious interconnection. (It would be well if the trivializing tyrannies of intimacy within a gender hierarchy would not immunize us against the poetics of love, even between the sexes.)

## Feminism and Process Thought

The germinal development of feminism inspired by metaphysical philosophy and philosophy of religion continues to sprout powerful insights, if the depth and darkness of the radix is understood. The genius of Mary Daly, the feminist philosopher and theologian, illumines the darkness most radically in her third book, *Gyn/Ecology*. She uses medical attitudes toward women's bodies and psyches as a complex metaphor and example of patriarchal theory and practice, not simply in relation to women, but as a *modus vivendi:* "In contrast to gynaecology, which depends upon fixation and dismemberment, *Gyn/Ecology* affirms that everything is connected."[13] In the final "Passage," she spins a mythic texture of webs, of weaving, of Arachne's unfair defeat by Athena at the loom, of Penelope's secret *art*, of every manner of "cosmic tapestry" spun to span the "split consciousness" that separates women from each other and from insight:

The mindbinders and those who remain mindbound do not see the patterns of the cosmic tapestries, nor do they hear the labyrinthine symphony. For their thinking has been crippled and tied to linear tracks. . . .

Since they do not understand that creativity means seeing the interconnectedness between seemingly disparate phenomena, the mindbound accuse Hags [a very good word for Daly] of "lumping things together." Their perception is a complete reversal.[14]

Daly has been articulating something like a feminist ontology: "the women's revolution, in so far as it is true to its own essential dynamics is an ontological, spiritual revolution."[15] Yet the instances where she evokes the image of connection display rather an epistemological concern to overcome the disconnecting, dismembering way of knowing by which women are cut up into "pieces," fetishes, and to do this by a methodology (or "methodicide") which sees the connection between seemingly innocuous or benevolent phenomena (from the trinity to therapy, from higher education to high-heeled shoes) and the cultural edifice of patriarchy. Her gynocentric metaphors evoke a vision of the fundamental texture of things, yet one for which she has cleared the way dramatically, without quite going there. She would not want to be involved in any apparently neutral metaphysics or purportedly open "dialogue." But she is not beyond acknowledging, tentatively, certain affinities. Not coincidentally to the present work, the strongest such affinity, less problematic finally than that with Tillich, seems to be with the process metaphysics of Whitehead and the process theology of John Cobb.[16]

Inspired by the germinal visions of the new physics to synthesize science with religious sensibility, Whitehead's philosophy of organism represents perhaps the most imaginatively ambitious attempt to articulate the intuition of interconnectedness as worldview admitting no exclusions. He accomplishes his megalithic metaphor of a universe-in-process by a pan-subjectivism which intends in a single wide stroke to eliminate every manner of classical dichotomy, without idealistic reduction to human subjectivity or materialist reduction to physical objectivity. In fact Whitehead hardly speaks of selves, performing as he does a cosmological deconstruction of that *anthropos* who has dominated thought as its Kantian subject, rendering all knowledge epistemological to the exclusion of the inchoate "knowing" by which the vague play of interconnections might approach consciousness. And precisely because he evades anthropocentrism while stressing subjectivity as the very nature of actuality, he sheds fresh drops of insight on the character of self. It must be, as subjectively immediate, strictly momentary: myself here-and-now. And it includes as its very stuff its inner objects, the previous subjects: all those occasions of being which have become up to the point in the universe at which the new subject is emerging. Thus each individual includes and is included by the perspectively spread cosmos of all other entities. Then the continuum of objects potentially part of new subjects "is present in each actual entity, and each actual entity pervades the continuum."

Within process thought itself, feminism is beginning to play a major role. This is so far most clearly signalled by the papers of *Feminism and Process Thought*,[17] in which consonances of process emphases with feminist intent, such as the mutuality of relation, non-dualistic organicism, non-hierarchical theology and the authority of the experiencing subject, are developed.[18] Process feminism so far, however, has been largely derivative from process concerns and categories, which are then taken and applied to feminism—as they are to ecology, to liberation, or to the interfaith dialogue. But discussion in these terms could rapidly become one-sided if the general theory and especially its methodology is understood to be already settled by an essentially male system, however sympathetic. Yet this need not be the direction this dialogue, or rather symbiosis, takes, for the insights which account for any preestablished harmony are firmly located within feminist sensibility. This alone should suffice to unsettle any theoretical imperialism.

I have suggested that both feminism and the metaphysical attempts to articulate a new paradigm require each other. *If this is true, it may be because at base the gesture of disconnection and the gesture of misogyny are one and the same.* This is only to restate the opening hypothesis, or koan. We will keep the issue of a new paradigm focused on the concept of self, for it is in the shaping of selves that every institution of culture, every philosophical presupposition or intention, at once roots and rests its case. However cosmological the ramifications of a self viewed as a process of interconnection, as point of intersection in a net or the net itself, the concept must curve us back through the regions of intimately political and densely psychological reflection if the discussion is not to drift into outer space. Spacey ladies and spaced-out selves do not express the ideal of interconnected liberation, which has an entirely different force, than, say, declarations that "all is one"—to which one may politely or profoundly nod, or vehemently protest that no, all is dangerously fragmented and at the best plural. Connectivity will not take us far unless it expresses a mode of self, or selving, or self-creation that has its merit not as a romantic panacea but as a realistic assessment of and attunement to the ambivalent and ambiguous nature of things. This brings us right into the heart of the question of subjects and objects, selves and their Others.

## Feminism in a Broader Philosophical Context

We need now to ask some methodological questions, first about the nature of the feminism being undertaken. Two converse queries naturally arise: (1) whether feminism is being generalized beyond its proper and legitimate claims as a socio-political movement aimed at establishing equality of rights for women in any dimension in which such equality has been abridged; and (2) whether in the process such an extension of its claims does not endanger the concentrated focus of the feminist project, threatening to reduce feminism to abstract issues such as "human self-hood" or "paradigm shifts."

Regarding the first concern, Morgan has attempted to draw a relevant distinction in explaining her own growing commitment to the analogy of the new physics:

For almost two decades, I've written about, lectured on, and organised for the ideas and politics of *feminism for the sake of women,* with the emphasis on women's right to freedom, access, self-determination, and empowerment—as a matter of simple justice. If, in fact, these were the sole reasons for and goals of the movement and consciousness we call feminism, they would be quite sufficient unto themselves as such. It might not even be necessary to try to envision . . . what the ripple effects might be from that single dropped pebble releasing the creative energy of more than half the human species after so long. Nor is it necessary to apologise for feminism's concerning itself "merely" with women, or to justify feminism on the "please, may I" grounds that it's-good-for-men-too, and therefore-won't-you-let-us-have-it? In the long run, it *will* be good for men, but even were it permanently to prove as discomfiting for men as it seems to be in the short run, that wouldn't make women's needs and demands any less just.

So the fact that I place feminism in a "larger context" is neither an apology nor a justification. It is simply to show, once and for all, that feminism is the larger context.[19]

"Feminism for the sake of women" need not, but does, expand into the feminism of the "larger context" because, according to

Morgan, it *is* the larger context. This claim states in positive terms the sentiment of Mary Daly's claim that "patriarchy is itself the prevailing religion of the entire planet,"[20] or of Ruether's analysis: "Sexual symbolism is foundational to the perception of order and relationship that has been built up in cultures."[21] That is, inasmuch as the system of sexual dominance which we call patriarchy precedes and performs every expression of cultural diversity in known history, and inasmuch as the vast contexts of "culture" are construed as fundamentally problematic, requiring a "foundational" metamorphosis, then feminism as the critique of the patriarchal basis of culture provides, indeed, the "larger context." At that point something very different from the feminist reductionism that could be interpreted from such a syllogism suggests itself. As Robin Morgan explains her intuition:

Feminism is, at this moment and on this planet, the DNA/RNA call for survival and for the next step in evolution—and even beyond that feminism is, in its metaphysical and metafeminist dynamic, the helix of hope that we humans have for communication with whatever lies before us in the vast, witty mystery of the universe.[22]

Hers is a powerful, poetic, and cosmological claim, yet one that may be no more outrageous than the simple fact of the virtual universality of male dominance for the past several thousand years. In the growing awareness of this fact lies a hope generating its set of firm projects and proposals, reflection and poetry, that potentially draws upon an enormous population—if the "gynergetic continuum" be touched, with its flow not only through all women but into all touchable men, through their relations with mothers and friends and lovers, and through their awareness of an insoluble sterility. In this continuum lies still untapped psycho-political power. Precisely this continuum is severed in the severed self.

In answer to the first query, whether the claims of a legitimate feminism are not being overstepped, we can say at the very least: if one begins to analyze the sources of sexism one is quickly led down a root system embracing the intimacies of love, the nuclear family, and the symbolism of all major religions. Unless one is prone to accept the self-description of classical philosophy as disinterested, dispassionate transcendence of the conditions of its own philosophizing, then the most abstract of theories, metaphysics, cannot provide a more general context than can feminism. Metaphysics itself must be seen in the light of the patriarchal context which enables it; the sort of self, or selves, it has described must be seen through from the perspective of its own unexamined presuppositions. (This does not dismiss metaphysics, which itself unfolds as the critique of prior unexamined presuppositions—and lives.) For this reason, perhaps, Morgan speaks of feminism *as,* not merely *in,* the broader context. There can indeed be no basis, no firm ground, for articulating a yet broader context. But while she distinguishes feminism for the sake of women from this wider variety, I would want to suggest that the concrete demands of women will be fulfilled—at best for an upper-economic, white fringe of society, where social experiments can be afforded and to some extent always have been—until the larger context shifts. The larger context, drawn by the interaction of world-view, social structures and natural environments, must indeed become (recognize itself as) feminist. But it is not *only* feminist.

When we speak of feminism as the larger context, it has begun to point beyond the concerns which first name it "feminism": feminism itself becomes a transparency, a trope, for a set of possibilities that would, if fully actualized, obviate itself by eliminating patriarchy. In any but the most affluent of circumstances, which affluence is now dwindling in even the wealthiest nations, rudimentary issues of sexual equality will be put to the side, by revolutionaries and reactionaries alike, unless the priorities of value transform themselves. And finally, feminism becomes an issue of what sort of selves, out of what sort of familial, educational, vocational, ecological, economic and spiritual environments, we want to be and to reproduce.

Such a broadening of the feminist context gives rise to the converse query: rather than reducing generalities to feminism, do we risk reducing feminism to generalities? Does such a move shelve the specific cries of stifled female selves under "issues of human liberation," "humanism," "selfhood"? We would then be contributing to the ongoing refinement of the tradition of subsuming women under the normative Man. I believe we succumb in the case of this thesis to precisely this pitfall if finally the symbolism and fact of sexism itself were to be unilaterally derived from some concept or set of categories, i.e., as an exemplification of a more "general" problem such as original sin or an ontological schism or psychological split. Yet the opposite train of thought, which would explain sexism itself as the original sin, deriving all known evils from the evil of sexual caste, would underestimate the energies of human ambivalence. For it is impossible to imagine a place of no evil without elimination of the *possibilities* for evil which belong to freedom. A feminist utopian vision cannot delude itself into the hope of overcoming all evil. Patriarchy represents a master paradigm of oppression, not evil itself. It is a particular, global but not universal, evil.

This would be the temptation to a feminist reductionism—which then allows no perspective from which to explain sexism itself, except as the spontaneous necessity of some innate male aggression—hardly a promising or encouraging vision for transformation! This larger perspective permits an understanding of what went wrong without merely reacting against patriarchy. Feminist methodology is becoming ever less reactive, ever more creative, as women find their voices and their vision.[23]

## The Self, the World and God

The three generalities which have dominated the history of western thought, evoking ever new formulations, rebellions and experiences—except from women—have been those of the soul or man, the world and God (the three transcendental limits of thought itself, according to Kant). Echoing this long tradition, in protest against the exclusivity of its epistemological dominion, Mary Daly declares that "to exist humanly is to name the self, the world and God."[24] I would suggest that these ideas have been not only named by men, a truism that needs no arguing, but that they have been increasingly external, presupposing separateness. This fragmentation includes, for instance, the separation of self from other selves, which appear before oneself as the world. That this three-way disconnection could be ill-afforded is proved by the tendency of self, world, and God to disappear. That the notion of "God" is in mortal danger, if not already dead, is a fact that the most convinced theist will not question. The psychological and anthropological systems that describe the self have with rare but notable exceptions (e.g., analytic psychology) excluded the divine from their parameters as anything but a morally regressive or useful idea to be replaced by more mature categories. The scientific systems that trace the natural world, the sociological and political systems that analyze the human world, have invested prodigious work in clearing—sometimes too vehemently—theological rubble from their view.

Referring to science, Buddhism, and feminism as three great challenges to the concept of God, one theologian suggests "we can understand the manifold criticisms of theism not as obstacles or enemies but as resources for the resolution of the problem of God."[25] "God" causes many of his own worst problems of worldly credibility; in fact, the secular tradition that produces the greatest challenges to him and his direct Judeo-Greco-Christian descendants. The tendency of "God" not to exist for us, to be excluded from systems of explanation of world and self, surely has something to do with the Supreme Deity's tendency to exclude himself, while ironically exacting exclusive fealty from his subjects. The great doctrines of divine transcendence —aseity, impassionability, immutability, *creatio ex nihilo,* and election—all may have metaphoric multivalencies springing from the originative experiences of something utterly sacred and novel, provoking self-transcendence. But their univocal and stubborn effect has been to seal God and world off from each other, except through institutionally sanctioned and dogmatically controlled relations. If in polytheistic religions divine and worldly realities mingled freely, as divine genders do even amid pagan patriarchy, a trajectory emerges in the Hebrew tradition lifting God outside the world of his unilateral creation, stressing the discontinuity between creation and creator.[26] Yet a mixed tradition charged with multiple metaphors mitigates the sheer transcendence of YHWH, even as the walls fall about his city and then his prophets. In early Christianity the incarnation and the trinity carried impulses of immanence, insight into a mode of connectivity in which persons can be both one and many, both human and divine; the countervailing impulse seemed invariably to be successful, foisting onto scripture the doctrine of an absolutely independent, immovable deity defined by a displaced Greek metaphysic.

In its theological systems, the Protestant schism, unleasing a flood of schisms, carries ever further the emphasis upon transcendence and discontinuity. As logos takes control, and the last halos of mythos dim—releasing no doubt certain new possibilities for conscious enlightenment and individual strength—the so-called secular world emerges, turning logos into the logic that will gradually pare the residues of the sacred out of the science of world and self.

If the disconnective, abstractly transcendent quality always prevailed in this trajectory, otherwise so ridden with internal conflict and contradiction, if the tendency of God to become the Outsider, the absolute Other, became stronger and stronger until with massive portions of the educated public he became almost irrelevant— then, according to the initial hypothesis, the fact of his He-ness would be precisely to the point. And this is a point that implies a much more radical critique than do the issues of exclusive gender language and male images of deity.

If God has become exclusive of and excluded by world and self, it is also true that world has succumbed to a radical severance. This becomes clearest in the trajectory moving from the Greeks and Romans, in which the goddesses and gods were gradually filtered out of *physics*—like so many nymphs and nyads out of streams—in order to make room for an utterly symmetrical *kosmos,* reflecting with legal regularity a single divine order. Even this capacity of cosmos to reflect *theos* dims with the Aristotelian attempt to come to terms with the real individual as substance. This historical process can be viewed as the gradual defeat of "animism." The tendency in Greek cosmology toward order and division links up, as though by pre-established harmony, with the Jewish apostasy called Christianity to generate western culture. I do not mean to underplay the difference between Athens and Jerusalem; but theology, especially of the Tertullianist variety, and most especially Protestant, never tires of making the distinction for purposes of de-Hellenizing. In fact, this form of biblical chauvinism and exclusivism pits itself precisely against those elements of continuity among nature, self, and deity that persist through the Hellenic influences on early Christianity. In Greece, rationality (*nous*) dominated as that highest human capacity by which the hierarchically ordered distinctions within the harmony of the cosmos, anthropos, and theos could best be perceived, that which made a self itself. By contract, the Christian synthesis subordinated this epistemological capacity to that gift by which the Otherness of God, in his separateness from the experienced world, is to be known: faith. The pre-epistemological meaning of faith as radical trust, which should precisely oppose the disconnection of God from self and world, however frequently recalled, seemed ever doomed to become again a form of propositional knowledge, belief, by which the participatory, active exploration by reason, feeling, or mystical sense could be controlled.

During the Christian epoch, the world operated according to natural laws as immutable as the One in whose mind they are primordially conceived. The move into Newtonian mechanics only heightened the precision of the laws and their independence of operation from the creator. Now the interaction of deity and human subjectivity with matter, world, under the image of the Thomist *organon,* moves readily through a coalescence of Protestant and Cartesian dualisms into the image of the machine. The world finally becomes the sole province of science; "natural reason" and any recrudescence of animism is roundly defeated.[27] Now not only is the physical world cleanly disconnected from the percipient subject, and from the absolute subject, but is itself a mechanism of intrinsically separate parts, cooperating in orderly fashion:

The principal feature of this (mechanistic) order is that the world is regarded as constituted of entities which are *outside of each other* . . . separately existent, indivisible, and unchangeable "elementary particles" which are the fundamental "building blocks" of the entire universe. . . . The theory of relativity was the first significant indication in physics of the need to question this mechanistic order.[28]

Now there is with world no process quite analogous to that of the obsolescence of God, whereby separateness leads to a tendency to disappear. The concept of world is very much with us. Here something perversely different has occurred: whereas the death of God is in our hands only inasmuch as God is concept, the death of our world, through the particular genius of a mechanistic worldview in its very transition into atomic relativity theory, has been taken into human hands. The scenario of the end of the world shows its biblical roots:

Since myth functions as self-fulfilling prophecy, it is especially interesting to consider the fact that Christian myth promises what is popularly known as "the end of the world.". . . In every age there have been Christians convinced that they were living in Apocalyptic times. . . . The development of modern technology, however, has facilitated movement beyond mere passive expectation to active enactment of the envisioned horror show.[29]

When things have grown outside of each other, when they do not take part in each other, when I look at the brazenness of the evening star, the tenderness of a spring snow, and I do not care— then what does "the world" matter? And what does this state of separateness with its self-destructive mechanism have to do with the state of woman? This has not been our world; we have not been of it. Yet we have been identified with its very matter, the stuff into which everything—God, world, self—collapses as materialism: the magna mater created of masculine shadows, Jeremiah's yearning for return to the grave-mother (Jer. 20).

But it is the notion of self with which we are concerned. For it is in the acquisition by human selfhood of the attributes of the Newtonian atom that the historical walls of separateness are guaranteed. For finally it is ourselves we experience as "separately existent, indivisible, and unchangeable," as "outside of each other"—inasmuch as we experience ourselves as normatively, normally human. As "Man," we aspire to independence, individuality (indivisibility) and separateness of being as women precisely because these traits had been, have been, continue to be, denied to us, because their opposite—dependency, undifferentiated nonentity, and self-definition by relation—have been required of us by an inside cultural agent effective long after the outer voices have been named and muted. And here the paradox for feminism emerges, in which is a secret for all selves. If the state of separateness is a fundamental characteristic of patriarchy, do we as women and as men striving beyond patriarchy want—can we afford—to acquire its goods based, finally, on the "private properties" of individuality? Can we not risk a radical alternative, which by its stress on connection may indeed spiral us close to the old confinements of patriarchal subject and objects, but only with a momentum which spins us beyond their boundaries?

In the whirling world beyond the walls, selves dance in a pattern of relations untrammeled by clumsy gestures of subjection, reflexive subjectivity and schismatic desperation. Among the destructured citadels, amazing graces of feminism choreograph self anew in its field of worldly and divine connectivity.[30] With regard to God, feminism has the amazing grace of a radical apostasy, for, as Whitehead said, "the progress of religion is marked by the repudiation of gods." With regard to world, feminism has the grace of a radical marginality, so that it is not of this world as constituted by the disconnective complex, but wields a lever upon the entire world by virtue of the universality of patriarchy. With regard to self, it has the grace of a radical self-interest, that capacity to make the very concept of self interesting again, a source of disclosure and relation rather than the strange, alternately shrinking and imperialistic entity which is the ghost of the substantial soul.

# ═══ NOTES ═══

1. Susan Griffin, *Pornography and Silence: Culture's Revenge Against Nature* (New York: Harper & Row, 1981), 260.

2. Alfred North Whitehead, *Process and Reality* (New York: Free Press, 1978), 67.

3. Sheila Ortiz Taylor, *Faultline* (Tallahassee: Naiad, 1982), 8.

4. Alfred North Whitehead, *Symbolism* (New York: Putnam's Sons, Capricorn, 1959), 44.

5. Doris Lessing, *Four-Gated City* (New York: Bantam, 1970), 537.

6. James William Whedbee, "The Quest of Gilgamesh: Death the Journey's End and the Walls of a City." Paper presented to the Pomona Alumni College, Claremont, Calif., 1979.

7. John Cobb applies Jasper's theory of "axial age individuals" to the structures of consciousness evolving simultaneously among the Hebrew prophets and the Greek tragedians and philosophers. John M. Cobb, Jr., *The Structures of Christian Existence* (New York: Winston, Seabury, 1979), 52–59.

8. Lessing, *Four-Gated City,* 488.

9. David Bohm, *Wholeness and the Implicate Order* (London: Routledge & Kegan Paul, 1980); Alfred North Whitehead, *Modes of Thought* (New York: Capricorn, 1938), 225.

10. Charlene Spretnak, "Introduction," *The Politics of Women's Spirituality* (Garden City: Doubleday, Anchor, 1982), xviii. An example of a "male ally": Fritjof Capra, *The Turning Point: Science, Society and the Rising Culture* (New York: Simon & Schuster, 1982).

11. Robin Morgan, *The Anatomy of Freedom: Feminism, Physics and Global Politics* (Garden City: Doubleday, Anchor, 1982), xv.

12. Robin Morgan, *Going Too Far: The Personal Chronicle of a Feminist* (New York: Random House, Vintage Books, 1978), 300.

13. Mary Daly, *Gyn/Ecology* (Boston: Beacon, 1978), 11.

14. Ibid., 412.

15. Mary Daly, *Beyond God the Father* (Boston: Beacon, 1974), 6.

16. Ibid., 188f.: her response to Cobb.

17. Sheila Davaney, ed., *Feminism and Process Thought: The Harvard Divinity School/Claremont Center for Process Studies Symposium Papers* (New York: Mellen, 1981).

18. John Cobb represents an instance of a male ally who considers feminism a topic of central concern; thus his article in the *Symposium* and in the recent *Talking About God* advance the dialogue of a metaphysic committed to a vision of the cosmic webwork with concrete feminist concerns (e.g., God-language). David Tracy and John B. Cobb, Jr., *Talking About God: Doing Theology in the Context of Modern Pluralism* (New York: Winston, Seabury, 1983), 75–91.

19. Morgan, *Anatomy of Freedom*, 282.

20. Daly, *Gyn/Ecology*, 39.

21. Rosemary Radford Ruether, *New Woman New Earth* (New York: Winston, Seabury, 1981), 3.

22. Morgan, *Anatomy of Freedom*, 283.

23. "Hearing each other to speech," Nelle Morton has taught us, we find our voice. Do we also see each other, out of our social invisibility, into vision? For *theoria* is a matter of *seeing*.

24. Daly, *Beyond God the Father*, 8.

25. Tracy and Cobb, Jr., *Talking About God*, 40.

26. See Peter Berger, ed., *The Other Side of God: A Polarity in World Religions* (Garden City: Doubleday, Anchor Press, 1981), 28–47; and cf. Michael Fishbane, "Israel and the 'Mothers.'"

27. On the relations between the rise of modern mechanism and the defeat of the original Renaissance sciences of Neoplatonism, alchemy and witchcraft, see David Griffin, "Theology and the Rise of Modern Science," paper written in 1982.

28. Bohm, *Wholeness*, 173.

29. Daly, *Gyn/Ecology*, 102.

30. "Religion deals with the formation of the experiencing subject; whereas science deals with the objects." Whitehead, *Process and Reality*, 16.

# Notes On Contributors

**ROSE HORMAN ARTHUR,** Dean and Associate Professor of Religion, Heritage College, Toppenish, Washington, U.S.A.

**ANNE BANCROFT,** Writer and Lecturer, Bridport, Dorset, England

**HARRIET ERICA BABER,** Assistant Professor of Philosophy, University of San Diego, San Diego, California, U.S.A.

**CHRISTIAN R. GABA,** Professor of Religious Studies, University of Cape Coast, Cape Coast, Ghana

**WALTER GARDINI,** Professor of Comparative Religions, School of Oriental Studies, Salvador University, Buenos Aires, Argentina

**CATHERINE KELLER,** Associate Professor of Theology, Xavier University, Cincinnati, Ohio, U.S.A.

**URSULA KING,** Senior Lecturer, Department of Theology and Religious Studies, University of Leeds, England

**KIM KNOTT,** Community Religions Project, University of Leeds, England

**FRIDAY M. MBON,** Lecturer in Religious Studies, University of Calabar, Nigeria

**SARAH PETERSEN,** M.T.S. Candidate, Harvard University, Cambridge, Massachusetts, U.S.A.

**RICHARD QUEBEDEAUX,** Author, Berkeley, California, U.S.A.

**KENDRA SMITH,** Clinical Psychologist, Berkeley, California, U.S.A.

**GEORGE H. TAVARD,** Professor of Theology, Methodist Theological School, Ohio, U.S.A.

**E. JANE VIA,** Attorney, former Associate Professor of Religious Studies, University of San Diego, San Diego, California, U.S.A.

**THE CONTEMPORARY DISCUSSION SERIES**

# Women in the
# World's Religions,
# Past and Present

# Index

# Index

# Index

Eberz, Otfried, *Sophia und Logos,*
26–27
Effutu (Ghanaian people), 15
Elizabeth, in Luke's gospel, as vehicle
of revelation, 39, 40–41
Engler, Jack, 224
Episcopal Church
full clergy rights in 1976, 132
ordination of women as priests,
controversy, 145–57
Epulu Pygmies (Zairian people), 18
Equal Rights Amendment (ERA), 129
Evangelical feminism
basic teachings, 139
centrality of biblical authority, 141
growth of movement, 137–38
history, 135
importance of movement, 141
leaders of movement, 138
nature and significance, 138–42
publications, 137–38
Evangelicalism, 133–34
declaration of social concern, 136
women's role, 136
Evangelical Women's Caucus
conferences, 138
newsletter, 138
Eve
birth of, 33
as carnal woman, 27
as heavenly instructress, 27
saving figure within proto-gnostic
myth, 31–34
separation from Adam, 32
symbol of life, 33, 34

feminine consciousness, repression of,
in patriarchal societies, 26–27
*Feminine Mystique, The* (Betty
Friedan), 130
feminism
androgyny and, 207, 211–12, 214
critique of patriarchy, 237, 242
critique of religion, 201–2, 203–4
evangelical. *See* Evangelical
feminism
goddesses in, different meanings of,
207–8
goddess worship and new
spirituality, 204–5
*Lady Unique* (magazine), devoted to
goddess worship, 207

metaphysical philosophy and, 238
metaphysical physics and, 237–38
methodology trend as less reactive,
244
multidimensional in character, 201
paradox of, 248
philosophy of religion and, 238
religious inclination, 201
self and, 232
theology, 203–4
transformation of religious
consciousness, 202–3
witchcraft movement, 205–7
*Woman Spirit* (magazine), devoted
to women's spirituality
movement, 207
women's spirituality conference,
207
*Feminism and Process Thought* (Sheila
Davaney), 240
femininity, cluster of properties,
146–47
feminist theology, 131–32
Fiorenza, Elizabeth Schussler, *In
Memory of Her,* 24
*Four-Gated City* (Doris Lessing), 233,
235
Freud, Sigmund, psychoanalytic view
of sexuality, 73
Friedan, Betty, 131
*The Feminine Mystique,* 130
Fromm, Erich, 64

Gaba, Christian, 109
Gardini, Walter, "Feminine Aspect of
God in Christianity," 4
Ghanaian people
Akan, 15
Ashanti, 15
Effutu, 15
gnosticism, roots as syncretistic
religion, 28
*Gnostic Religion, The* (Hans Jonas), 28
God
challenges to the concept of,
244–45
feminine attributes, 147
masculine attributes, 146–47
natural symbols of, 145–53
obsolescence of, 247
God, in Christianity

255

# Index

# Index

# Index

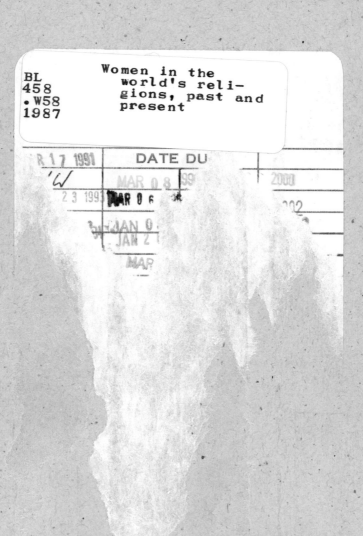